MAKING
RUMOURS

MAKING RUMOURS

The Inside Story of the
Classic Fleetwood Mac Album

Ken Caillat

with

Steven Stiefel

WILEY

John Wiley & Sons, Inc.

Photo credits: pp. 2, 19, 20, 33, 59, 167, 170, 176, 177, 179, 180, 181, 217, 241, 243, 282, 283, 321, 329, 335, 341,342, 343, Ken Caillat; pp. 6, 7, Biff Dawes; p. 10, Jeffery Husband; pp. 12, 13, 28, 29, 30, 31, 32, 40, 41, 60, 138, 184, 190, 197, 198, 202, 210, 211, 212, 214, 234, 237, 239, Herbie Worthington; pp. 18, 21, 24, 26, 27, 153, 158, 178, Nina Urban Bombadier; p. 34, Sally Fleetwood; pp. 35, 46, Record Plant; p. 53, Christina Conte; pp. 55, 163, 207, 326, Cheryl Geary; p. 191, Sam Emerson

Published by John Wiley & Sons, Inc., Hoboken, New Jersey
Published simultaneously in Canada

For general information about our other products and services, please contact our Customer Care Department within the United States at (800) 762-2974, outside the United States at (317) 572-3993 or fax (317) 572-4002.

Wiley also publishes its books in a variety of electronic formats and by print-on-demand. Some content that appears in standard print versions of this book may not be available in other formats. For more information about Wiley products, visit us at www.wiley.com.

Library of Congress Cataloging-in-Publication Data:
Caillat, Ken.
    Making Rumours: the inside story of the classic Fleetwood Mac album/Ken Caillat with Steven Stiefel.
        p.   cm.
    Includes index.
    ISBN 978-1-118-21808-2 (cloth : alk. paper); ISBN 978-1-118-28460-5 (ebk);
ISBN 978-1-118-28236-6 (ebk); ISBN 978-1-118-28286-1 (ebk)
    1. Fleetwood Mac (Musical group). Rumors.   I. Stiefel, Steven.   II. Title.
    ML421.F57C35   2012
    782.42166092'2—dc23
                                                                    2012004081

Printed in the United States of America

10 9 8 7 6 5 4 3 2 1

To Mick, John, Christine, Lindsey, Stevie, Richard,
and of course my mentor, Wally Heider

Contents

Foreword

by Colbie Caillat

Whenever I hear a song from Fleetwood Mac, I get a big smile on my face. Hearing their music reminds me of my childhood growing up in Malibu. My family lived in a little brown house on a cliff overlooking the ocean (the hill right above where the restaurant Duke's is, which used to be the Sea Lion back then). My big sister, Morgan, and I would play in the backyard in our blow-up pool with our golden retriever, Laz, and we'd blast "Second Hand News," "Go Your Own Way," "Songbird"—all my favorites! Whenever I hear those songs my eyes fill with happy tears from beautiful memories with my family when I was a little girl! Those were the days.

Because of Fleetwood Mac, I learned to write meaningful and honest music with soaring melodies, and the importance of being able to listen to an album from start to finish. Working with my dad has been such a fun experience. I feel lucky that he's been a part of my last two records. I've learned so many things recording with him.

Every song of mine that he's produced has honestly been my favorite. He's such an enthusiastic producer and puts his heart into every project he works on. He has so much fun making music and wants every record he does to sound classic and timeless. He brings in unique and creative ideas, sounds, and instruments to each song.

I know he learned so much from being a producer on the classic Fleetwood Mac records *Rumours* and *Tusk*, and he's sprinkling some of that into the music of today.

Today when I hear "Second Hand News," it makes me want to get in my car and drive up the coast of California on a beautiful sunny day, windows down, hair blowing in the wind, singing this song at the top of my lungs!

I hope you enjoy my dad's book as much as I did.

—Colbie Caillat, Grammy Award–winning singer

Foreword

by John Shanks

Rumours is an album I carry with me emotionally: the sound, the songs, the playing, the tension. It's like *Dark Side of the Moon*: perfect as a whole, but with songs that stand alone as individual moments and that are hits. It's one of the records that made me want to be a producer, a writer and, without a doubt, a guitar player.

It not only has some of the greatest guitar playing, the drums and the bass are haunting and beautiful and strong, the arrangements add up to pure sonic perfection, and the singing and harmonies are some of the most beautiful ever.

It's amazing that a record that features three singers feels so connected. Even though the band members were each hurting and falling apart, they turned their personal pain into collective grief and love.

In this way, *Rumours* exemplifies what great records should be. You bare your soul for all to share.

There is such joy and sorrow in the record that I still feel when I listen to it. From the darkness of "Gold Dust Woman" to the hope of "The Chain" and "Don't Stop," each song is its own movie.

Every day as I scan the radio dial for something to listen to, I always stop and reflect on the songs from *Rumours* when they pop up, because they still sound great and they're better than most stuff out there.

I'm sure it was not an easy one to record and make, but Ken and Richard made it seem effortless.

The record still sounds as fresh and as important today as it did when it was released. And it will sound the same way tomorrow. So thank you.

—John Shanks, six-time Grammy nominee and
Grammy Producer of the Year

Preface

Making Rumours is about the journey that a handful of people, myself included, took during the mid-1970s. It's about how being part of the phenomenon of the *Rumours* album not only changed our lives but touched millions of other lives around the world forever. It is also the story of a perfect album, made out of flaws in the human spirit, sometimes through agonizing determination, love, lust, and a force of will that made failure unthinkable. It's a success story of epic proportions—not always pretty, but a dramatic illustration of greatness delivered, of passion embraced. It is my story, and I want to share it with you.

Yet this book is not really about me—it's about the music on the album. I want to take you on a journey so that you can understand what it was like being in the studio making *Rumours.* Imagine the control room of the recording studio being similar to the cockpit of a plane, nearly airtight, soundproof, and cramped. Imagine the band and the engineers all coming into that room, taking their seats, adjusting to get comfortable. Then I start the engines. The lights go down, and I turn up the speakers, as we leave everyone and everything else outside. We're alone for the next ten to fourteen hours. I spin around in my chair, look back at the band, and say, "What do you guys feel like working on today?"

What happens next is magic.

After *Rumours* was released, the world went insane over what we'd created, and everyone wanted a piece of us. We were famous—myself in the industry, the band all over the world. We weren't just fifteen-minute famous either but forever famous. What we had wasn't just success, it was *crazy* success.

Suddenly, my world changed—money flowed and offers rolled in from other bands that wanted the producers of *Rumours* to work with them. Life became insane and exciting, and my path, like everyone else's, changed, sped up, and flew by.

Today, more than thirty years later, when people meet me they still say, "Hey, you recorded *Rumours*. I love your work. Thank you!" *Rumours* sat at number one on the charts for thirty-one weeks and, as of this writing, has sold more than forty million copies. It's taken me all of those thirty-plus years to complete my journey. It has culminated with the certification of my first number-one album since making *Rumours*, my own daughter Colbie Caillat's second album, *Breakthrough*.

Rumours thrust my life into a great detour, one filled with the music I had worked so hard to be a part of, filled with the force of great personalities, splendid talents, and iron wills, and the current of that music has carried me through a life I never expected.

In January 1976, Fleetwood Mac's personal catharsis, brilliant artistry, and technical innovation all came together to create *Rumours* at the Record Plant studio in Sausalito, California. After winning the Grammy for Best Album in 1977, it would come to stand as the defining rock-and-roll masterpiece of its generation. *Making Rumours* is my story of that remarkable, serendipitous time.

Most people who were paying attention to music back in the seventies can tell you where they were the first time they heard *Rumours*. The album boasted ten hit songs out of its eleven cuts, and the creation of the record spanned twelve months, employed seven recording studios, and cost nearly one million dollars to make.

Its emotional cost was even greater. In making the album, three couples in the band were destroyed. Yet in listening to the album, countless others fell in love. Maybe, ultimately, that makes everything worthwhile.

Musicians are a lot like children. Every day when they come to the studio, they're unsure of what lies ahead. They're extremely fragile. The process by which they imagine and create is almost inexplicable. They draw from their ideas and their emotions and from one another. Sex and drugs, hope and love, and fear and heartbreak are only parts of the story. It's what a musician does with those things that creates magic. That's how greatness is developed and measured.

By vanquishing, ignoring, and burning through the personal tragedies and turmoil, sacrificing the connections that each band member lost, the members of Fleetwood Mac created one of the greatest rock-and-roll albums in history. It's a success story of epic proportions, and I was there to witness it and help make it happen. Not bad for a jobless kid who had arrived in Los Angeles five years earlier driving a VW minibus. I was lucky to be that guy, and I knew it.

1

Ken's Wild Ride

Quit sniveling. You're doing the job!

—*Mick Fleetwood*

You never know when you're going to be a part of history.

It was Tuesday, January 27, 1976, the midst of one of the wettest winters in Northern California's history. After five years in Los Angeles, I had upgraded my VW bus to a '72 Audi 100, and now I was driving it up Interstate 101, heading four hundred miles north with my best friend, Scooter, who was riding beside me in the passenger seat. Scooter was a brown-and-white beagle mix, and he was very, very smart.

We were going to Sausalito to record Fleetwood Mac's new album, *Rumours*. Amazingly, twelve days earlier, I had never heard of the band. I know how crazy that sounds in retrospect, especially considering that I was already something of a music industry insider. But Fleetwood Mac had yet to have a hit song in America. By the end of my journey making *Rumours*, though, I knew that my life would never be the same.

Scooter Brown, the Regal Beagle, was my constant companion.

As I headed north, I could see dark clouds gathering on the horizon. These storm clouds are typical of Northern California's winters, bringing heavy rain and a cold chill that goes right through you. Scooter and I were driving straight toward the storm. I'd grown up in San Jose, about fifty miles or so from my destination, so the clouds didn't portend anything dark or ominous to me. They just made me feel like I was heading home. Scooter sat on the passenger seat looking ahead, ears up and alert in typical beagle fashion.

I had just taken a leave of absence from Wally Heider Studios in Hollywood, where I had been working as a recording engineer. Five years earlier, I had left a law internship in San Jose to follow my dream of becoming a successful songwriter in Southern California. I had taken a job with Wally at his recording studio shortly after arriving in Los Angeles, hoping to advance my songwriting career. While I hadn't exactly blown the doors off the songwriting world, I had become, all things considered, a fairly successful up-and-coming recording engineer.

Now I was leaving a job with security to engineer the new Fleetwood Mac album at the famous Record Plant studios up in Sausalito, right on the edge of San Francisco Bay. As I was driving back up to the Bay Area, I realized how much I had grown accustomed to the nearly year-round warm Southern California climate.

Rumours would be Fleetwood Mac's second record since the band had brought Stevie Nicks and Lindsey Buckingham on board, and it was slated to follow the release of their self-titled album—often referred to as the White Album, the one with the hit singles "Over My Head" and "Rhiannon." These songs weren't hits yet, but they would be soon. That's where my good luck comes into play. I can't say I have always counted on good luck, but I'm never surprised when it happens.

Fleetwood Mac itself was already an unlikely mix of opposites: old and new, English and American, male and female. What was to come were even more dichotomies: the contrasts between being unknown and famous; blues and rock; alcohol and pot. All of these contradictions were wrapped up in each of the band members and their relationships with the others. The one constant from every member of the band was each individual's relentless talent.

The core of the band was drummer Mick Fleetwood and bassist John McVie. These two had met in 1966 when they were playing backup in John Mayall's band, the Bluesbreakers. Guitarist Peter Green also played in that band. He'd replaced Eric Clapton when Clapton left to found Cream.

Back then, Peter had been called the "Green God." He dubbed Mick and John "Fleetwood Mac," and soon the three of them were recording together. A few years later, songs such as "Albatross," "Black Magic Woman," "Oh, Well," and "Green Manalishi" established Fleetwood Mac as a premier blues act in England. Yet they still hadn't really gained much traction in America.

In making the move to Sausalito, I had some apprehension. I was twenty-nine, single, and not as outgoing as I wanted to be, and I would be living with rock musicians for the next several months. I would have to share a large two-story house with all of the guys in the band. I didn't know what to expect from living with a bunch of musicians, but I suspected things might get pretty crazy.

During the previous week and a half, I had spent two full studio days mixing two versions of "Rhiannon" with the band. Even though I didn't know the band members very well, I had already learned that they could really play and write songs.

The band had gone through some ups and downs since their time with Peter Green. John's wife, Christine, had joined the group in 1970. They had gained and lost Bob Welch, their guitarist and lead singer, and, finally, they had recently hooked up with Lindsey Buckingham and Stevie Nicks. So, the current five members of the band were all still getting used to one another, too.

Stevie and Lindsey were virtual unknowns, despite the fact that they'd put out their debut record, *Buckingham Nicks*, and they'd recorded the White Album with the current Fleetwood Mac lineup. Stevie and Lindsey had grown up in the Bay Area, in Palo Alto, close to where I had lived, in San Jose. After a promising start in the Haight-Ashbury scene, they were discovered and encouraged to move to L.A., where they landed a record deal with Polydor. Stevie and Lindsey cut a brilliant debut album that had only one problem: it flopped. Because of this, Polydor dropped them as recording artists. Undeterred, the duo continued to pursue their dreams. With no money and no record deal, Stevie and Lindsey went right back into the studio, working after hours with their good friend and sound engineer Richard Dashut.

At that time, their studio had been the same one—Sound City in Van Nuys, California—where Fleetwood Mac was looking to cut its next album. A producer there, Keith Olsen, the guy who had brought Stevie and Lindsey down to L.A. and produced the *Buckingham Nicks* album, played Mick Fleetwood some of his handiwork. But it wasn't Keith's engineering that caught Mick's ear, it was Lindsey's brilliant guitar playing.

When it came to music, Mick had superb intuition and a flair for taking risks. So, when Bob Welch announced his intention to leave Fleetwood Mac, Mick made a phone call that would change the lives of all of the current members of the band. He asked Lindsey to join Fleetwood Mac. By default, this included Stevie.

With the offer already on the table, Lindsey and Stevie didn't even have to audition. Suddenly, Fleetwood Mac had something more than a new lineup; they had a new sound. Fleetwood Mac now had that indefinable combustion of elements that separates a truly great band from a thousand pretenders. They cut the White Album in just three months, took to the road, and played the hell out of every cow town and college campus in America, introducing the current version of the band to a new generation of fans. On that tour, in the summer and fall of 1975, the musical chemistry of this new Fleetwood Mac lineup started to come together, but the bonds between the band's couples began to fall apart. This was when I met the band.

Back on the road with Scooter, as we headed toward the storm clouds, I said, "Geez, Scooter, what have I gotten us into?" Scooter wagged his tail. "This may change our lives."

Scooter didn't care where we were going. He was just happy to be along for the ride. He stepped onto my lap and licked my face as if to say, "Everything will be okay." Scooter was definitely a smart dog.

I nearly didn't get the job. On Thursday, January 15, 1976, twelve days before I headed up to Sausalito, I got a call from Gail, my studio-booking manager at Wally Heider's in L.A. She told me that Fleetwood Mac had booked studio 1 to mix a one-hour show they'd recorded for the syndicated *King Biscuit Flour Hour* radio show.

Later that day I was standing with two of my co-engineer friends from Heider's, Biff Dawes and Dennis Mays.

Biff asked, "You're gonna do it, right?"

"Do what?" I asked back.

"You're going to do the Fleetwood session?"

"I'm not sure," I said and shrugged. "I don't know their music. Are they any good?"

"These guys are great. Have you heard 'Rhiannon'?" Biff asked.

I shrugged again. "Eh, maybe."

"Ken, go buy their album," Dennis said. "You're an idiot if you don't take this job."

So I bought the White Album. I liked it, and I took the gig.

The Biffer worked with me at Wally Heider's.

On the day of the mix down for the *King Biscuit* show, Saturday, January 17, 1976, I was feeling really good. It was one of those sunny mornings in Los Angeles when you know that everything is going to go great.

Around 10 a.m., Richard Dashut, the band's close friend and also their live engineer, walked into studio 1 with the tapes of the show. I gave them to the maintenance engineer to align the 24-track tape machine so we could mix down the twenty-four channels of vocal and instrument tracks for broadcast into a flowing, exciting mix.

My job was to blend all of the tracks into the best stereo mix possible, to find and bring out the best licks, to adjust the bass and treble settings of each instrument, and to blend in the proper amount of audience mics and their live ambience to make the listeners feel as if they were watching the band in concert, sitting in the best seat in the house.

We added effects to enhance the listener's experience, and it just so happens that I was really good at this. In mixing, I'm creating a sonic painting, adjusting the colors to make it beautiful. The knobs and the

Dennis Mays, "the hit man," was another of my
Heider's buddies.

faders on the console are my brushes; the speakers are my canvas.
I already knew how to do this really well.

Richard Dashut and I hit it off right away. He was Fleetwood Mac's
ears, and he was a very likable guy. One of us said to the other what you
heard in nearly every recording session back in those days: "Wanna get
high?"

"Absolutely," the other agreed.

So Richard and I smoked a joint as we prepped for the band. We
were co-engineers, and—eventually—we both became coproducers on
Rumours. He had entered the music business as an assistant janitor at
Crystal Sound Studios, a competitor to Wally Heider's, the studio where
I worked. Like me, Richard listened and waited for his time. He was one
of the kindest, most empathetic souls I've ever met. He was also a very
funny guy to have around.

When I was in college, I'd considered becoming a psychiatrist, so I called a couple of prominent shrinks in the San Jose area and asked whether I could talk to them about their career choice. One of them said to me, "You hear other people's problems all day long, and you have to be careful to let it go at night, or else it will stay with you and build up inside you. And that can destroy you." That was all I needed to hear. I immediately looked for a career that would lift people up, something positive. So I chose a career in music. Richard Dashut, I think, in the way he handled everyone in the band, chose a career in both.

My path to engineering records was fairly direct. I grew up as one of two children of a normal, conservative married couple in San Jose. My dad worked for NASA, and he also had a business making home models. My mom and dad worked hard and often into the late hours. They taught me not to be afraid of hard work, that I was smart and that Caillats can do anything they set their minds to.

Meanwhile, I had taken up guitar, and suddenly some of the ladies were interested in me—music looked to me like a much better alternative than angry clients and law school.

After graduating from Santa Clara University with a degree in business, I decided to move to Los Angeles to get a job at one of the recording studios or record labels. I figured I'd land a job, record my stuff in my spare time, get a quick hit record, become wildly famous, and live happily ever after. Right.

I drove the four hundred miles down to Los Angeles in my VW bus in January 1971. At that time, I had long hair and owned two suits from my law office days. My mom had helped me write a résumé (she was an executive secretary), and it turns out that this was the first step that led to my success in the music business.

When I got to L.A., I parked my sleeping bag on the floor of my ex-girlfriend's mother's house for the night. The next day, I pressed and dressed and hit the big studios. Everywhere I went, I heard the same thing: "No jobs here, but you should go to Wally Heider's studio. They do location recordings for all the top bands."

Not exactly what I wanted to hear, but what the hell? Off I went to Hollywood, long hair, beard, three-piece suit, and all. Wally's place was less than impressive from the outside, and parking was a bitch, but there were a couple of cute girls out front as I tried to maneuver my VW. I got wedged into a place I couldn't back out of. I finally parked (much to the amusement of the previously mentioned hot girls), marched myself into the studio office, and delivered my résumé. I left it with the manager, Ron, and he told me they'd be in touch.

Wally was a big man and brilliant. He was so smart that his brain ran ahead of his mouth, and he was always correcting what he was saying, so it actually sounded like he was stuttering, instead of editing in mid-sentence. When he got excited, the words came out faster than his tongue could process them, like Lucy and Ethel trying to sort chocolates. He peppered his dialogue with "uh," a habit that, like whispering, seems to be contagious. In his early years he was an avid fan of the Big Bands, and he had bought a trailer and recording equipment to allow him to follow his favorite bands around, recording their live shows. He became one of the first to record live concerts. Eventually he bought the building on the corner of Selma and Cahuenga in the heart of Hollywood and converted one of the rooms into a mix studio where he could process his live recordings.

About 7 p.m. that night, Wally himself called me at home. "Uh, is this K-Ken Caillat?" he said into the phone.

"Yes, it is," I said.

"K-Ken, this is, uh, Wally Heider. Uh, I read your résumé, and I'm very impressed with you. Uh, I'd like to see you right away." I could hear the excitement in his voice.

"Great," I replied. "I'll be down first thing in the morning."

"Uh, c-can you come down right now?"

Suddenly, I began stuttering, too. "Uh, uh, ya-yes, sure. Now's good!"

I jumped into my VW bus, dressed in Levi's this time, and off I went to meet the famous Wally Heider. I walked into the same trashy office I had been in earlier. Draped over the couch was Wally himself.

As I opened the door, he looked up at me and said, "Uh, you must be Ken." He was 6'3" or 6'4" and about 260 pounds. I shook his large hand, and then he stood. We walked into his office to talk.

Later, I would learn that Wally was generally a happy man, but he had no patience for human error. He really liked that I was a college

Wally Heider relaxes on the job.

graduate with a typed résumé, and I think he got a kick out of my suit-and-tie delivery earlier that day.

We talked for a while, then he said, "Ken, I have a real good feeling about you. I don't have any room for you, but I'm so sure about you that I'm going to fire one of my new boys and give you a job."

What? This had been so easy that I figured there must be a catch. At the very least, I expected the recording studio must be a dump.

"Thank you so much, Wally," I said. "But before I say yes, could I see your facilities?" Cocky, huh?

Wally looked at me and smirked a little, then, very slowly and deliberately, he said, "Why sure, Ken, just follow me. We have three studios here and a remote truck." I knew immediately that he was going to enjoy this.

We went downstairs, passing the traffic office, and came to a studio.

"This is studio 3, but unfortunately it's booked now with Crosby, Stills, and Nash, so I can't show it to you." My heart skipped a beat. Crosby, Stills, and Nash were my idols. "Let's go around the corner to studio 1. It's open now." Wally continued the tour.

He opened the door to studio 1, and I saw a small mixing room, about twenty feet by twenty feet, with the biggest console I had ever seen. It must have had a thousand knobs—it had dials and switches all over it. The console was more than six feet long, and I was stunned. CSN in one studio and now this!

"Wow, Wally, this is great, we don't need to see any more. I love this place!" I backpedaled fast, hoping I hadn't blown my chance.

"So, you've decided you do want to work here?"

"Yes, sir! I definitely want to work here, if you still want me to." I was done being a wise guy, and I desperately wanted the job.

Wally put his arm around me and said, "Ken, I like you. Be here at nine sharp tomorrow morning."

So, yes, I got the job, and Wally said I was a "real go-getter" (one of his favorite phrases).

Wally had me stock the studios with supplies, move tape machines around, load the remote truck, go on live recordings, and sit behind clients' engineers as their assistant. He became my mentor. I was always taking notes, watching, learning, and listening.

During the next four years, I worked with some big names: T-Rex, the Fifth Dimension, CSN, Joni Mitchell, George Carlin, and Paul McCartney—sometimes as assistant and other times as first engineer. With Crosby and Nash, I learned what the brilliance of production and artistry can do. With Joni, I learned that if I was given the perfect set of colors, I could paint a masterpiece.

When I was asked to record the strings for *Venus and Mars*, I decided to get the best string sounds Paul McCartney had ever heard. Before Paul arrived, I played back the instruments, and the session leader told me they sounded like he was hearing them from his seat as first chair.

When Paul got to the studio, he came up to me and said, "Hello, I'm Paul McCartney."

"Yes, I know," I said. "Nice to meet you."

One of the Hudson Brothers once said to me, "Ken, you're a great engineer. When are you going to learn how to talk?"

During that time at Heider's, I learned how to make the big consoles sing in those three studios. I had a blast. I made a lot of new friends. My girlfriend and I broke up. I traveled, and the L.A. women were beautiful. I was single and a recording engineer in the seventies in Los Angeles! Yahoo!

Back in the darkness of studio 1 on that Saturday *King Biscuit* mix down of the radio show, Richard Dashut and I were alone with the beautiful music in a soundproof room, protected from the distractions of daily life. Studio 1 had a double-thick door that opened directly to the street and flooded the small room with light and sound whenever anyone entered. We sat in that quiet, guarded cocoon and began to mix the show.

About an hour later, the members of the band started to arrive and immediately began moving to the power of our mix.

The first band member to arrive was Mick. Before he could even get his coat off, he shouted over the loud music, "Yeah! Sounds fucking great!" That's a good sign, I thought.

Richard (on the right) and I make music.

As the rest of the band showed up, I greeted each of them. Over the weekend, I had taken Dennis's advice and studied up on Fleetwood Mac. I thought I knew my way around their music and their names. The White Album sounded wonderful. Keith Olsen, their engineer-producer, preferred a softer sound than I did, in part because he used an English console, a Neve, that's known for its warmth. The console I was using was an API, which gave me a red-hot, edgy sound that I liked better. But at this early stage, I really wasn't thinking about that. I was just having fun, and I really wanted to impress Fleetwood Mac.

When Stevie walked in, I said confidently, "Hi, Lindsey! I'm a big fan."

"I'm Stevie," she said politely. "Nice to meet you."

I felt like an idiot. I didn't know that on their album cover, Lindsey's and Stevie's pictures were reversed. And they both have androgynous names. So much for doing my homework.

With the full band assembled, Richard and I kept working on each song as they listened to our work. When we got to "Rhiannon" Stevie stopped me. "Ken, this has to be a great mix." Stevie had an amazing

Christine and Stevie wait and listen while we mix their song.

smile; the corners of her mouth turned up in a very cute way. She looked so young, sweet, and happy. "This song is very special to me." She turned away but then turned back to me as if for emphasis. "It's magic," she said.

"Don't worry, Stevie, the song is so good it's almost mixing itself!" I shouted over the loud music. Later, Stevie would introduce the song in concerts as being about a Welsh witch. She had written the song for her second album with Lindsey but ended up recording it with Fleetwood Mac. Even though I was working on a live track and not the studio version that would be released as their single, it was still really important to the band.

Stevie danced around the room to the music with her arms above her head. I didn't know it at the time, but she believed that she had magical powers. Later, I understood that she probably thought that she was chanting up a good mix from Richard and me.

One day, a few years earlier in my career, when I had been an assistant working with the great engineers who came to mix in studio 1 at Wally Heider's, a very pompous engineer abruptly stopped the tape he was working on, held up his hands, wiggled his fingers, and said, "Sorry, no magic today." He stopped the session and just went home.

"No magic? He thinks he has magic!" I chuckled to myself.

He was a conceited jerk—but I learned later that he was also right. Sometimes you have it, and sometimes you don't. That day Richard and I had the magic. Good music does that to you. It lifts you up, and you do things you didn't know you could do. We mixed "Rhiannon," and by the time we were done, the whole band was dancing. Stevie was twirling around the console, completely elated. It was a great day.

The band was heading up to Sausalito in a few days to record their new album. They had already hired another engineer from the Record Plant in Los Angeles. Though they all told me how much they would have liked to work with me, Mick said that the other engineer had much more experience than I did, and he was already under contract.

The band was going to work with him for the first time the next morning to create a new radio mix of "Rhiannon" from the album's original twenty-four-track tape. Of course, I wanted that gig, but it was a done deal. So, we all hugged one another good-bye, and the band left the studio. Easy come, easy go, I thought. It had still been a great day.

● ● ●

The next night, after the band's first session with their new engineer, Kelly Kotera, I got a call from Richard. He told me that things had gone terribly wrong. The studio had a brand new computer-automated console to help the engineer make things work more smoothly, but the console automation had crashed, and Kelly had had to mix manually. He wasn't able to get it right. To make matters worse, I later found out that apparently both Lindsey and Richard had spent the day hovering over his shoulders while he tried to find the sweet spot in the mix.

I can tell you from experience that this is the worst feeling. Sometimes clients would come in to work with me, and they were so close to their music—so protective of it—that if they saw me reach for a knob or a fader to change anything, I could hear them gasping behind me. I would solo an instrument to hear what it was doing, and they would immediately tell me all about it and why it was that way. Of course, I couldn't listen to the track while they were talking to me, which kept me from being able to change it. Often, I believed that this was their intention—to keep me from changing anything in the original recording, even though my job was to improve it.

Anyway, Kelly, with those two guys hanging over his shoulders, was screwed from the start. He should have told them to leave him alone, but I guess he didn't.

Richard, who would soon become my good friend, told me what had happened after that session. Mick walked with Richard out to the parking lot and put his arm around him.

"Looks like you'll be in charge of our next record," Mick said.

"You must be out of your mind!" Richard said. "I'm an engineer, not a producer."

Richard didn't want to produce the record, because he thought producing was the wrong job for him at this point in his career. He wanted to grow into the job of producer, because he felt that it was too much responsibility for his knowledge and experience at this stage.

"You're the right man for the job," Mick reiterated. Mick was right about Richard. He had an uncanny ability to spot talent.

"Three years ago, I was cleaning toilets," Richard told Mick. "I can't do this by myself!"

Mick said, "Dashut, quit sniveling. You're doing the job!" Sniveling. I love that word.

"Okay," Richard said and shrugged. "But can I bring in Ken Caillat as the project engineer?"

"That is a fantastic idea," Mick said. "Which proves to me that I've made the right decision in hiring you."

In retrospect, I have to shake my head. Fleetwood Mac hadn't hassled me one bit that Saturday morning at Wally's—maybe because it was a low-intensity gig to mix a radio show, not their all-important radio single. Or maybe because I was already in a working groove with Richard when the rest of the band arrived.

Anyhow, that Sunday night Richard called me. "Ken, we didn't get the mix today. Everything went wrong, Can you come in tomorrow and mix it?"

"You bet I can," I said.

The next day, Monday, January 19, 1976, we were back in studio 1 and blew the doors off the mix for the radio edit of "Rhiannon." Richard and I got started early. The fidelity of these studio tracks was far superior to that of the live radio show's tracks, so it really made my job a lot easier. I knew the song. I knew the structure, and, in this version, the instruments sounded huge. I knew this would be a great day.

Keith Olsen had produced and mixed the album version of "Rhiannon." He had a particular talent for mixing, and one trick he liked to use was to emphasize the bottom end of the instruments. I, on the other hand, preferred to emphasize the midrange so that the instruments jumped out of the speakers more. I would compensate by increasing the volume of the bass instrument to support the extra mids and highs. Keith's tracks were a pleasure to work with.

By the time the band arrived, the track already sounded pretty damn good.

"My God, man," Mick said when we walked in. "That sounds amazing!"

Lindsey came in right behind him, took one listen, started rubbing his hands together in excitement, and sat down next to me to roll a joint.

Heider's had great speakers in studio 1: Altec 604 Es, also known as Voice of the Theater speakers because they were big cabinets hanging from the ceiling, about five feet by four feet with a fifteen-inch, full-range speaker that could easily handle the power from the 300 watts being delivered from each of the classic Macintosh tube amplifiers. When you walked in, they overwhelmed the room. We turned up the volume a little more, just to feel their power.

We mixed the song for about seven hours, playing it over and over, looking for every hook in the song and bringing each one out to build excitement. For about the last half hour of that session, we started recording our mixes to the Ampex stereo two-track tape recorder.

The last mix was the one. We all had our hands on the board, moving the instrument faders up and down until everyone performed each move perfectly. As the song was ending and I was doing the final fadeout, we all looked at one another. We knew we had done it.

As the last of "Rhiannon" disappeared into the speakers, I stopped the 24-track and the 2-track. We all jumped to our feet with excitement. We knew this would be a hit. Even Scooter was dancing!

Then Mick came over to me and asked, "Want to go to Sausalito and do our album?"

I was young, and I took this in stride, Okay, I thought. I've been asked to go up to Sausalito and record an album with Fleetwood Mac. It didn't matter to me that I had never done a major album before, only pieces. I was ready. As I said, I've always been lucky, and I had always followed my instincts.

The next day, back at work, my friend Chris "Chiggy" Chigaridas said, "Do you really think it's a smart move to leave this great job to go do this album? Good jobs don't come easy."

I told Wally about my opportunity, and he said, "Ken, you deserve it. Go ahead and go. Uh, they live here, don't they? Try to bring them, uh, back here to finish the album. I'm, uh, proud of you!"

Eight days later, on Tuesday, January 27, 1976, I was driving up the coast from L.A. to San Francisco. The warm sunny skies gradually faded to gray and by the time Scooter and I crossed the Golden Gate Bridge, it was already raining.

We approached the Waldo Tunnel and passed under the famous rainbow that was painted over the entrance. That rainbow welcomes travelers to Marin County. I believed it was a sign of good things to come, an omen of riches and success, and it made me smile. Of course, when I came out the other side, it was pouring like hell.

After a couple of wrong turns, I came down the steep hill past the stilt houses that were stacked in rows leading into Sausalito proper. I have to say, it was with some difficulty that I eventually found the Record Plant. It probably wasn't unintentional that the studio was hard to find, because it was the secret haven for celebrity musicians.

Scooter and I were the first of the group to arrive at the studio. Located off a small descending side road, the Record Plant, Sausalito, was tucked away from sight, hidden in the crook beneath the main road. To ensure its anonymity, the wooden studio was obscured and camouflaged by the tall trees around it, and there were few parking spaces in

The entrance to the Record Plant in Sausalito.

I'd stand and look through this porthole outside our studio while my ears cooled off.

front. The only thing that betrayed the building's identity was the 2200 in large white numbers over the door.

Leaving Scooter in the car, I raced through the rain to the front door. It was then that I noticed the door had a band of carved-wood animals playing instruments in a forest jamboree. Without stopping to admire it, I quickly turned the doorknob, which was located in the middle of a fox's bass drum, and stepped into the foyer of the Record Plant. This studio would become my second home for the next three months, and that would seem like an eternity.

In the entrance, I noticed the fine woodwork on the walls. Just inside was a small office. A beautiful young woman stepped out to greet me. Shaking the water off, I extended my hand to her and said, "Hi, I'm Ken Caillat. I'm going to be engineering the new Fleetwood Mac album."

Her face lit up with a wide white smile. She shook my hand. "Hi, I'm Nina, the studio manager. Did you have any problems finding us?"

Wow, she was stunning! "Nah, just the damn rain," I said.

Nina Urban was a transplant from New Jersey, and I was instantly smitten with her. Yet I could never reconcile her thick East Coast accent with her Southern California good looks. She was a ray of sunshine on this otherwise gloomy day. Suddenly, everything felt comfortable, and I could see my stay in Sausalito working.

The staff at the Record Plant did everything they could to make it a wonderful place to get away to, and musicians loved the vibe. Nina told me that engineers, roadies, and rock stars alike needed to feel as if they were escaping from the world that they had to deal with on the street or in restaurants or after a show. The staff worked hard to make us feel as if we were in our living rooms or bedrooms while at the Record Plant. The staff members were there to be our caretakers, careful not to intrude on our creative space.

Nina loved her work, and she was great at it. She showed me around the building. Surprisingly, I found it a little claustrophobic. Recording studios back then were designed to feel like a cocoon. They tried to seal you in a soundproof world where you could forget about things outside, where you could drop into the music and lose yourself for as long as it

One of the dark halls, lit up by the flash. Imagine this hall dimly lit.

The Record Plant house with guesthouse in front.

took to get things right. The walls of the Record Plant were a mixture of yellow and blue cloth and redwood strips. There were two individual studios and a lounge. The company's cooks made food for us daily in the kitchen. The building had a sunken pit that served as a conference room. It even had a Jacuzzi adjacent to a shower with multiple jets and a playroom featuring a stand-up Pong machine.

The connecting hallways were narrow, dark, and uneven, like something out of a Tolkien story. Just outside our studio was a door with a porthole. When we were recording the album, I would often take a break and look through that round window. I wondered what other people were doing, and my sense of separation from the real world would increase. It was like looking out an airplane window while flying over a foreign land.

The company also owned two big beautiful houses in the hills of Sausalito, with great views and lots of trees, but that day it was still raining San Francisco–style. Nina told me to follow her to the house where I would be staying. It was a nice place in the hills near the studio, completely furnished with everything we could ask for.

Richard and Lindsey arrived soon after I did, arriving in Lindsey's blue Mercedes. Richard and I decided to share a room, and, naturally, Mick and John each took one. Lindsey spent the night at the house, but he decided to stay in an apartment a few miles away, on his own.

The house we stayed in had five bedrooms and a big kitchen. A woman who lived in a cottage on the property came down and cleaned up after us every day. The house was very comfortable, not high-tech, not palatial, not gilded, but it was a spunky, groovy, colorful place to hang out.

At the house that first evening, the guys kicked around a while, settling in. Then I suggested we drive into town to check out the studio so that they could see it before we started recording in the morning. We hopped into my good old front-wheel-drive Audi to make the twisty fifteen-minute drive to the studio. I couldn't resist showing them what front-wheel drive could do. I had bought the Audi four years earlier, because no American car at that time had front-wheel drive.

Lindsey, Richard, and I got into my Audi. Richard rode shotgun, and Lindsey got in the backseat. We took off out of the driveway and downhill on the winding road to the studio. The first curve came up quickly. I slowed down into the curve and accelerated out of it, past the tall, dense Mill Valley trees that lined the narrow street, the front wheels pulling the car forward around the curve. In my rearview mirror, I could see that Lindsey looked a little pale.

"Pretty cool, huh, guys?" I said, beaming from ear to ear.

Richard went into his Rodney Dangerfield voice, "Uh, Ken, at this speed we'll arrive at the studio before we actually leave home."

Lindsey gave a nervous, guttural laugh.

From that point on, Richard, Lindsey, and I often drove to the studio together, in what would become known as Ken's Wild Ride. Door-to-door service: a fifteen-minute drive in ten minutes flat.

2

Starting *Rumours*

God knows, if the drums aren't right, then the song is not survivable.

—*Mick Fleetwood*

I walked into the Record Plant, Sausalito, around 11:30 a.m. on Wednesday, January 28, 1976. I'd seen the studio the day before, so I knew they had all of the best equipment: a console more than six feet long, all of the latest tape machines and microphones. I was impressed. And since Nina had given me a tour, I knew the layout.

I was the first one to the studio that morning. Well, to be honest, Scooter was the first one, charging ahead of me to sniff out the place. I liked to get to the studio a few hours before I worked with any band, when things were still calm and sleepy. It allowed me to get to know the space, set up the equipment with the other techies, and get started mic'ing the instruments before the band arrived. Band members often have opinions about how their instruments should be mic'ed, so even

Nina Urban was the Record Plant, Sausalito, manager.

back then my solution was to get to the studio and start my setup work before any rock star could give me his or her two cents.

This also gave me an opportunity to talk to the lovely Nina. Her office was just inside the front door. As I walked in, the morning sun flooded the area, illuminating Nina. She was twenty-three, and her shoulder-length brown hair reflected the sunlight.

"Well, good morning," Nina said, smiling widely. "You're an early riser!" This, even though it was already close to noon. Nina knew all about bands and their schedules.

"Just trying to stay ahead of the wolves," I said. "You look great."

Her smile widened. "You just haven't had your coffee yet. Come on, I'll show you the kitchen."

I tried to make small talk, but I was clearly captivated by her and a little tongue-tied. The Record Plant kitchen was rustic, redwood-lined, and, like everything else inside, dimly lit. The intercom came on; Nina had a call waiting for her in her office.

"Okay, I gotta go. See you in a little while." She disappeared down the narrow south hallway.

I took the north hallway up toward studios A and B and went into studio A. I sat down in the chair, in front of the big API console that would be mine for the next three months. I'm sure it had well over a thousand knobs on it—scary for a novice, but thrilling for me. This is the big time, I thought.

I sipped my coffee for another moment before I started dealing with the equipment. I was trying to wind down and crank up at the same time. I was just shy of my thirtieth birthday, and I was working for a band that had already put out ten albums, but they'd had no big hits in the United States. Their latest record, the White Album, had been given the eponymous title *Fleetwood Mac* because of the new lineup and because of the controversy with the "fake" Fleetwood Mac. The band's former manager, Clifford Davis, felt that he owned the name Fleetwood Mac. While the real Fleetwood Mac band was in the United States touring, Davis had assembled a fake band to tour, creating all sorts of controversy and lawsuits that the band was dealing with.

I was a little nervous but eager to wow the band with my great recording skills. I'd already had some success with my two days of mixing with the band back in Los Angeles, but I still felt that I needed to prove myself to them.

Moments later, Cris Morris came into the control room. Cris was twenty-nine, about 6'1", and he had a brown afro-style hairdo. He was employed directly by the Record Plant, Sausalito, and he would be an assistant engineer on *Rumours*. Cris was an Atlantic City boy, and he had already worked with many San Francisco bands that had come through the studio in that era.

"Morning, Ken. Ready to get started?" Cris lit a cigarette. Soon I would learn that Cris was a fully capable engineer on his own, and he was a great asset to have in our arsenal.

"Let's do this," I said. "First, I'd like you to plug in my Revox reel-to-reel tape machine so I can listen to the speakers." No sooner had I said it than it was done.

"Just tell me what mics you want and where, and I can start setting up the studio while you listen to your tapes," Cris said.

Cris Morris was the Record Plant's assistant engineer.

"Great idea." I turned over a track sheet and started drawing where I wanted the instruments to go and what kind of mics I wanted on each. "Where do you recommend we set up the drums?" I asked. "The room sounds pretty dead out there."

"Yeah, we have a wood portion on the north wall. Most guys put the drums there."

I walked out into the studio, stood in front of the decorative wood portion of the wall, and clapped my hands together. "Still pretty dead," I said. "Do you have any plywood I could set the drums on, instead of setting them on the carpet?" Carpeting absorbs all of the sounds of the drums, and I wanted Mick's drums to have a big sound.

"Absolutely," Cris said. Off he went to get that project completed. I kept sipping my coffee and continued to work on the mic chart.

Over the years, I had developed preferred combinations of microphones to use to get my favorite sounds. I jotted them down quickly, listing a combination of ten American and European mics for drums and two to three mics for each of the other instruments, totaling about thirty mics altogether. I took one of my reference tapes out of my leather man-bag, threaded it onto my trusty Revox, and pressed PLAY. The meters started to move, but no sound came out of the speakers. I looked at the big console and found the input selector. Then I turned up the volume knob. The sweet sound of Steely Dan came out of the speakers.

"Wow, that sounds really great," a voice said from behind me.

"Yeah, but it's a little bright in the midrange frequencies, don't you think?" I turned to see Richard Dashut. His eyes looked a little funny, and I could tell that he had prepared for the day by smoking some pot so that he could "zone in" on the sounds. His eyes were like little slits. He had obviously ridden in with Lindsey or one of the road crew.

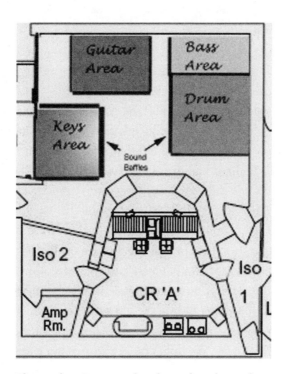

This was how I put together the studio A layout for the band.

John McVie was the quiet, rhythmic soul of the band.

Richard and I listened to the speakers a little longer, then I hit STOP. They sounded fantastic. I showed Richard my mic list and setup. He looked it over and nodded his approval. Our control room looked out into the studio through a giant soundproof window. On my chart, I had set up the instruments so that the band members could face one another and still see us as well. Richard had experience recording with the band, so I was curious to know whether he thought my setup would please them.

On our right against the north wall would be Mick, playing his giant drum set. Moving counterclockwise, as close to Mick as possible, I had put John's bass setup. Left of that was Lindsey's electric guitar setup. On the south wall was Christine's electric keyboard station for her clavinet, Fender Rhodes, and Hammond organ. We had a mic in front of each instrument so that she could sing while sitting and playing. Stevie would stand in the middle of the studio, waving her tambourine over her head in time with the music. We didn't bother to give her a mic, opting to have Mick play her parts later. As with everything Fleetwood Mac did, it all had to be perfect, including the tambourine. Stevie played for the "vibe," but only Mick's tambourine parts were recorded for the album. Stevie played the tambourine in the studio to entertain herself. She also played the tambourine onstage, but we never mic'ed it.

Directly to the left and right of the control room were two isolation booths that also had large windows, so you could see out into the studio and the control room. The one on my left was where I would record acoustic instruments, such as the grand piano and Lindsey's acoustic guitars and quieter things such as vocals and tambourines. The one on the right was for loud guitars, bass amps, and organ speakers. Each of the instruments was surrounded on all sides by sound-restraining, movable barriers called baffles.

Richard and I talked about how it would all work. He was the funny guy, and he chattered incessantly while I worked. Cris sat behind us and kept notes, listening to everything, anticipating our needs before we could even say them out loud. So, since we really had three engineers, we knew that we should be able to solve any sound problem.

What's ironic is that throughout the *Rumours* journey, Fleetwood Mac went from one end of the fame spectrum to the other. That day

Mick Fleetwood, the leader of the band, enjoys another Heineken on the job.

in Sausalito, when we walked into the studio to start recording, they were an established band, but you could hardly say they were rock stars. Before we even released *Rumours*, that had changed dramatically.

At the start of that first day of making *Rumours* in Sausalito, I was more eager than nervous. I knew my mic choices were tried and true. I had just used them to record Joni Mitchell's live album *Miles of Aisles*. I had a great support team at the Record Plant, and Richard was by my side. Along for the ride, once again, was Scooter. I felt that this was my time, and I couldn't wait to show everyone what I could do, because I knew it always worked. That may seem arrogant, but I couldn't help it—I had a good background, and I was young. I really liked my mixes, and I knew that other people did, too.

Christine McVie was talented and tough.

Lindsey Buckingham was brilliant but difficult.

Richard became a lifelong friend, and he was the perfect guy to help keep things light when the dark clouds formed. He was close with every member of the band, and they all told him their problems. But he only shared these problems with me when he felt that I needed to know. Sometimes this information helps you figure out how to approach a difficult rock star (or even one who isn't that difficult), when you know what's going on in his or her personal life, but other times it's just gossip. Richard knew the difference.

His insights, in addition to his empathy and humor, made him every bit as important to the success of the record as any individual member of the band. Making a blockbuster record is a team sport, and it can fail whenever a key player wanders off the reservation. Richard helped keep all of the players, if not sane, at least focused on the bigger picture.

During the early hours of recording sessions, John and Christine were civil with each other, but as the hours wore on and the booze flowed, John would start buzzing around Christine, and their conversations became shorter and more tense. Because I was in the control room, often I wasn't able to hear how their arguments started, but I could hear how Christine usually ended them. "John, you're being ridiculous. You've had too much to drink. Now leave me alone and just concentrate on your bass part."

They weren't the only broken couple: Stevie and Lindsey were right in the middle of ending their relationship. At this point, I wasn't even aware of it. I thought they just had an open relationship. When they joined Fleetwood Mac, though, their happy days as a couple had ended. They often turned to Richard for advice: Stevie whispered to him about Lindsey, and Lindsey whispered to him about Stevie.

Then there was the third, lesser-known breakup: Mick's wife was about to leave him for his best friend back home.

Mick had two beautiful daughters with Jenny Boyd, who was the sister of George Harrison's wife, Patty. Mick was a womanizer and a workaholic, so his relationship with his wife was doomed because he couldn't change his ways. Richard listened to Mick's secret pain and carried it with him. I think Mick would only tell Richard because everyone else in the

Stevie Nicks wrote Fleetwood Mac's only number one single, "Dreams."

Richard Dashut was the band's brilliant
engineer, therapist, and friend.

band still viewed Mick as their leader, manager, and father figure. When
all of this turmoil was going on, he just shouldered the brunt of it, sharing
with me only what he felt I needed to know.

From these very early, unsettled days, it seems as if all of these
doomed love affairs should have consigned *Rumours* to the discount bin.
In retrospect, it's a miracle that we were able to finish *Rumours*. But
later, I came to understand that *Rumours* probably succeeded because it
was brilliant group therapy in which we all—wittingly or unwittingly—
participated. It's possible that if it hadn't been for all of the sexual and
relationship turmoil in the band, you wouldn't know this record any better than some of the previous Fleetwood Mac records.

So, for the most part, once I'd gotten to know the band and we
started to play and record, I just sat there doing my job, steering clear of

Mick and Jenny Fleetwood would divorce,
remarry, and divorce again.

the band's personal dramas. If I had had to contend with what Richard dealt with, I probably would have run like hell. Then again, he didn't have to do what I had to do: stay serious and focused (and relatively sober) so that we could complete the record.

On that first day of setup, though, I was oblivious to all of the drama going on in the band. With my coffee finished, and the mics all set up and tested, the band's road crew arrived and began to unpack the instruments. They spent that time getting to know the rooms and the people at the Record Plant.

The good news was that the studio was state-of-the-art seventies technology. It was designed to be very dead acoustically. This means that the sounds from the band would be radically absorbed, instead of bouncing and echoing all over the place. With a "dead" studio, every instrument sounds lifeless, as its sounds disappear into the absorptive walls. This can make recording individual instruments difficult. Imagine

This was the band's view of the control room in studio A.

if you heard only the pluck of a piano string without the sound resonating through the piano's wood frame. Not so pretty.

The reason for designing a dead room comes down to personal taste, and the studio's co-owner, Gary Kellgren, the producer-engineer for Jimi Hendrix, must have preferred this type of studio.

The studios where I had learned had had a more balanced sound, with some sonic reflections allowed. To illustrate, imagine the sound in a small tiled bathroom, compared to an overloaded clothes' closet versus your family's living room. Wally Heider's was the living room, and the Record Plant was the clothes closet.

It was a top-notch room, but it was still foreign to us. An engineer has to adjust to every new studio, because each one has different sounds that are often unapparent at first. Sometimes you're really impressed by the openness of the studio or the aesthetics, where you can see the band and get a sense of everything that's going on. Other times, studios feel a little cramped and claustrophobic. Yet no matter how good the studio is, you still have to get used to it before it feels like home and your work becomes second nature.

The band's studio techs got the instruments in place, and Cris and I made sure all of the mics were positioned properly and tested.

The band employed two young kids as drum and guitar roadies, who traveled with them to keep the band's instruments in perfect working order. Now that we were in the studio, they were an integral part of the team: Ron (Rhino) Penny, twenty-one, was the drum tech, and Ray Lindsey, twenty, was the guitar tech.

Rhino and Ray set up the equipment while we continued to work on the mics. We spent about an hour to an hour and a half doing this, then the band started to arrive—first Christine and Stevie, who had been put up in a deluxe hotel, where they each had their own room and could be properly pampered.

We knew we were a long way from finishing with the equipment setup, but Christine and Stevie were glad to see us, and Richard and I were happy to see them, too. It was hugs and kisses all around. Each girl brought her small dog, respectively, Duster and Ginny, and Scooter welcomed them in his usual way, smelling their private parts before Christine and Stevie could scoop up the little dogs in their arms.

"Scooter, leave her alone!" Stevie said.

"Typical man!" Christine added.

I laughed to myself and thought, Nice one, Scooter. Stevie and Christine never warmed up to Scooter, even though most people really liked him.

At the time when we started recording *Rumours*, Stevie was twenty-seven, and she was our newly added songwriter and vocalist. This was only her second album with Fleetwood Mac after her debut with Lindsey on *Buckingham Nicks*. Stevie would, arguably, become the best-known member of the band.

Yet at this point, she was content to be a member of a band with a record deal. When we started to record, many people thought of Stevie as the weakest link in the band, because she was somewhat of a sweet hippie chick, and she didn't have a lot of technical knowledge about music and instrumentation. That's not to underestimate her. Ultimately, her ethereal songwriting and vocals added a dimension to Fleetwood Mac that was every bit as essential as any other band member's contribution. She also wrote the band's only number one hit, "Dreams."

Christine was the thirty-three-year-old keyboardist and a longtime member of the band. Her recent separation from John resulted in some very strained moments in the studio. You see, John was still in love with Christine, but he continued to choose booze over her. So Christine had decided to end their marriage. But they were pros, and they had a job to do. They were polite to each other when they were in the studio. Sometimes, though, when John drank, he wanted her more, and things became difficult. I was never sure what he wanted from her, maybe to get back together, but he never flirted with her or brought her flowers. He'd only look at her or stand close to her.

In some ways, I found Christine the most intriguing member of the band. She had a very sharp tongue. One time I was walking through the studio, whistling something to myself. "I *hate* your mindless whistling, Ken," she said. "I hate when people do that!" So, from then on, I tried not to mindlessly whistle.

Christine drank like one of the guys, and she swore like one, too. The only woman I ever met who could do it better was Grace Slick. Christine smoked up a storm, but she played killer keys and sang great hooks. Christine is quite possibly the queen of English blues.

I gave Christine and Stevie a tour of the studio while we waited for the other members of the band to arrive. I remember thinking that they seemed a little prudish and that having two women in the band could certainly change the all-guy dynamics I was used to—but I had no idea how much.

Lindsey came striding in right after that, rubbing his hands together, his long coat flying behind him. This meant he was happy and enthusiastic—ready to go. This was the happy Lindsey who I wished would walk through the door every day. I soon found out that Lindsey could be very unpredictable, depending on which side of the bed he woke up on. If his first thought was positive, he was off to a good day; if he had a negative one—say, he awoke doubting the quality of yesterday's track, we would have to scrutinize it for hours.

I found (and still find) Lindsey to be extraordinarily talented, extraordinarily opinionated, and extraordinarily annoying. He was twenty-six when I met him, a little younger than Stevie, and he had recently been added as a songwriter and a guitar player. *Rumours* would be his second album with Fleetwood Mac. Mick had hired him and Stevie Nicks based on what he'd heard on *Buckingham Nicks*, which was well crafted but, all things considered, a relative bomb.

Lindsey was an integral part of driving Fleetwood Mac into the stratosphere, but, creatively, he was the band member who had the most conflicts with others. I had more conflicts with him than with any of the other band members. Yet I have to admit, Fleetwood Mac had put out nine albums before Lindsey joined, and I'd never heard of the band. With Lindsey's contribution to the White Album and *Rumours*, everyone in the world who'd ever heard a song on the radio would eventually know who Fleetwood Mac was by the time *Rumours* had run its course. Personal relationships aside, I can't say for sure that this would be true if Lindsey Buckingham hadn't been part of Fleetwood Mac.

Finally, Mick Fleetwood and John McVie—the beating heart and the soulful groove of the band—brought up the rear. This was the duo's eleventh album together as Fleetwood Mac, yet it was another beginning. I could see they were both in a good mood.

"Morning, lads," said Mick, standing tall and proper.

"Morning, mates!" said sailor John.

Mick was somewhere between twenty-eight and thirty-four, but who knew? He was 6'6", and that, somehow, along with his long hair and beard, made it hard to tell his age. He was a founding member of the band. Mick was very aristocratic. The way he formed sentences was impeccable. When he spoke, everyone stopped and listened. He was quiet and wise, and he had a great sense of humor. He loved to laugh, but he was also a straight shooter.

Mick is still one of the most amazing drummers I've ever met. He had his rack of tom drums arranged back to front. Most drummers place them from high to low (in pitch) from their left to right, but Mick chose to place his mid, high, low. I think perhaps this helped him develop his unique style.

He hit his drums very hard, except for his kick drum. For some reason, when he played his high hat, it distracted him. He would keep perfect beat with his kick, but he played it so softly that we could hear his mouth noises through his kick mic. "Ol' Feather Foot," Richard and I began to call him. He'd be singing, "Muaa, muaa, muaa," in time with the music to help him play.

Mick liked his Heineken, and he definitely liked to get a buzz on in the studio. He was rarely a problem, and his intoxication caused only occasional inconvenience and slightly more frequent mischief.

John, thirty, was also one of the founding members of the band. He had played bass on all of the band's previous ten albums. John was one of the sweetest guys you could ever meet; he was quiet, shy, and probably insecure. I liked him very much. He has a great ear and plays a smooth bass line. He also has a great sense of humor.

John is probably one of the best bass players in the world. He could play a new song twice and come up with the most amazing melodic bass lines. He and Mick formerly were with John Mayall and the Bluesbreakers, playing their favorite kind of music—blues. Later, I found out that when John joined Mayall, he had a day gig as a tax inspector.

When John started with Mayall, he listened to B.B. King's records. He also had a unique collection of basses from the standards, such as the Fenders, to the classics, including Paul McCartney's P-Bass, and he was always on the lookout for new additions to his collection.

John was pretty quiet when he was sober. He was British. He could be quite the gentleman—smart, funny, and warm. Yet soon he would show his darker side; he had always been a heavy drinker, a problem he was repeatedly fighting.

Richard had a drumstick in his hand, and he immediately thrust it into Mick's left side, like a sword. Mick allowed it to go between his arm and his side, capturing it with his arm, leaving it protruding out of his chest. He gasped and clutched his chest with his right hand around the sword and staggered backward as if he had a Shakespearean actor buried inside him.

"That will teach you to be last to a session!" Richard said. "Now off with you to tune your drums."

Mick still had a lot of hair back then, and, in some ways, he looked like Rasputin with his dark full beard. At his height, he could seem a little intimidating, but to know him was to love him. He broke out in a big laugh at the prank. "I shall not be last a-gain, Sir," he proclaimed.

Rhino handed Mick a cold Heineken and the day began. I was a little surprised at the skit I had just witnessed. I wondered if participating in these pranks would also be part of my job. I hoped not.

The band was assembled, ready to rock and roll, but Richard and I still had to finish the setup. We had everything in place; the next thing was to get the drum sounds, because the drums are the center of a rock album. I have a rule that I don't press RECORD until the drums are perfect. For the next thirty minutes or so, Mick went through each of his drums, hitting them and adjusting the tuning pegs until they sounded right to his ears.

When Mick was ready, Richard and I went into the control room to listen to his drums through my mic setup. We were in search of that perfect sound, which we knew would be key to the overall sound of the music. I opened up Mick's kick-drum mic, and it sounded like a toy drum, small and unimpressive. I brought up the volume fader of his snare mic, and the same thing happened—it had no bite.

Mick goes for it, so we can hear what his drums sound like.

The drums sound weak, and frustration begins to set in.

We turned up the volume of the control room speakers, but we got the same limp effect. Mick's huge tom drums sounded embarrassing. The cymbals sucked, too. Everything that came out of the instruments just disappeared into the brightly colored, tie-dyed baffles that hung on the walls around the room, sucking in the sound. We were doing something very, very wrong, and we didn't know how to fix it. We moved the microphones. We rearranged the baffles. We changed every setting on the console. Nothing helped. This was my winning setup. It always worked! But not that day.

What's different? I wondered. The speakers, the room, the console? I didn't know the answer.

Lindsey came into the control room and pulled out his bag of pot. Then he asked us for a tape box, which he liked to use to roll his joints. He picked his favorite producer's chair and sat down as if he were there to oversee the process.

John had Ray bring him his favorite bass and a breakfast cocktail, a screwdriver, heavy on the vodka. Christine's keyboards were already set up, and she asked for a glass of Blue Nun to be brought promptly to her as she sat on the couch in the rear of the control room. Stevie came into the control room and took a puff off Lindsey's newly rolled joint.

A few minutes later, Mick followed the others into the control room. "What's up, guys? How do my drums sound?"

"Pretty weird, Mick," I said. "Your kick has no balls. We're going to need to work on this some more. Do you feel like going out and playing them again?"

"Sure." Mick signaled for Ray to get him another Heineken, and out he went to hit his drum kit. The other band members decided to go somewhere else, rather than listen to drums being beaten. Mick was a real trooper: he'd hit; we'd listen; we'd make suggested changes; he'd hit again—but the drums just didn't sound right.

This went on for five days—five excruciating days—while the band sat around and drank, smoked, and grew more silent and anxious at how long it was taking us to finish the setup. I could almost hear them thinking, Did we hire amateurs?

Never before or since in my career have I spent this much time on drums. In the end, it was a good lesson learned.

"God knows, if the drums aren't right, then the song is not survivable," Mick said at some point. Richard and I knew he was right.

The more we worked on the drums, the more Richard could see how much it was working my nerves. Richard was worried, too. On the White Album, he had used Keith Olsen as engineer. Keith was a real pro, but he had also been working in a studio that he knew intimately. In Sausalito, Richard had to help me solve this problem or go down with the ship.

On the surface, the band seemed to be patient, and they continued to cooperate while their engineers floundered. I was sure that they felt as if they'd made a huge mistake in hiring us.

I started to hear subtle digs in the tone of their voices. "Ken, should we bring in one of the other Record Plant engineers to help you guys?" Mick asked politely.

"No, we got this. We just need to find the key, and we'll be good to go," I said. I knew my mic choice was good, so I thought it must be something in the room or Mick's drums.

Nevertheless, I could feel dirty looks coming at me from across the room. The pressure was practically suffocating. I was sure that I was going to get fired. I had just gotten the biggest break of my career, and I was blowing it in the first few days.

On the fourth day, Richard put his jokes into overdrive. He and Mick played the lawyer game. Richard would say to Mick in the most accusative voice, standing almost a foot below the giant Mick, with his finger pointed up at Mick, "Isn't it true, *Mr. Fleetwood*, that you are knowingly withholding cocaine from your friends?" I knew that, in part, Richard was doing this to keep the focus off me and the drum sounds. The drums became my epic challenge.

Later that day, I was in the studio, cramped on my side with my head in a kick drum when Mick came bursting into the room with news. Big news. He called us all into the control room.

"'Over My Head' is in the top-twenty singles in *Billboard* this week!" Mick said. The song had been released about nine weeks earlier, and it was now Fleetwood Mac's biggest hit in America. Ever. The White Album was also still surging up the charts, propelled by the success of "Over My Head," which was now getting a ton of radio play. "Over My Head" would soon peak at number five on the Billboard top 100 and would help the White Album sell more than 4.5 million copies, reaching number one several months later.

Christine giggled, then said in her Dame Edna voice, "Well, for fuck's sake, break out the champagne. I want to celebrate!"

Stevie and Lindsey both congratulated Christine, because "Over My Head" was her song. "Thank you, guys. I love you. I couldn't have done it without you." They all hugged.

For me, sitting up at the console and looking back at them during this historic moment, I just thought, Wow! How great is this? These were great numbers for a band that had had only marginal success in America. The sales pointed in only one direction: toward the top of the Billboard pop chart.

I couldn't wait for my radio mix of "Rhiannon" to be released. I figured that things would really get crazy then! I was proud of that mix—after all, it was the reason I had this long-term gig. My radio mix was shorter than the album version, and I had mixed it to bring out maximum sound quality from car speakers. Keith Olsen had mixed the album version, but because the band had had a falling out with him, it had opened up the door for me.

The band felt jubilant, but this only ratcheted up the pressure on Richard and me to get our shit together. Now, as they say, it cranked up the intensity to eleven. Of course, the pressure was also building on the band, too. The band's photographer, Herbie Worthington, had recently taken a picture of Lindsey sitting on the floor at the departure gate of an airport, innocently playing his guitar. This type of youthful anonymity would soon be gone.

The band knew that their record label would expect them to follow up their current success with an even bigger hit, which meant more fans, more fame, and more money. Meanwhile, they were sitting around watching three young engineers with their heads stuck in a drum. I could feel the band's anxiety in every clipped comment.

"So, do you guys think we're going to be ready to record . . . today?" Lindsey asked, the celebration over. I could see the veins pounding in his neck. He was starting to lose it. I stared at Mick's lifeless drum set, and I didn't know what the hell I was going to do.

Of course, there's a huge upside to working with a rock band with a hit on their hands, even if you're on their shit list. Wait till the girls in town hear about this! I thought, with a big smile on my face. I looked down at Scooter and rubbed his head behind his ears. Scooter loved that. He stretched out his front legs and pushed his butt in the air.

The first chance I got, I went out to tell the girls at the front desk, especially Nina, about the band's success.

Nina looked up at me as I stood before her. "Well, hi," she said.

"Did you hear about 'Over My Head?'" I asked.

Nina was sharp, and she always had her ear to the ground. "Yeah, I did," she said. "Top twenty." She stood and gave me a big hug—as if I'd had something to do with the band's current success. I didn't stop her.

Yep, things were looking pretty good. Now, if only I could get some decent sounds out of that board.

While we were settling into our studio in Sausalito, Don Henley, Glenn Frey, and the rest of the Eagles were dug in at the Record Plant,

L.A., recording their monster album, *Hotel California*, which *Rumours* would eventually supplant at the top of the charts. The title song of their album, with its sense of lost, hopeless decadence, its eerie, druggy claustrophobia, was written about being trapped in the studio, panicked and sweaty and unable to get out. The Record Plant, L.A., was their Hotel California.

Soon, the Eagles and Fleetwood Mac would be grouped with other artists as members of what became known as the Southern California sound. This always fascinated me, because the Eagles' first album, *Eagles*, was recorded in London. They actually brought the tapes to L.A., and I helped edit the album during my first years in the industry. So, even though Fleetwood Mac recorded *Rumours* for the first few months in Northern California, the time we later spent in Southern California would come to define the band.

Our Record Plant stay in Sausalito was something different from the Eagles' experience, unique to us. Yet our recording sessions certainly shared a lot in common with their experiences: they were druggy, claustrophobic, and there were days where I felt that I could never leave. Which is probably why the band had chosen this studio—to get away from all of the daily distractions of home and to be thrust together, for better or for worse.

Having worked through the weekend and now on the fifth straight day of dicking with the equipment, I realized what was wrong—you can't just listen to one instrument and tell how it sounds. That's like looking at a beautiful painting through a microscope. I decided that the band should just go out to the studio and play together and work on something new and forget about the sound.

"Fuck this," I said to Richard, beyond desperate to overcome this initial hurdle. "Let's go for it."

The band started playing a new song written by Christine that at this point was called "Keep Me There." It would later become known as "The Chain," and all of the band members would eventually be credited with writing it, which was unique in all of Fleetwood Mac's writing credits.

The API console at the Record Plant was very similar to Heider's studio 4 console. To get these consoles to sound good, I would have to

My view from the control room.

open up the mic pre-amps and back down the faders. When I did this, the console sounded best, but it wasn't conventional wisdom.

Now that the band was playing together, though, I started twisting the console knobs to their extremes. I wasn't listening to only the drums now, but to how everything fit together. I shoved up the bass to sit even with the kick drum. I pushed the electric guitar off to the left speaker and turned up the treble so that it stung like a bee.

Then I pushed the organ to the right speaker and made it bright. I put Christine's vocal right down the middle with some reverb on it. Those troublesome drums were spread wide apart, and I shoved them up so that they supported the whole band.

It took me about five minutes before we were ready to record our first version of our first track after five long days. Richard and I had been so intent on getting every sound perfect that we had forgotten about the big picture: the instruments have to sound great together. It doesn't really matter that much what each one sounds like alone.

As it turned out, that was all Richard and I needed to do—get pissed off, not take any shit from the console, and put it all together. It was an attitude that would serve us well during the next year, helping us muscle through much greater obstacles to come.

We were finally ready to record a song. The band played "Keep Me There" twice, from top to bottom, while we listened to the basic foundation of the music: the drums, John's new Alembic fretless bass, the electric guitar, the organ, and the work vocal—wow, a superstar foundation! Later, Richard named this guitar of John's "the Bay Bridge" as a joke, based on our time in Sausalito, and especially for its all-stainless-steel neck.

In the control room, Richard and I began to get really excited. And when I get excited, I can't sit down. I stood on one long leg with the other knee on the console. Richard was dramatically bobbing his head to the beat of the music. When his head bobbed like that, I knew we were doing well. I looked at Cris, back by the twenty-four-track tape machine, and he was moving and grooving, his brown afro trying to keep up with the movement of his head.

Something magical was happening while the band was playing down the song—I could see that they had started to feel the excitement, too. Mick was smiling, and he gave me a thumbs-up. He liked what he was hearing in his headphones. John was standing in front of Mick, so he could feel Mick's drums in his chest, and he locked into his famous Mac groove. Lindsey stood playing his Fender Strat, suspended from his shoulders, nodding his head from side to side. Christine, at the organ, also gave us a wink. Stevie was playing tambourine in the vocal booth on my left. She looked so young and fresh in her layers of silk cloth.

For the first time since we'd arrived at the Record Plant, Sausalito, music pulsed throughout the studio. Finally, I was hearing not just one or two instruments or a sound check, but a complete rock band playing a potential hit song. The frustrations of the last five days instantly disappeared in that moment, and we all felt our adrenaline rise. I could practically see the anticipation in the atmosphere. Our family almost felt like it was whole.

"Keep Me There" was a fairly typical Christine McVie song, with verse, chorus, verse, chorus, instrumental break, chorus. Except, as the band played it down, a musical tension developed that needed to be released from the song. So, after the last chorus, they started playing a jam or tag out, where everyone played hot and heavy. John started it with an amazing bass line in the break before the tag. Then Christine and Lindsey started playing off each other for about three minutes. Each time they played the song, it got better. Something amazing was taking shape. I was trembling with excitement and anticipation.

Ready for the band to play the song for the third time, I looked at Cris. There was new tape loaded on the machine. I armed the 24-track recorder into all twenty-four tracks: RECORD ready. Richard pressed the talkback button to open the console mic to the band.

"Guys, it sounds fucking great. Let's put one down."

As Richard released the button, the index and ring fingers of my right hand pressed PLAY and RECORD simultaneously on the 24-track remote box, sitting next to me, and that big beautiful tape recorder started rolling. The one-pound roll of two-inch-wide tape started turning at the same time that the twenty-four vu meters, mounted above the tape, lit up bright red. This meant we were recording. With my left hand, I pressed the talkback again.

"'Keep Me There,' take one," I said. "Somebody count it off." And that was recorded at the beginning of the take.

I released the talkback button. "Wheels up," I said to Richard. We both sat down in front of the console to ride levels, if necessary. This was it. We were finally recording *Rumours*.

Mick sat at his drums. He took another hit off his cold Heineken. Then he handed it to Rhino. He quickly adjusted his headphones and raised both of his arms up high above his drums, then hit his sticks together as he counted aloud, "One, two, one, two, three, four . . ." Suddenly, the most beautiful sound I had ever heard, a wall of music, came out of the speakers as every member of the band hit on the downbeat of one.

I had ten mics on Mick's drums, two on John's bass, two on Christine's organ, three on Lindsey's electric guitar, and one for Christine to sing the "ruff" lead vocal into. On that downbeat, when that tsunami of sound hit, all of the meters on the console flared to life, and I could feel my blood run with the sounds that came out of that room.

I checked the levels on the board. Yep. I looked back at the 24-track in the rear corner of the studio. Yep. Everything was turning or bouncing or rolling the way it was supposed to, the red lights of the 24-track glowing steadily. The big roll of tape turned; the music poured in, and the sound was perfect. That's the moment that makes a recording engineer love his job. It just doesn't get any better than that. Richard nudged the main speaker volume up a little bit.

"Oh, yeah!" I yelled to him over the blaring speakers.

Richard gave me a thumbs-up and closed his eyes, and his head began to bounce with the music.

The song felt fantastic and, about halfway through, the band got even more inventive, jamming and loosening up. At the break in the middle, John played this amazing bass line that we kept in the final recording of "The Chain": "Dum, da da dum, da da dum, da da dummmm." Then Lindsey lit into a minute-and-a-half screaming guitar solo out of the blue. Richard and I just looked at each other. Holy shit. Where did that come from?

To this day, I still think John's bass is one of the most memorable moments on the record—and one of the few pieces that survived from its first incarnation.

As the band finished the song, I held up my hands, signaling everyone not to talk. As soon as I stopped the tape, Richard hit the talkback and excitedly exclaimed, "You've got to come in and hear this!"

The band members took off their headphones and piled into the control room, finding places to sit so they could listen to what they'd just laid down. Lindsey was visibly excited, rubbing his hands together. Christine was giggling with excitement. Stevie said, "You guys, that felt amazing!"

John and Mick sat up by us at the console to hear it better. Cris rewound the tape to the top of the song. I pressed PLAY. Richard cranked up the speakers, and this talkative bunch sat in silence as the track they had just recorded blared over the big studio speakers. When it was over, everyone jumped to their feet, dancing and high-fiving. It was great, and we all knew it.

Mick looked down at Richard and me from his great height, wearing a grave expression. Then he broke into a huge smile. "So, what took you guys so fucking long?"

Richard and I got a big hug from every member of the band. And *Rumours* was under way.

3

Go Your Own Way

There was a part of me that was very offended by the lyrics of "Go Your Own Way," but the album really needed that big, up-tempo song.

—Stevie Nicks

After working so hard to get a recording of "Keep Me There," we all heaved a sigh of relief. We had the template down now for that track, and when we wanted to work on it again, we could put the tape back up and lay the next brick on the foundation.

I didn't know it yet, but for the next year, we would go through every song we recorded over and over again, listening for the perfect piece of each sound, each voice, until we had perfection or as close to it as we could get. Sometimes we would get on a roll and do a couple of parts in a day, but that day, the end of a very long week, we broke early to celebrate.

Christine and Stevie went back to their hotel, and the boys—well, we went to see what Sausalito's nightlife was like. We had heard about the famous Trident Restaurant—a rock star hangout—from the staff at the Record Plant. The Trident was also famous for its waitresses, who were supposed to be knockouts. The heart of Sausalito was about a five-minute drive south on Bridgeway Boulevard toward San Francisco.

As we drove, the empty warehouses gave way to the lights of San Francisco Bay on our left and small shops and restaurants to our right. I liked this quaint little town a lot. It was right on San Francisco Bay, overlooking Alcatraz, San Francisco, and the Bay Bridge. When I was younger, I had come here many times with my family.

The last time I had been to Sausalito was when I turned twenty-one. My parents had taken me up to San Francisco to celebrate my birthday at Fisherman's Wharf. We decided to take the ferry over to Sausalito and spend the night. I was about to turn twenty-one the next day. My dad bought me a beer on the boat to celebrate, but the bartender carded me and refused to serve me.

The next day when we returned on the boat to Fisherman's Wharf, I was twenty-one, and I decided to buy my dad a beer. I couldn't wait for this other bartender to ask for my ID, but he looked at me and said, "'Certainly, sir." Damn! When you're a kid waiting your whole life to be legal, it's really important to show that license the first time. Yes, I liked Sausalito, and I think the band did, too. When Richard, Lindsey, and I got to the Trident, it was busy. We went in and noticed that it was very dark, and the view through the restaurant was completely obscured by numerous decorative cloths hanging from the ceiling. We realized that if we sat down in one of their booths, we would be completely isolated, with no hope of meeting any of the town's women. The Trident had been designed by the same people who had designed the Record Plant, and it was meant to be a romantic place for couples to go. Disappointed, we went to Agatha's Pub across the street.

Agatha's was a quaint single-story restaurant/bar carved out of a converted house with a panoramic view of the Bay and the San Francisco skyline across the water. We hadn't been inside for more than two minutes when a beautiful waitress walked past Richard. She slowed down to look at us, then she said, "Well, hi there! Just sit anywhere, and I'll be back in a moment to take your order."

We all just stared at her. Suddenly, another equally gorgeous wait-ress passed between Lindsey and me. We looked at one another, and Richard said, "Oh, yeah." We knew we had found our new home away from home.

There were about twenty round tables at Agatha's. Each table had a white tablecloth and a small vase with a rose. A short bar stood opposite the front door at the back of the building, where the food and drinks were made.

We sat just about in the middle of the little restaurant/pub. As I looked out the many panes of glass facing the Trident and past to the Bay Bridge, I could see the magnificent lights of San Francisco shining on the tranquil bay. This did feel like home. There was something very calming about this place, very right.

The women of Sausalito seemed magnificent! They were all so fresh, healthy, and happy looking. I'm not talking only about the waitresses, which to my count were about seven or eight—all stunning—but the clientele were beautiful, too! The three of us felt really alive at that moment. We were like kids. Remember, this was the midseventies, and hair was all the rage. Most guys had long hair and beards, and the girls seemed to have either long straight beautiful hair or long curly crazy hair.

We met three girls that night, Christina, Rachel, and Ginger, who would all become more than friends during our stay. Crazy Christina came over to our table and took our order. She had such a happy smile, and her hair was like Lindsey's, a full Afro head of hair that bounced and swayed as she walked. She would eventually play a small role in the his-tory of *Rumours*.

Lovely Rachel brought our order moments later. I think they were all trying to meet us.

Still glowing because the day had gone so well, we toasted one another and talked excitedly about what tomorrow had in store. I was starting to get to know these guys a little better, and we all got on great. An hour later, we got the boot from Agatha's because they were closing. Before we left, we somehow managed to let it slip that we had a top-twenty hit on the U.S. singles charts (I might have said "world").

Christina Conte dated Lindsey during our stay in
Sausalito.

We headed back to the house, and everyone was so happy that nobody
complained about my wild driving. I had made a two-track recording of
the day's work on my Revox, a small reel-to-reel tape player. For the rest
of the night, the boys sat at the house and drank beer, and we listened
to that tape of "Keep Me There" over and over and over until we all fell
asleep.

The next day, Tuesday, February 3, 1976, we arrived at the studio
about noon, the time I had suggested as we were leaving the day before.
It was another gray day, and the drizzle closed everything down, making
us feel as if we were stranded in some alien land. Inside the cozy studio,
we decided that the next thing to do was to sing a good lead vocal on
"Keep Me There."

But it was not to be. While Christine was warming up, she noticed that the piano needed tuning, and, fortunately, the piano tuner was still in the building. We called him in, and he went to work on the piano. We left the tuner alone and went inside the control room to listen to "Keep Me There" a couple more times.

Although the song had sounded great the day before when we were in the studio—and even better when we were drinking beer back at the house—now I realized that "Keep Me There" had a long way to go before it would be finished.

The Record Plant had a full kitchen equipped with two girls who would make anything we wanted, but when we called for lunch, it wasn't ready, either. We milled about, looking for something to do. We were off to a slow start. These things happen.

In the control room, Christine and Stevie were making small talk. Also with us were John and his new girlfriend, Sandra (pronounced Sondra). Christine and Sandra were sitting on the couch behind me, drinking champagne and talking pleasantly. Sandra was also British, and she was a real sweetheart. Even though Christine and John's marriage was breaking up, Christine liked Sandra, and they were becoming fast friends. I guess John had good taste in women.

Maybe Christine didn't have a problem with Sandra because Christine was seeing the band's lighting director, Curry Grant. Christine wasn't jealous of John's relationship with Sandra, but John was jealous of hers with Curry. To make matters worse, Christine wanted Curry to come visit her that upcoming weekend in Sausalito, and John wasn't happy about it.

John started arguing with Christine about Curry coming. "Chris, I don't want you bringing Curry up here to the studio," John said quietly, almost as if he was trying to make it so that only Christine could hear him.

"I don't have a problem with you bringing Sandra here," Christine said, her voice louder than his. "Why should you have a problem with me bringing Curry here?"

Both of them began to raise their voices, and I spun my chair around just in time to hear John say, "Yeah, but Sandra means nothing to me!"

Sandra stood up. *Splash!* She threw her full glass of champagne right into John's face and stormed out of the studio.

Christine fumed. "John, you are a fucking asshole!" She charged out right behind Sandra.

John, more than a little drunk, followed them both, flinging curses around the room like confetti.

Richard and I looked at each other. We were both in shock, but he was less surprised than I was because he already knew about Christine's ongoing affair with Curry and also about John's drinking problem and his temper.

When John was sober, he was a kind, gentle person, but his world soured when he drank. I was still ignorant of all of this, and it was weird to see Sandra dash out, followed by Christine and John. I wasn't even sure whether Christine was angry at John because he was having an affair or for being so rude to Sandra, his new girlfriend. How bizarre was that?

In fact, in my short stints on projects with Fleetwood Mac and other bands, I had never seen any personal problems, especially nothing that

John and Sandra go for a walk in Sausalito.

would have prepared me for the storm that we were about to fly into. There was one time when I was working with Loggins and Messina in Wally Heider's studio 3, and Jim Messina got really pissed at Kenny Loggins.

Jim started yelling at Kenny, saying he had no talent, was useless, and was nothing, and Jim was the real talent! All of this with me only about three feet away. Kenny just let Jim rant and didn't even argue. Later, when Kenny had so much success as a solo artist, I had to think, Good for you, Kenny!

Richard shared with me a little about John and Christine's relationship, explaining that they had decided to split up a while ago. They were still married, but both were dating. On good days they were amicable with each other; on bad days, not so much.

Christine once said to me, "You know, Ken, I used to be perfect until I married John." John was sitting in the room at that time, watching her laugh at a joke that I didn't get. Shit, here we go again! I thought.

Then Christine explained to me that her maiden name actually was "Perfect." Before she married John, she had recorded a solo album (*Christine Perfect*), one album as a session player with the early incarnation of Fleetwood Mac with Peter Green, and two albums with Chicken Shack, which had a hit in Britain called "I'd Rather Go Blind" that Christine sang lead vocals on. She won Melody Maker awards for female vocalist in 1969 and 1970.

Needless to say, we didn't get much work done that day. The booze was already out, and John had taken Sandra out to try to patch things up. We got a vocal out of Christine on "Keep Me There," and then she left. Lindsey and Stevie were off talking somewhere—probably about their relationship. When one couple began fighting, it became contagious. Even Mick didn't seem quite himself that day. After Sandra threw champagne in John's face, Mick seemed to go deep into his thoughts. The whole Sandra, Christine, John thing had put everybody off, and I was still in the dark about most of it.

That was the eighth day in a row of work. Of course, I should have known that nobody can work that long every day, nonstop, without starting to crack. We all needed a break. So, that night, Richard and I headed back to Agatha's. On the way we stopped at a 7-Eleven across from the studio on Bridgeway Boulevard. Inside, we met a very hammered Denis Lambert, of Lambert and Nuttycombe, working behind the counter. Lambert and Nuttycombe had had some great folk hits in the late sixties and early seventies that helped me get through a lot of college boredom. Richard and I chatted with Denis for a while.

On the counter in front of Denis was a large glass jar full of twelve-inch round chocolate chip cookies. Suddenly, I needed a chocolate chip cookie, and I promise you it was the best tasting cookie I have ever had. I asked Denis where I could get them, and as it turned out, the Pine Street Bakery, just up the road, was responsible. It was closed, but the sign in front read, "Open at 4:00 a.m."

"I bet this will come in handy sometime," I said.

"Definitely!" Richard agreed.

When we left the 7-Eleven, I couldn't get past the fact that a famous recording artist whose records I had at home was working behind the counter of a 7-Eleven. It was a sobering thought about our own prospects.

At 6 a.m. the next morning, Wednesday, February 4, 1976, Cathy Callon, who lived at the Record Plant house as the caretaker, knocked on my bedroom door, frantic. "Ken, wake up! Come quick! I need your help."

I jumped out of bed with a headache after only about three hours of sleep. I could barely open my eyes. I put my hand up to my head.

"It's Scooter," Cathy said, pulling my arm as I followed her outside into the searing bright morning light. "Look," she said, pointing to my dog.

Scooter had been humping Cathy's dog, but the little female had gotten bored and had tried to walk away. Yet Scooter was stuck inside her. I didn't know this was possible. Her dog was walking around with Scooter being pulled backward by his "ouch."

"I bet that hurts," I said.

Cathy laughed hysterically. Me, not so much. I needed my shades. All I could think was, The first time the sun comes out since I've moved to Sausalito, and it has to be now?

I grabbed a garden hose and turned it on full, blasting Scooter with a steady stream of water until the cold water had its effect on his male member, and he and Cathy's dog were free to go their own way.

"Damn it, Scooter, get in the house!" I was kind of laughing to myself. I think Scooter was the first of the guys in the house to score!

It took me a while to dry off Scooter and get back to sleep. While I was sleeping, Richard went to breakfast with Lindsey.

Everyone dragged themselves into the studio late that day, around twelve-thirty or so. I pulled into 2200 Bridgeway just as Lindsey and Richard walked in, both of them very excited.

I was disappointed that I hadn't been invited to go to breakfast with them. Richard and Lindsey were thick as thieves and full of ideas, and I wanted to be in the loop. They'd brought in a cassette of one of Lindsey's songs, "Go Your Own Way," something he'd been tinkering with since a few months earlier when the band had been on tour in Florida. They had been playing it all morning.

Richard asked Cris Morris to play the cassette for everyone so they could get an idea of how the song went. Cris obliged, and Richard cranked up the volume on the big control room monitors. Lindsey played a hard-strummed acoustic guitar and sang loudly. Being that we were listening to a cassette, the fidelity was pretty bad. The lyrics weren't fully worked out on this tape yet, so what he sang on the tape were only partial words and sentences. The rest was just Lindsey singing musical notes.

I was a little surprised at the intensity of his vocal, almost angry, and I wondered what Lindsey was driving at. This version was pretty raucous, compared to what it would end up sounding like. At this point, I thought it was kind of a stinker of a song; however, I couldn't wait to hear what would happen when everyone played on it. The rest of the band seemed to like the song. This was only the third day of real recording and our second song, so we were really only establishing our work ethic at this stage.

The band took their usual spots in the control room. Stevie usually sat on the sofa with Christine and both of their dogs, Duster and Ginny. Mick and John perched in their rolling chairs, and Lindsey sat up at the console with Richard and me. Scooter, a very independent dog, would be either with me, under the console, or out of the studio trying to get fed by someone. The guys were sipping their coffees as they listened to the rough tape.

John, being a bassist and used to working off others, wanted Lindsey to play "Go Your Own Way" on acoustic guitar, instead of playing it from the cassette. I hit the talkback and asked Ray, Lindsey's roadie, who was in the studio tweaking the previous day's setup, to bring Lindsey's acoustic into the control room with us. John asked Ray to bring in his bass. Lindsey, sitting in front of me and about five feet away from John, began playing. John joined in with a great bass line almost immediately—as if he had already mapped it in his head during the first playback.

A lot of Fleetwood Mac's songs began their evolution this way, and I was starting to get a sense of how the band worked together to create a song. No one in the band could read or write music. They did it the hard way, by memory. Someone—in this case, Lindsey—would come in with an idea. He'd say something like, "'Go Your Own Way' is verse, chorus, verse, chorus. If you get lost, just stop and ask."

This is the view John had of the control room from his seat, with Mick to his left and Lindsey and Christine to the right.

That was usually enough for everyone to get going. I'd often ask whether Lindsey was going to play electric or acoustic, which bass guitar would sound best for the song, and what keyboard Christine should play. Finally, I'd ask if there was anything for Stevie to do on the song.

Then the fun began. All of the members of the band went out into the studio's recording area on the other side of the large double-sided glass separating the control room from the studio, and sat down at their starting instruments: Mick with his eight-inch Ludwig snare, John with his Fender Bassman, and Christine at her Hammond B3 organ. Lindsey chose his 1959 Fender Stratocaster, and Stevie picked up her tambourine, festooned with long black ribbons.

Lindsey started out playing the electric guitar, instead of the acoustic, because he liked playing in the same room with everyone else, and, best of all, we wouldn't get any leakage from the other instruments into his electric guitar. He could look into everyone's eyes, so communication was easier.

Stevie makes her musical contribution to the band.

I had set up a vocal mic so that he could sing a rough vocal and at the same time call out the chord changes for the first couple of rundowns. He started playing the verse licks in eighth notes, then after four bars he sang the verse in his piercing tenor.

He nodded, indicating that the chorus was here, and sang out the lyrics he was sure of: "You can go your own way . . ." Then Lindsey stopped. "Okay," he said, "That's the song. Play two of those, then solo, chorus, and out." Everyone nodded. John was already halfway to having his bass line figured out.

"What are you hearing for the drums?" Mick asked Lindsey.

On the ride in that morning, Lindsey had told Richard that for this song, he heard an unusual, tribal-sounding drumbeat that would have Mick's tom-toms playing a powerful rhythm, something like the drums in the Stones' "Street Fighting Man." Lindsey started playing the guitar and singing the drum part he envisioned Mick playing, "Bam, ba, bam, bam, bam, ba, bam." In his head, Lindsey heard a thundering, offbeat rhythm for Mick to play on his toms. Mick wasn't sure what Lindsey was looking for exactly, but he knew he didn't have it yet.

Richard and I went back into the control room to work on sounds, while the band worked the kinks out of the song's arrangement. Lindsey started playing the song again from the top, and Mick was slowly getting it, but it was very rough. Then John came to the rescue with his bass, and I could hear that they were onto something.

"Chorus!" Lindsey shouted, and Christine brought in the organ at the top of the chorus. Stevie shook the tambourine loudly, and Mick, as if by instinct, played the chorus this time in straight 4/4, making for a dramatic change of feeling. "You can go your own way, go your own wa-aay!" Lindsey sang with a huge smile on his face.

Just then I noticed Stevie. She was playing her tambourine, but she didn't look like she was having much fun.

John, out of nowhere, came up with another of his classic hook lines and played it through the chorus.

"Verse!" Lindsey yelled, and Mick fell back into his thundering tom beat. Now it was starting to come together.

I whipped around and looked back at Cris. "Clean tape?" I mouthed. He gave me a thumbs-up. "Good to go," I said to Richard. We didn't want to waste a second. I was busy working on the sounds, and Richard's head was bobbing up and down with the beat, which we all knew meant that the groove was right. It was perfect.

Suddenly, the band screeched to a noisy halt, as Lindsey jumped up, turned, and screamed at me at the top of his lungs, "Damn it, Ken! Let Richard fucking get in there and do something!" He was screaming at me so hard that his face had turned bright red, and I could see the veins popping out of his neck.

Flabbergasted, I hit the talkback and blurted out, "I'm not stopping him!"

I stepped away from the board so Lindsey could see that I was making room. Richard sat down and just looked at Lindsey as if to say, "Everything's fine in here, idiot."

I didn't know what to make of it. Everything was going great, and then, out of nowhere, blind rage. Over nothing. "Is it me, or is that guy crazy?" I asked Richard.

"You're fine." Richard smiled. "Never mind Lindsey."

I was shocked. Everybody went back to what they had been doing before Lindsey's freak-out without so much as batting an eye. Little did I know that this was the real Lindsey coming out in front of me for the first time. The others were simply used to it.

In truth, it wasn't just that they were used to it, but they allowed it. They understood it. That day's outburst—like the verbal and physical outbursts that would follow—was just the most extreme manifestation of the obsessive character that every member of the band possessed.

Successful musicians are not normal. Your average person doesn't have the kind of single-minded, relentless determination it takes to spend three hundred days a year on the road playing dive bars and half-empty clubs in pursuit of some elusive, vaguely defined dream of stardom.

Each member of the band had his or her obsession. I was quickly learning that it was my job to cater to all of them, even though it often meant being the first one to the studio and the last one to leave every day.

Stevie's obsession was her words. That's where her passion started to verge into mania. Lord help anyone who suggested changing or cutting so much as a syllable of anything she'd written. She was defiant about keeping the tone, rhythm, and meaning of every last syllable in her lyrics—even if nobody else could actually understand them.

For Christine, it was her piano. She had perfect pitch, and the nine-foot Steinway grand piano she played had to be perfectly in tune. This would cause us a lot of angst during the next few weeks. Lord, how we suffered for her piano. To show you how picky she could be, if she didn't like what I was wearing, out of nowhere she'd say something like, "Ken, I hate that shirt!" Christine and I always got along very well, but she never withheld an opinion.

Anyone who saw us in our little Hobbit hole might have looked at Christine's piano tuning or Lindsey's outbursts and decided that they were the most fanatically obsessed members of the band. Outwardly, maybe that was so, but beneath his madcap persona, the most methodically and meticulously fanatical member of the group was undoubtedly its leader: Mick Fleetwood.

In Mick's mind, no amount of hours worked was enough. I guess it was his "No rest for the wicked" theory. This personal philosophy, through the years, had distanced him from his wife and two daughters, and it would ultimately lead to the undoing of his marriage. As the recording progressed, Mick still wasn't happy with his part on "Go Your Own Way." He was determined to do it just as Lindsey heard it in his head.

"Just be an animal, Mick!" Lindsey yelled at him.

"Just get on with it, mate," John said, in a reassuring tone to his rhythm partner.

Mick smiled and nodded agreement. Suddenly, he got this shit-eating grin on his face that I came to know as his Okay-now-watch-this look. Mick reached down and grabbed his just-opened Heineken. (The motto of a good roadie, like a Boy Scout's, is "Be prepared." A roadie understands what his boss needs before he asks for it.) Mick took a long pull off that beer, turned his drumsticks around so that the big ends were hitting the drums, adjusted his headphones, and gave Lindsey the nod.

"One. Two," Lindsey counted. I put the 24-track into RECORD, just in case. "One. Two. Three. Four," Lindsey finished his count in, and here came that wall of sound again. The meters were moving, red lights flashing. They quit after about thirty seconds. I stopped the tape machine and wrote down FS for Take One as a false start. Something wasn't right.

"Don't record for a minute until we figure something out," I said.

The band ran the song down nearly to the end, stopping here and there, making corrections. This gave Richard and me a chance to improve the EQ on our mics. Mick loosened his snares on his drum to make them pop a little more. I boosted 10k to his snare mic's EQ to brighten up the snare's high frequencies, sonically. You see, on a console we have what's called EQ, a small tone control section on each mic channel where I could add or subtract low frequencies, 50 hz to 800 hz (bass), from the sound of the instrument, or midfrequency, 1,000 hz to 7,000 hz (1k to 7k), and finally the high frequency, 8k to 20k, in the highest part of your hearing. This would help me shape each sound to make them all fit together best.

Christine asked for a little more reverb on her organ in her head-phones, and everyone wanted more bass in their headphones. In the studio, every member of the band wore headphones so they could hear one another more clearly.

In the control room, the sound engineers listened on speakers, but it was Cris's job to monitor their headphone mix and make sure it sounded as much like a record as possible. He had a panel of knobs that repre-sented every instrument, so that he could give each band member exactly the sound he or she wanted in the headphones. You'd think every mem-ber of a band would want to hear pretty much the same thing, but that wasn't the case.

For example, Mick was playing his loud drums, so he didn't want to hear very much of them in his headphones—he just wanted enough of his drums so that he could hear how they sounded with the rest of the band. Christine was sitting away from Mick, and her B3 Leslie organ speaker was in an iso booth in another room, so she needed a little of Mick's drums and a lot of her organ, John's bass, and Lindsey's guitar and his vocal. Inside the control room, we made all of the changes so that each person in the band could hear what he or she needed to hear.

"Okay, I'm ready," I said to Richard. "You?"

"Yep," he said, and pushed the talkback. "It's sounding fucking great in here. I think we should start putting them down now."

Everybody nodded, but Mick still wasn't happy with his headphones. This tended to happen after he'd had a few beers. As per his request, we gave him a little more snare in his headset, trying to keep it moving so that all of the band members would stop focusing on their headphones. Clearly, they were working fine because the last takes had been nearly perfect.

Let's get 'em going before we lose 'em! I thought. "Okay, let's do a few!" I said on the talkback. "I have a good feeling about this—I think I smell a Grammy!" Then, without pausing, I put my right hand down onto the talkback button, jumped into RECORD on the 24-track, left hand pressing PLAY and RECORD simultaneously, "Okay, 'Go Your Own Way,' take two, count it off, and kick some ass!"

This time Lindsey counted in at the top of his lungs, "One, two, one, two, three, four . . ."

Mick hit his drumsticks for the last four counts. The guitar started. "Lovin' you . . ." Lindsey sang. The drums were magnificent, the bass incredible: second verse, first chorus, third verse, second chorus, solo section.

"Go, go, go . . ." Richard and I were rooting for them to finish the last chorus.

We were into the tag, the home stretch, and it was just the chorus chord, over and over. They just kept playing, round after round, leaving room for something extra special, should someone think of it. At about six minutes they finally stopped playing. I gave Cris the cut signal, with my hand moving across my throat.

"Do you want to come in and hear that last take?" I asked, but all of the band members had had so much fun that they wanted to play it again.

"If it doesn't feel better, then we'll come in and listen to it," Lindsey said, raring to do another take.

We ended up recording nine takes that day. By that time, it was about 4 p.m., and John was getting grumpy, so we put a lid on it for the afternoon. We hadn't had the energy to get it perfect that day.

That night John went to dinner with Rick Turner, his friend the fine guitar maker. The rest of us took a break for a homemade Record Plant dinner. The two girls in the Record Plant kitchen were real California hippie chicks, and they were always concocting something healthy for us. Well, almost always, anyway.

That night's meal was herb-baked free-range chicken, baked country potato wedges, and a big green spinach salad with mandarin oranges and walnuts. The Record Plant kitchen was rustic and only big enough to hold a picnic table and the two girls who prepared the meals. Christine and Stevie sat at the table and ate. Mick, Lindsey, and Richard dished up and joined Ray and Rhino in the lounge. I filled my plate and took it to the reception area to see the last of the daylight and, of course, Nina.

So far, my progress in getting to know Nina was moving slowly. I'd had no time for flirting during the last nine days, but I knew that Nina knew I was interested in her. I was pretty sure that she was interested in me, too. It was only a matter of finding the right time; however, I also had to consider the other women in town.

I got to the foyer of the Record Plant, plate in hand, and looked out toward the patio.

"Hello, stranger!" Nina said. "So, you finally decided to take a break?" Her comments were warm but professional. After all, she was the studio manager, and she had an image to maintain. "Would you like to sit at my desk and eat your dinner?" she asked.

"Is there somewhere we could go?" I wondered aloud.

"Sure, let's go out to the patio table."

"Why don't you get some food, too, and join me?" I suggested.

"Good idea. I'll be right back."

Nina met me on the patio in a few minutes with her dinner and two beers." Excellent idea!" I said, as she handed me an open brew.

Nina and I sat together for about a half hour, sharing time under the big eucalyptus tree above the patio. It felt nice, just sitting there looking at her and listening to her as we got to know a little about each other for the first time.

We fed Scooter as we talked. Nina's plate was much "greener" than mine, so Scooter stayed close to me. If I lived here long-term, I could really see something happening with Nina, I thought.

Just then, Ray returned from a booze run with plenty of Heineken, Pouilly Fuissé, and Courvoisier for Stevie's vocals (just in case she wanted to sing later that night).

It was starting to get dark, and I figured I should go back inside and check in with the band, because I knew they'd want to work more that night. This had been the longest break I'd had since I had arrived.

I put my hand on Nina's warm hand, squeezing it gently as I stood up. "Thanks for sitting with me," I said. "I hope we can do it again, soon."

"We will," she said, smiling at me.

I thought, Oh, yeah. If I can just take her out on a date or two, then I bet I can move this relationship along.

Nina and I headed back inside, to our respective duties. It had been a nice moment. I hoped that there would be more. Many more. I already liked her a lot.

I greeted the band members at the table on my way back to the studio. They had finished their dinners, too, and they were ready to indulge in Ray's booze stash and, eventually, other things that evening.

Stevie sipped at a Courvoisier in hot water with honey. Aside from the relaxing properties that the booze offered, Stevie claimed that it made for an excellent singing potion.

I headed back to the studio, and the rest of the band came in shortly after that. Ray had told Richard that Nina and I had had dinner on the patio, and I could tell that the boys were proud of me.

Mick came over to me and said, "Nice one, lad!"

"Thanks, Mick," I said. "Good news travels fast around here."

After dinner, Stevie announced, "Okay, now it's my turn. I have a song—it's called 'Gold Dust Woman.'"

She had written "Gold Dust Woman" a few years earlier, before she joined the Mac, back when she didn't do drugs. The song was about the L.A. drug scene, but it was also about Lindsey being too controlling.

That night, we all went back to studio A and settled into our usual places. John was still at dinner. Stevie had a cassette of "Gold Dust Woman." She gave it to Cris to pop into the cassette player, and he reached past me to choose the appropriate switch on the console to crank up the volume.

Interestingly, "Gold Dust Woman" had a strong country feel. It's a little-known story that Stevie's grandfather, Aaron Jess Nicks, was a wandering, boozing, honky-tonk singer, and he taught Stevie how to sing on his lap in these bars.

A.J. lived out of two trailers in the Arizona mountains, and he played guitar, fiddle, and harmonica. He was a pool shark, and he didn't own a car. He took freight trains all over the country. Unfortunately, A.J. never made it in the music business, but Stevie started singing at the age of five when her late grandfather would take her with him to his local gin mill gigs. She once told me that her granddad sang country music to her most of her life. Later when her band, Fritz, opened for Janis Joplin, Stevie's new inspiration became Janis and San Francisco's Grace Slick of Jefferson Airplane.

As the speakers played "Gold Dust Woman," our third song contending for the album, we all listened as Stevie sang lead vocals, swaying back and forth to the rhythm of the music. This was a typical Stevie song, with a couple of piano chords changing back and forth, coupled with her distinctive nasal vocal. I liked the melody against the chords.

We listened down to the song's end, nearly eight minutes of Stevie's music. The cassette version was very plain and uninspiring, with none of the screams and howling that are in the final version; however, the lyrics caught my attention.

What the hell? I thought. How can she sing those lyrics country style? "Silver spoon, dig your grave?" The song had a lot of space, a lot of room for other fun sounds, which during the next twelve months we would fill in. But for now, we were only building the song's foundation.

A lot of people think that when a band goes into the studio to record an album, they simply bang out every song from top to bottom, including background melodies, harmonies, guitar solos, finished lead vocals, and all of the other parts of the song, as is typical of so many Hollywood dramatizations. I'm happy to explain that that's not how it works. As you know from learning how Fleetwood Mac recorded their first song, this process is painstaking. First we laid down the basic track, then we carefully filled in the space with the perfect instruments. Then we added the lead vocals, and, finally, we layered in all of the background vocals.

In the case of "Gold Dust Woman," when we finally got to that point, we realized that this was a very special song that could handle extremely unusual sounds to complete its journey. This is how that process evolved: Lindsey first started to learn the guitar part of the song by playing his acoustic along with the song in the control room. Then we turned off the cassette, and Lindsey played the guitar part, and Stevie played the Fender Rhodes electric piano we had brought into the studio for this purpose.

Lindsey's guitar added a soothing rhythm color to her song. On the last rundown, John returned from dinner. All of the members of the band were now familiar with the song's structure, and they had an idea of what they would be playing, so they proceeded out to the studio to record another song.

Mick was on drums. John was on his new Alembic bass. Lindsey played electric guitar, his Strat again. Now Christine played the Fender Rhodes, and Stevie sang a rough vocal. We ran the song down a few times, this time with Stevie playing the piano and singing, while Christine played the organ. After a couple of passes, though, Christine knew the part and took over on the piano (being the better player), and Stevie was content to focus on her vocal track.

I noticed that John was acting a bit unusual. He must have had more to drink at dinner than he'd had to eat. I remembered that John didn't usually eat that much, maybe because he was a smoker.

He still had his attitude from earlier that day, but he hadn't lost his wit. In preparation for cutting the new track, Lindsey, Richard, and I had a hit of pot.

Noticing this, John said, "I'd rather have my drink than smoke pot and stare at trees!"

Among this group, we always had a battle between the smokers and the drinkers, divided by the Atlantic Ocean. Christine, Mick, and John liked booze—and later coke—while Richard, Lindsey, and I preferred pot. This was primarily because Richard and I couldn't drink alcohol and work the console. It screwed up our acoustic perception and made it impossible to do our engineering jobs. At first, it was pot or coffee, then sometimes we'd substitute a little coke for coffee. I say a little because when I'd had too much, I couldn't sit still.

On the other hand, Stevie was in both camps. She liked to drink and smoke pot. She had the most time on her hands of anyone, and she was always looking for the right inspirational input. Stevie was extremely prolific, and she was young and eager to compose. All she needed was the inspiration, which she got plenty of from her crumbling relationship with Lindsey.

What's interesting is that I later learned that the original band members hadn't been that excited to sign Stevie. Keith Olsen, the band's producer on the previous album, told me that Mick, especially, had wanted only Lindsey for his amazing ability with the guitar.

"I said to Mick that he was probably going to get a duo," Keith told me. "You're going to get a twofer because I don't think Lindsey will join without Stevie. In fact, I told him that he didn't want to split them up because they had 'the Sound.'"

Stevie had a lot to celebrate and a lot to cry about. She and her soul mate were going their own ways. It was a challenge for Stevie to keep everything in perspective. That was her ever-elusive quest. Like most musicians, Stevie would arrive at the studio every day not knowing whether she'd find that magical moment. So, like many of us, Stevie learned to fudge with her emotions with a shot of this or a hit of that, always walking that thin line, looking for her own "gold dust moment."

Stevie, seeing that Lindsey was rolling a joint, joined us for a couple of hits. She asked Ray for a glass of hot water and honey with a decent amount of Courvoisier. John, Christine, and Mick each got refills on their drinks. John had a tall screwdriver; Christine, a large glass of wine; and Mick, his usual, an ice-cold Heineken.

Then Mick signaled Ray to come over to him, and Ray proceeded to bring a small bottle out of his jeans pocket. He unscrewed the top, put what looked to be a tiny spoon down into the white powder, and carefully lifted it up to one of Mick's nostrils. Mick inhaled it and screamed loudly, as if in pain. Mick's hearty laugh followed. Christine looked at Mick and indicated that she wanted some, too. Ray obliged and eventually made the rounds to everyone, including the control room team.

Cocaine had entered the building for the first time in more than nine hard days of work. I had tried cocaine only a few times prior to this and only late at night after a long gig. I didn't really ever remember feeling its effects, just a little wake-up nudge, warding off sleep in the late hours. But that night, coke seemed to have an upside. Everyone in the studio was primed and ready to play Stevie's strange song.

We spent about an hour running the song down, allowing everyone in the band to learn his or her individual part. I noticed that I was feeling a little anxious, as if I'd had too much caffeine, but without the stomach pangs that often accompany too much coffee.

I had another drink, a couple of cigarettes, and, funny thing, everyone was ready for another hit of coke. Stevie made the request to Ray this time, and he made the rounds again.

We ran "Gold Dust Woman" down a couple more times, and we liked it enough to start recording. That night, we got eight takes in the can, but still something just wasn't right. John went home a little before 11 p.m. After that a "transcension" broke out, and the rest of us stayed for three more hours, continuing to record the song. Mick coined this term *transcension* to describe the moment when most of the band members were at just the right buzz point where they were ready to play or record anything, even if they were missing a couple of band mates.

Often, I felt that these "transcensions" worked against our bigger goal. I would try my best to reason with the band to keep on schedule. I seemed to be the only one who understood the twelve-hour rule. I knew that musicians didn't return to the studio after they left until at least twelve hours had passed. They had to go home, wind down for at least a couple of hours, go to bed, then get up and head back to the studio. Not many people could do this in fewer than twelve hours.

I liked to start studio sessions between eleven and noon, but when we would "transcend," we would usually go until two or three in the morning. So that would mean a late start the next day. Of course, the exception was John, who usually went home first and would be up early and pushing to get started the next day. This meant that on most days, I would have to get up and go to the studio early, too. John had no problem waking up Richard and me and dragging us to the studio for some bass repairs.

So, after we finished our first transcension, there was no stop at Agatha's. By the time we got out of the studio, fog had shrouded the forlorn building. The clear day brought the night fog. The quiet in the car was almost painful. Scooter, Richard, and I sat and listened to the strange silence the fog seemed to create. As we drove home, our ears were still ringing from "transcending" for hours after we should have stopped.

"Where the hell did all that come from?" Richard asked.

"Just our punishment for working late and letting them waste our time again!" I said, very annoyed. I hadn't made the connection yet, but the addition of cocaine had had its effect.

As I lay in bed a little while later, I thought again about Lindsey's freak-out earlier that day. "Scary . . . ," I muttered, as I fell asleep. I was right. There was much more drama to come from Lindsey.

4

Oh, Daddy

> Ken hadn't been living with all of us, so he was able to step back and see things more clearly. He could be more of a grown-up.
>
> —*Stevie Nicks*

The next morning, Thursday, February 5, 1976, I looked out the living room window, and everything had a dusting of snow on it. A rare storm had blown through Northern California overnight, turning Sausalito into a snow globe and dropping about a half foot on Mt. Tamalpais, the highest point in the area. The top of Mt. Tamalpais was a favorite hippie hangout in those days. You could park and look out at the ocean and the San Francisco Bay while you relaxed, contemplating pretty much anything you wanted. The snow was a surprise for me—let me tell you, you never see snow in L.A.!

As I scraped the frozen snow off my Audi, Scooter was busy making last-minute yellow marks in the snow. Scooter and I drove to the Record Plant alone that day. As we made our way down the hill, the sun broke out, and I could see the bay and the snow-covered Mill Valley glowing brightly below.

In the distance, a row of motley houseboats lined the edge of the bay. The houseboats had no building codes to follow, so many people built whatever they wanted and lived their bohemian lifestyles on the edge of the water. Long walkways protruded out into the marshy land that would rise and fall with the tides. The city was constantly worried about sanitation issues, as well as plumbing and electrical codes. Mill Valley wanted to build proper piers and walkways and have decent housing. The morning papers called this battle the "Houseboat Wars." Ultimately, the city won a few points. My brother-in-law still lives there, and it's a very rustic place to this day.

We all got to the studio around 2 p.m. that day because of the transcension the night before. I hated that our starting time had slipped back two hours.

Out front at the Record Plant were the remnants of the snowman that Nina had made to greet us. One of the roadies had given it a carrot for a penis. Of course, they would think that's funny, I thought. Inside I did, too. As the day warmed up, the snowman became unimpressive. Scooter mistook him for a fire hydrant.

Inside the warm studio, we all talked about how amazing it was to see snow. Sausalito hadn't had snow for almost sixteen years. Snow always made me think of Christmas, because we would usually go to my grandparents' home in Lake Tahoe, Nevada.

Christine and Stevie had dressed in their warmest clothes. They both wore long silk mufflers wrapped around their necks. Sailor John wore a full-length navy blue pea coat, and Mick was adorned with a fine silk muffler, tucked into what appeared to be an elegant English dinner jacket. Richard and I were just wearing our everyday Levi's and tennies.

Christine announced that she had a new song, "Oh, Daddy," and we were back to work. She had written the song about Mick and his wife, Jenny.

" 'Oh, Daddy' is a lesson in less is more," Mick told me later. "It's one of my favorite songs that Christine has ever recorded. I think it's a fantastic song."

Since we had kept all of the instruments mic'd and set up, and the board was always in RECORD-ready mode, the players went straight to their instruments. We only had to have Christine play down the song so that everyone else could learn it. Then we would decide what instrument each member of the band should play.

John had several choices of Alembic basses and also a couple of standards. Mick only had to decide which cymbals to use—the bright ones that covered up everything or the ones with rivets that hung loose, making a sound like rain on a plastic sheet. Mick also had a number of snares, ranging from thin to thick ones. He could tune the heads so that they would crack or thud more, but we never knew what we wanted from his drums until we had heard the band run down a song.

Lindsey, for basic tracks, would usually play his Fender Strat or his Gibson Les Paul through his Marshall amp. Christine would choose electric keys or organ. She had a midseventies Yamaha Electric piano, an early '70s Fender Rhodes, a Wurlitzer, and a clavichord in her electric arsenal.

We ran "Oh, Daddy" four or five times, stopping only for the band members to change out an instrument or comment on the tempo. John usually knew what bass he wanted to play, and Mick just needed to check on how his cymbals and drums sounded in the control room.

"Ken, before we start recording, can you record a little bit and let me hear it back?" Mick asked. John had all of his basses surrounding him, so he could easily try out different ones.

Lindsey discussed guitar-sound ideas with us, looking for more growl, edge, or atmosphere. As we, the sound engineers, became more comfortable with the band, one of us would sometimes suggest a specific guitar to Lindsey, and he'd look up and smile, while Ray went for the guitar. By this time, I think Lindsey had about fifteen electric guitars and maybe ten acoustic guitars, and Rick Turner was always adding more to his collection.

Rick lived in Northern California, and he made very unique basses and electric guitars. They all had an incredible sound and very high output. This meant that they tended to jump out of the speakers at you. Technically, Rick made a small amplifier that he would build into the Fender Stratocaster's output connector that would boost the output by

15 decibels. I liked them so much, I had Rick build me one in a box so that I could use it with any instrument.

"Oh, Daddy" was a beautiful, airy song, and the tempo was critical. When we played it too fast, it felt rushed and congested; when we played it too slow, the song became lethargic. Like "Gold Dust Woman," which we had recorded a day earlier, "Oh, Daddy" had a lot of space to play with. Having a diverse array of sounds to fill it was key.

Christine wrote the song while she was in the studio. Nobody told John what to play on the song. He just came up with his own bass lines, as he often did. I wanted to make sure the song had an open sound but that it was still propulsive. With all of our instrument choices made, we were ready to record.

Because Richard and I had both been hired as sound engineers, we focused strictly on the technical side of things, recording the sounds coming from the live area into the control room. Very soon after we started recording, though, it became clear that the band needed far more than two technicians turning knobs and pushing faders. They also needed a producer, someone who could be their eyes and ears in the studio. Our journey toward producing started innocently.

On the second pass of the recording of "Oh, Daddy," Christine stopped playing. "Did you like that tempo or was the first better?" She looked directly into the control room at Richard and me.

Neither of us was prepared to answer her. We were completely focused on trying to get "Oh, Daddy" to sound great, not on doing what producers do.

Instead of keeping quiet, as I usually did, I said, "Why don't you come in here and listen to both takes? Then you can decide."

"We don't want to have to come in and listen every time we try out something different," Christine said firmly. "We want you guys to start paying attention to tempos and keys and tuning and other important things and help us out here." Her comments clicked with the band, and Richard and I understood them, too.

"Okay. We get it," I said. "We'll start keeping track of that."

"Great," Lindsey said. "Now, let's do this."

Richard and I dove in. "Learn while you earn," Richard said to me.

After that point, I began taking even more meticulous notes about what we were hearing. Richard and I began to provide the stabilizing force that the band needed to stay on track, musically, professionally, and emotionally.

At first, though, Richard and I toppled over each other, both of us at the same time answering questions or suggesting changes or ways to play a song differently. Eventually, the difference in opinions became more rare as we started to get in sync. Very soon after Christine's outburst, Richard and I were on the same wavelength most of the time. The band was, for the most part, unaware of this.

From that day forward, Richard and I had more responsibility. We were the control room team, listening for everything good and pointing out everything bad. That was what we faced every day while we were making *Rumours*.

Every song was written or produced on the spot in that studio, often when we'd had little sleep. It was part of my job, along with Richard's, to manage the feelings of the band. Sometimes their emotions were volatile, and we always had to juggle their temperaments. In retrospect, I can say that it was almost like being a parent, trying to raise your kids the right way, all the while working hard not to screw it up.

At the time, I just did what I had to do. Looking back now, with many more albums under my belt, and as a father myself, I realize what a huge responsibility I had, trying to manage a dysfunctional, talented group of musicians without having any real authority over them. I tried to do this without falling into the same drug-and-alcohol trap that they were headed toward, on one hand, and on the other, without seeming as if I wasn't "going with the flow" when substances showed up in the studio. This caused some problems between Lindsey and me at times. He became uncomfortable if I didn't get stoned with him. Richard always smoked with Lindsey. I guess Richard could handle it better than I could, but I needed to pace myself.

So, with our "learn while you earn" philosophy established, Richard and I started to feel like real producers.

"Chris, you and Lindsey seem to be playing in the same register," I would say. "Can you move up or down in the scale a little so we can hear what you're both playing more clearly?"

Or, "Hey, guys, the tempo seems to be picking up in every take. I think it was better before. Can you try it a little slower?" Richard and I were giving directions to the now-famous Fleetwood Mac band! How cool was that? That's what they wanted, and that's what they got. Later we started using a metronome, so we could play them the right tempo.

"Lindsey, your E-string is a little flat," I would say. Or simply, "Lindsey, can you check your tuning for me?" Richard and I began to give them feedback that was more demanding than questioning, and they liked it.

We were getting close to putting our 24-track into RECORD on "Oh, Daddy."

"How does my snare sound, lads?" Mick asked.

"Can you loosen your snares a little?" Richard asked.

"The more you can make your snare drum crack, the better it sounds," I added.

"Oh, Daddy" was a dark-sounding and spacious song, with many of the instruments playing long lines and some of them filling the dark musical voids within the music. We immersed Mick's snare in reverb, making it swirl in the fog surrounding the track.

Everything with this song depended on Christine's organ part. It carried the entire track. Christine played her organ with her spinning Leslie speaker set on slow rotate, turning only a few times a minute. I had mic'd the speakers so that the organ moved eerily between each of my big control room speakers.

John's moving bass line, similar to the newly discovered whale call, supported the whole sonic structure like the foundation of a house. Finally, Lindsey's electric guitar, his Fender Strat—set in reverb and multiple delays—penetrated the sonic soup much as low-beam headlights cut through fog.

Mick's freshly washed Zildjian cymbals sparkled like rays of sun breaking through Sausalito's morning fog. Okay, so I might have smoked just a little that day.

Stevie sat up at the board with Richard and me. She patiently took an occasional hit off the joint that she found in Lindsey's tape box/converted pot rolling area. She liked to sit between Richard and me but slightly behind us. That gave her the dead-center listening position and the best viewing position for all of the action.

"Let's do this, guys," I said on the talkback.

I could see that everyone was ready. Ray had reloaded Mick's Heineken, and John and Christine also had refreshed glasses.

"'Oh, Daddy,' take one." I slated the new tape.

"Mick, count it off," Richard said.

Mick obliged. "A-one, two." *Click, click, click, click.*

Lindsey began his guitar part; it was a mixture of strumming and his unique picking style on electric guitar.

A very interesting thing about Lindsey's unique guitar style is how he learned it. Instead of using a pick to play his guitar, he primarily uses his fingernails. Now this isn't that unusual. Many folk guitarists use their fingernails when they're picking guitar strings, but they do it by plucking the strings in an upward direction, one string at a time.

Lindsey, however, developed a style that can play more than one string at a time by using the backs of his fingernails in a down stroke, as well as up strokes. The result is that he can play multiple notes at nearly the same time.

This remarkable and unusual talent came to him years before he had joined Fleetwood Mac. When he was young, Lindsey came down with a bad case of mononucleosis, and he was bedridden for six months. He occupied his time by playing his guitar. While Lindsey lay in bed all of those months, weak with mono, he found that he couldn't sit up and play his guitar in the standard fashion, so he developed a style to play his guitar while lying down, in a hybrid downward-picking style.

Lindsey's like that; his guitar is truly his best friend. You rarely saw Lindsey when he wasn't noodling around on his guitar. He told me that he combined the thumb in his playing, similar to banjo picking, and his thumb can play a pseudo bass line on the lower strings of his guitar, while his first three fingers create rhythms. He can have two different rhythms going on simultaneously, as well as two different melodies.

Next on "Oh, Daddy," Christine's vocal came in, then the whale-call bass, and then Christine's sparse organ part, topped by Mick's cymbal glisses. Mick's detuned snare crack came at the top of the second verse. Richard and I looked at each other and nodded in approval as they played. I had never heard anything like this before! It was spooky, haunting, and beautiful at the same time. We recorded four more takes after this one, each one better than the one before it.

On the last take, very near the end, Christine thought that she had made a mistake, and she tried to get our attention by hitting some odd notes on the organ at 3:42 into the song, trying to stop everyone from playing so that we would do another take. But nobody noticed. We finished that take, and it had the magic we were looking for.

We ended up leaving those *Bep! Bep! Bep!* moments in the final version of the song on the album. They were random at the time, but they really worked for us, even through the final edit. They just added something that we all loved.

"Oh, Daddy" came out great. Take five was the master. It had the magic, that's for sure! Those odd notes—I enjoy them each time I hear the song.

After we finished that take, Christine re-sang the lead vocal without the drum leakage. That was the fourth song foundation we had cut. During the next eleven months, we would, as the spirit moved us, return to "Oh, Daddy" and ornament it with little touches that would make this lesser-known *Rumours* track a hidden gem. This song was one of the few on *Rumours* that didn't reach primary AM radio rotation.

We eventually added twenty parts to "Oh, Daddy," including additional vocals. It was during one of those early overdub sessions that I loaded up the big twenty-four-track tapes and started to rewind them to the head leader. Earlier, the maintenance engineer was setting up the tape player, and he had left a scope on the tape machine right where the reels went. So, before I loaded the tape, I moved the scope up on the meter bridge above the reels, out of the way.

As the big tapes were rewinding—really cranking—the scope vibrated off the machine and—luckily—fell backward away from the tape. As it fell, though, it landed on the power cord and pulled it out of the wall, sending the machine into a free spin, which snapped the tape in half before I could save it.

"Shit!" I turned around quickly and saw the stunned looks on the faces of the band, as if I had just mangled their baby.

It was destroyed. There was nothing I could do. I cut out the bad tape and spliced the good tape back together. I rewound it a bit, pressed PLAY, and hoped for the best. The tape had almost made it to the beginning of "Oh, Daddy" when it broke, so I thought we might get lucky. The organ started to play, and then, abruptly, we heard Christine's voice sing "—addyyyy." We had lost the "Oh, D———." Fortunately, when we heard her sing, "-addy," so adamantly, we all laughed. Even Christine.

"Make a note. We'll have to fix that," I joked, nervously. We didn't fix it for about a month. We got so used to it starting that way that we nicknamed the song "Addy."

Accidents happen. A couple of years before that, nearly the same thing had happened to me when I was seconding with Jefferson Airplane. The engineer was sick that day, so it was my big chance.

The maintenance guy at Heider's had left a portable oscillator on the back of the tape machine, and it fell on the tape while it was rewinding. The tape snapped. This time it happened right in the middle of their song. Not good at all. I removed the damaged tape and spliced it back together. After hitting PLAY, I immediately heard that most of the first half of the guitar solo had been chopped off. It had disappeared, completely destroyed! Shit! I thought. I could be fired for this!

Jorma Kaukonen of Jefferson Airplane looked at me. I must have been as white as a ghost. I didn't know what to do. I bent over and offered my ass to them for a good kicking, but he just shrugged and said, "You know, I didn't like that solo, anyhow. Just cut the first half out and leave the rest." I cut it, as he suggested, and played it, and it sounded great. I couldn't even tell that I had edited it. As I write this, I wonder whether he was just being nice to me, or if he ever fixed it. I don't know. I never worked with them again.

Accidents aside, "Oh, Daddy" was a great song and a great master track. Happy with the work we'd done, we decided to break for dinner. Mick had his dinner by himself somewhere else in the building and joined us toward the end of the meal. He'd told us that he had just gotten off the phone with Mickey Shapiro, the band's attorney and primary go-between with Warner's. "Lads, it appears I have good news to share," Mick said, standing as tall as a proper English lord. "The White Album is going through the roof, and Warner's is going bonkers."

Indeed, the numbers on the White Album were getting stronger every day. This was amazing, considering that the album had been released six months earlier. Back then, without the Internet, records often took a long time to build momentum, relying solely on the cycle of radio play and album sales to spiral up fan interest. As I write this today, the entire life span of a hit record can be little more than six months, from its release to its exit off the charts.

Mick continued, "Mickey says that it's imperative that we do our best on this record. That's because, if we can create two hit albums in a row, we'll be set for life."

That's how the music industry works. If your sophomore album is as successful as your debut, then you aren't a flash in the pan. You're accepted by radio, tour promoters, and the industry in general. You're in the club, so to speak. This was great news for all of us, but I soon understood that the bigger things got, the harder they were to hold together.

After dinner, Lindsey pulled out another song with a lot of possibility, but I could feel the energy from the other members of the band starting to wane. After all, we had been working nine straight days, and this was the fifth song we'd worked on in four days. I was really ready for a day off, and I knew that everyone else was, too.

Fate had other things in store for us. We had just recorded a fantastic song by Christine, and everyone had played brilliantly on it, but I could see the band members talking among themselves. They were starting to obsess about the phone call that Mick had just received from Shapiro.

John came up to me, and before he could say anything, I said, "John, your bass line on 'Oh, Daddy' was great. Was that meant to be an imitation of whale calls?"

Several years earlier, Judy Collins had recorded a beautiful album, *Whales and Nightingales*, where she brought to my attention the sounds of whales singing, and on that album Judy sang with them. I was sent by Heider's to help record Judy Collins's live concert tour. I remember thinking how amazing and haunting the whales sounded while they were played into those large concert halls.

"Yeah, mate, I guess. I think it was," John answered.

"Brilliant, mate," Richard said.

"Sod off, all of you!" John said. "I was just doing my job, playing this part!" He stormed off, with his back to us and his middle finger held high so that we wouldn't miss the gesture.

John didn't take compliments well. They seemed to embarrass him.

"Oh, yeah. I almost forgot," John added, looking back at us over his shoulder. "I want to start coming in with you at 10 a.m. to start listening to all my bass parts. I want to make sure they're perfect."

"I thought they were perfect," I responded.

"You just let me be the judge of that! Be here at ten sharp tomorrow morning," he snapped.

That one phone call from Mickey Shapiro to Mick was the start of the second-guessing from all of the members of Fleetwood Mac. From this point on, the relatively easygoing band would begin to review everything, to question and pick apart what they had already recorded. That's just what we needed—more paranoia.

How was I ever going to get laid if I could never leave the studio?

For his next song, Lindsey gave us only his chord ideas. The song that he played on his Martin acoustic with rapid strumming didn't have any lyrics for us to hear. At the time, I didn't understand why Lindsey kept his lyrics from us. Later, I learned it was because he knew that Stevie would get into an argument with him when she heard them, and he didn't want to have another fight with her over his song lyrics.

This song became known to us by its working title, "Strummer," for most of the year due to Lindsey's rapid strumming. When we finally had the lyrics, it became "Second Hand News."

To preserve the initial spirit and the optimal feel of this song, we wanted to keep Lindsey on his acoustic guitar. So we had to put him in the isolation booth to avoid drum leakage into his mics, and this also meant that he could see everyone in the studio. Lindsey wanted a strong, almost disco groove (he offered the Bee Gees' "Jive Talkin'" as an example) to propel the song. Although Mick and John were the best battery mates in the business, Lindsey felt that they were getting it wrong. Mick was playing a folk-y Irish press roll that Lindsey thought was out of place, and he was irritated that John's melodic walking bass flourishes strayed from the rolling rhythm he heard in his head.

To compound problems further, neither Lindsey nor Christine heard a keyboard part in the song. And since no one besides Lindsey had any idea what the words and the melody were, this gave Stevie nothing to do.

Lindsey was a brilliant songwriter and arranger, but as a band mate and producer, his communication skills weren't always what they could be, and our first attempts at "Strummer" were proof of this. We could see Lindsey's frustration in his face and in so many other ways, especially the way the veins in his neck throbbed. He would sit in his chair, alternately playing his unplugged Strat and rolling joints in his white tape box to release his nervous energy. At this point in his career with the band, Lindsey was caught between respect for the old pros and his young ego, telling him that something was wrong, that the band was ruining his song.

"Mick, play it straight. Don't get fancy," Lindsey said. "Just listen to the Bee Gees. John, keep the bass part simple." Lindsey paced nervously back and forth between Mick and John.

"Lindsey, you just let Mick and me play your song," John said with a slightly condescending tone. "That's what we do."

Lindsey came into the control room to roll a joint. He complained to Richard that it wasn't going how they had discussed earlier. "Mick's got it all wrong," Lindsey protested, "and John's got to play the part straighter." Richard dutifully agreed.

I thought the song was sounding pretty good, but I decided to sit back and see where it went from there. This, of course, wasn't the first time I had seen a session fizzle out.

Recording music is largely about the technical manipulation of sound, but it's also about the performance. No amount of studio wizardry can compensate for a lackluster take by the artist. The proof will always be in the pudding. When the production and the performance combine, it's an absolute thrill: like bottling fire. If you've ever seen a great band live, then you know what I mean.

In a live performance, there's often one moment that is unrepeatable and unique that you were there to witness. The trick—in the studio—is to capture that one moment on tape and then build on it. A song can take on a life of its own. When you start to get it right and all of the members of a band are adding their own unique contributions, there's an energy that swoops up and carries everyone away. This is what you live for when you're a recording engineer.

No such luck for us that evening. Maybe it was because the stakes had increased for everyone. It was already a somewhat harrowing and insecure situation to begin with—deliberately trying to make a hit album—but suddenly expectations were through the roof. This was my chance for a big break, but the hours just kept adding up.

My duties became more tedious as the days passed. At this point, I was supposed to help them produce the album, and they also expected me to come in early every day and recheck the work from the day before. What were we doing the first time? I wondered.

Of course, almost every day someone in the band wanted us to work late. Luckily for Richard and me that day, we got out of the studio without even a hint of transcension.

Everyone in the band was beat and ready for an early night. Richard, Lindsey, and I decided to make a quick stop at Agatha's. As we walked in, all of our favorite girls were there, except Nina for me. We let it slip that the White Album was climbing the charts, and the rest of the night was a blast.

Christina, the waitress, had gotten very friendly with Lindsey, but, frankly, Richard wasn't having much luck with Ginger. Rachel continued to draw my attention, but I wasn't having much luck with her, either. Fun, yes; luck, no.

"Why didn't you bring Stevie?" I asked Lindsey.

He just shook his head. "That wouldn't work."

"It seems like that's just what you guys need, Linds," I offered.

"Maybe," he said. "But I think that ship has sailed."

"Here's your next round, boys," Christina interrupted us, handing us our drinks. She had this way of smiling and looking at Lindsey at the same time, as she set the tray down on our table.

"I wished she looked at me that way," I said after she had left.

"You wouldn't know what to do," Richard kidded.

Lindsey smiled and rubbed his hands together, laughing in his guttural manner as if to say, "Oh boy, this is fun!"

The next morning, Friday, February 6, 1976, came way too soon. John had me get up earlier than everyone else so that we could go to the studio and record his bass parts. John often had me solo record his bass tracks, which I thought was unusual, because it's really better to hear what other members of the band are playing while listening to the bass.

Then I realized that this was how John was dealing with Mickey Shapiro's advice. He was literally trying to make sure that each of his parts was perfect. This was another sign that the tension had ratcheted up from the success of the White Album. Great. Just great, I thought.

After John was done scrutinizing his parts, Nina called me out to the office and handed me an envelope.

"What's this?" I asked.

"It's Friday, and it's your check for your first full week of work here," she said in her New York accent. She was so lovely, and she had a body to die for.

"My check? What for?" I asked, very confused.

"It's the Record Plant's policy to give the project engineer some payment for working here," she explained. I was pleasantly shocked. I was already getting paid by the band, but Nina explained to me that it was standard practice in the industry for the lead engineer to be compensated as an incentive to keep things working well and to keep everyone happy.

I opened the envelope. It was a Record Plant check for $1,500. I put it in my wallet, trying not to look too excited. So this is what it's like doing a big-time album, I thought. From that point onward, I treated Richard to a few drinks whenever the opportunity arose—my way of thanking him for helping me get this gig.

I went out to my Audi and put the envelope in my glove box just as Mick pulled up outside the studio. He looked awful.

"Hi, Mick," I said.

He acknowledged me with a brisk, preoccupied, "Kenneth." Then he walked into the studio.

I knew something was terribly wrong. I followed him, and eventually Mick came into the control room. I could tell he had been crying, because his eyes were red.

Christine looked up and said, "My God, Mick. What's the matter?"

"Jenny's left me." The words ripped out of him. He was having trouble maintaining his composure, and he walked out of the control room, Christine, Stevie, and John all right behind him.

I left them alone. Obviously, things weren't going to be any better that day than they had been the day before. We already had tears in the studio, and Mick hadn't even opened his first beer yet.

As fate would have it, Fleetwood Mac's road manager, John Courage—known as JC—had come up to Sausalito for a long weekend. JC was very British and very aloof—in other words, somewhat of a prick.

He ran the live shows with an iron fist. Sometimes, I imagined him holding a small whip in his hand. I always thought that he could have been a German SS officer in a previous life because of his frame and composure. He was an arrogant SOB.

On the road, JC liked to control everyone who worked for him. He had the typical road mentality that anything goes, and the show must go on. He once threw a television out of his tenth-floor hotel-room window because it didn't work well enough for him. The hotel didn't complain because the band was big, and they spent a lot of money at the hotel.

His arrival in Sausalito was timely, though, because Mick needed a strong shoulder to lean on, and that was JC. Although I didn't like JC or his pompous attitude toward those who worked for him, he knew how to deal with the band members when they needed support. He loved the band with all his heart, and I understood that he would do anything he could to help them.

JC took Mick into one of the offices and talked to him, helping him make plans for his future. Just the way he spoke made it sound so right and proper. JC was there for Mick at a time when Mick was in desperate need of guidance, and JC just did what he does best. After all, the show must go on!

Jenny was having an affair with Mick's best friend, Bob Weston. Mick's an unusual guy. "If somebody's going to have an affair with my wife, I'd rather have it be him than someone I don't know," Mick said to me at one point.

Mick took on the father role of the band very easily, but he acknowledged that Jenny felt that there was a lot missing from their marriage. He put much more of his energy into the band and their latest album than he did into his marriage and children. Still, he was devastated that Jenny was leaving him.

The peculiar thing was that in the studio, sadness seemed to be contagious. If one band member was breaking up, then it made them all think about breaking up. Richard and I tried to push on, to keep things on track.

"Where'd we leave off on 'Strummer' last night?" Lindsey asked. When he wasn't drinking, he never got too far off track, especially when it came to his songs.

I asked Cris to put up the recordings from the day before. He loaded the big two-inch reel of tape and rewound it to the head of the song. He pushed PLAY on the big machine, and I had about fifteen tracks playing back through the console. It was an early foundation, and we had only drums, bass, acoustic guitar, organ, and a cue vocal at this point.

I had already positioned the kick, bass, snare, and vocal in the center of the big fifteen-inch speaker array's sound field. These custom speakers were powered by 300 watts per side, and they sounded great, but they could get *really* loud if we needed them to. (I should point out that nobody needs to listen to music at 110 decibels, but sometimes it just feels good.)

I positioned the acoustic guitar to the left side, the organ to the right side, and I split the drum kit hard left and right to fill out the sound field. Yet no matter what I did, the song sounded limp. It didn't have the right energy, even at an ear-splitting 110 decibels. I put a little reverb on the organ and acoustic and then decided to add some EQ to the instruments. On the console, I had knobs that could add reverb or other effects, change the placement in the speaker panning, even change the sound of the instruments with tone controls. Each channel strip had special knobs that allowed me to add treble, midrange, or bottom end to every instrument, very much like those tone controls on boom boxes. I would add high frequency to Mick's snare so that instead of sounding like a thud, it would sound like a whip cracking.

"I don't know, guys, I'm not really feeling this. The energy just feels off," I said.

"I agree," Richard added.

"I think we need to get the rhythm section right," Lindsey said sternly.

"John's already left," Mick said, smiling. "He was over the top."

"Well, that's it then. We need to recut this song. How about an early night and a fresh start tomorrow?" I said, trying to sound as positive as possible. Surprisingly, everyone agreed. At last, an early night!

We called it a day around 6:45 p.m. I set a 10 a.m. start for the next day, and the night was mine!

Richard and Lindsey headed off together, presumably to regroup on "Strummer" and the best course of action to steer Mick and John in the direction that Lindsey wanted.

Scooter and I made a dash for my car, and, to my surprise, Nina was just finishing up in her office. Instinctively, I hit the brakes and stopped myself just past her door and got out of my car.

"Hey, you're still here!" I said.

"Hi, there. Are you done already? How'd you pull that off?" she asked, surprised.

"I decided to try logic on them," I said.

"Logic! Well, look at you, smarty pants." She smiled. It may have been my imagination, but it seemed as if she had moved closer to me during her last sentence. I was starting to sweat.

"Hey, why don't we get out of here and get some dinner? Let's see what the real world is doing," I said, gently pulling on her hand.

"I know what the real world is doing—being boring, that's what," she said.

I don't know if she had had other plans, but I was feeling happy and alive. "Come on, you—get in my car. You look like you could use a good meal, and Scooter and I need to talk to someone else." I put my arm around her, and we headed to my car. As we headed out, she put her arm around me, too.

Before she got into my Audi, I kissed her on the top of her head and impulsively said, "Thank you, thank you, thank you!" Scooter jumped into the backseat.

Nina was gorgeous, inside and out. She always had a smile on her face, and she had a great laugh. I was over the moon that night. I had a night off and a date. I was footloose and fancy-free!

Scoma's seafood restaurant was right on the bay, set a few doors down from the Trident. It was one of my favorites, and my parents used to take me to the Scoma's across the bay at Fisherman's Wharf in San Francisco. Their specialty was abalone. I thought that was the best tasting fish in the world. Having a Scoma's here in Sausalito made me feel comfortable, as if this dinner would be perfect.

I asked for the best booth, with a view of the San Francisco lights on the bay. I remember the red leather seats shaped in a half circle. Nina sat first, and I was going to go in the other way, but she slid in just far enough for me to fit in beside her. Fine with me! My normally shy self was giddy beyond belief, and somehow I felt kind of extroverted. I ordered a couple of margaritas and fresh baked French bread. We talked. A strange calmness came over me, as though things were really all right. I was in sync with the world.

Nina told me about how she had decided to come to California from New York, and I talked about how I had moved from Northern California to Southern California—and from pre-law to songwriter-engineer.

I put my arm around her, and we looked at the city lights twinkling on the bay. I could also see the lights of Alcatraz across the bay. We laughed and had a great time. It was so good to be normal for an evening. What a change my life had gone through!

By the time we finished dinner, I was noticeably tired from our long stint of recording, especially with no outside stimulants to boost my energy. The restaurant was closing. "Wow. It's getting late," I said. "I should probably get you back soon."

Nina agreed. I took her back to her car at the studio. I really wanted to kiss her, but I didn't because we were working together (or so I told myself), and I didn't want things to get complicated that fast. Plenty of time for that later, I thought. That night, I was in bed by twelve thirty. Alone.

Lindsey and Richard had gone to Agatha's, where Lindsey hooked up with Christina, again. He had begun to date Christina recently, and the rest of us were just beginning to figure this out. Richard got a ride back to the house later with one of the cooks from the Record Plant. He had tried unsuccessfully to pull the beautiful but elusive Ginger away with him.

After I'd been asleep a couple of hours, I awoke to Richard and JC arguing in our room. JC was pissed about something, and Richard was being his usual comedic self, laughing it off, which made JC even angrier.

JC demanded respect from everyone who worked for him, and I think that because Richard did sound on the road for the band, JC felt that Richard worked for him and that Richard needed to give him more respect, even when he wasn't reporting to JC.

Wiping the sleep from my eyes, I said, groggily, "Hey, guys, can you go someplace else and do this? I'm trying to sleep."

"Stay out of this, Caillat!" JC ordered.

"Oh, yeah, you're a big man!" Richard said, laughing at JC, who towered above him.

Then JC reached down and grabbed Richard by his shirt, shaking him. "Fuck you, you little prick!" As Richard moved backward, he reached the foot of his bed, and they both fell onto Richard's bed, JC on top of Richard, making the bed collapse onto the floor.

"You're crazy!" Richard said, no longer laughing. "What the fuck are you doing?"

I jumped out of bed and ran over to them. "JC, knock it the fuck *off*!" I yelled.

JC was clearly drunk, a problem he had then. I think he would have hit me and continued his argument with Richard, but he realized that his bosses—Mick and John—might hear him, and they wouldn't be happy that he was causing fights late at night. Besides, he was in our world now, and he had no authority here.

JC took a moment, composing himself quickly. Then he smartly straightened his clothes and tried to act as if his fight with Richard had just been a joke. He gave Richard a big hug, apologized to me, and left our room. Richard, who was clearly a little stoned, spent a peaceful night sleeping on his mattress on the floor.

The next morning, Richard was still sleeping on the floor. It was Saturday, February 7, and drizzling outside. Scooter was bugging me to take him out. The roadies were already up. They had heard the noise in our room the night before.

"What the hell was all that about?" Ray asked. I told them the story. They weren't surprised that JC had gone off.

"He's always picking on Richard, because JC hates that Richard's so close to the band and they protect him. As you can imagine, that really pisses off JC," Ray explained.

"Especially when he's been drinking!" Rhino added, laughing.

I told them that I was off to the studio and to make sure that they didn't forget to bring Richard, who was still downstairs sleeping.

Having a little bit of time to spare, Scooter and I left the house, heading out for some breakfast. I drove down the hill and decided to make a left, turning away from the studio toward Mill Valley. Mill Valley was just as it sounded, a very cute little town with a wide, tree-lined main street and shops on either side. Having been stuck in the studio for almost ten days now, I enjoyed being by myself with a little time to explore. I was looking for a McDonald's so that I could get some beef patties for Scooter and coffee for me. Suddenly, a silver 190SL Mercedes turned left in front of me and pulled up into the driveway of the local car dealer. Wow, what a beaut! I thought.

I whipped a double U-turn in the Audi and pulled up behind the classic car. Then I noticed the "for sale" sign on it! I parked and quickly walked up to the car to look inside. The red seats had a few tears, but it was in pretty decent condition overall. The owner, who'd gone into the dealership, came back out and saw me looking at his car.

"Pardon me, but are you interested in this car?" he asked with a hint of skepticism, obviously distrustful of my young and somewhat shaggy appearance.

A little offended, I confidently shot back, "Yes, I am."

"Well, let's get away from here, then. I was supposed to drop it off for consignment this morning, but if you're really serious, then let's go somewhere and talk."

We got into our cars and drove down the street to a McDonald's parking lot. On the way over, I couldn't help feeling good about how my luck never lets me down. I'd wanted a car like this, and there it sat, waiting for me.

When we got down to business, the owner asked for $2,500 for the car. My jaw nearly dropped to the ground. I couldn't believe my luck. Without a moment's hesitation, I pulled out my checkbook. To his surprise, I cut him a check on the spot, and I had his pink slip a few seconds later.

Scooter also got what he wanted, and he happily wolfed down his beef patties. I was now in possession of a classic car and a coffee to boot. I couldn't believe that it had taken longer to get Scooter's burgers than it had to buy my car. Thinking back now, I don't know what's harder to believe: that cars were so cheap back then, or that things had been that easy!

The car had been well maintained, so Scooter and I drove back to the house, and I got one of the guys to help me retrieve my Audi. Richard was up by the time I got home, and he was amazed at what I'd done.

Good-bye, Ken's Wild Ride; hello, two-seater! After all of the ups and downs of the last few days, we were two boys playing with a new toy. Excited and optimistic, Richard and I rode into the studio in my new car. All the way down the hill, I kept thinking, Twenty-five hundred dollars! I can't wait to show Nina. I'm sure Richard was thrilled at the speed decrease!

When we arrived, I called to Nina, asking her to come outside and inspect my new wheels.

"Very cute!" she said and then added slyly, "When do I get a ride?"

"Damn well anytime you like!" I said.

Just then, Christine and Stevie pulled up, and that meant it was time to get back to work. First, they both took turns admiring the car. I offered to let them sit in it. Ever the critic and never afraid to speak her mind, Christine said, "I'm not sitting there, the seats have some tears in them.

I'll get your stuffing on my new outfit! Do you like it?" she asked, changing the subject to her new clothes.

"Hmm, what? Oh, yeah, very nice," I muttered.

Stevie, who would have looked great in a Mercedes but couldn't drive due to her nearsightedness—a fact that her last producer learned the hard way—merely agreed. (Stevie once drove Keith Olsen's stick shift car back home for him after taking him to the airport at 6 a.m. one day. She had forgotten her glasses, and parked his car in his driveway on a hill in Coldwater Canyon. She put the car in neutral and only partially set the parking brake. It rolled down the hill and into someone's bedroom. Stevie was a terrible driver, but she always blamed it on her nearsightedness.) "It will take forever to get that stuff off," Stevie said. "Chris and I each got new outfits this morning."

"Very nice, ladies!" Nina said, complimenting Stevie and Christine.

"And I bought my new car! We're all winners!" I said.

"Very nice, Ken. I'm going inside. It's cold out here," Christine said, and just like that, they were gone.

"Thanks again for dinner last night," Nina said, kissing my cheek as she went back inside.

Something told me that I wasn't going to be taking the women of Fleetwood Mac out on the town any time soon, but Nina was another story.

Still, inside the warm studio I was feeling pretty good. I now owned a 1956 Mercedes, I was working with a hit band, and I had a check for $1,500 in my glove box. What could go wrong?

The rest of the band arrived, and we were all very joyous. It was Saturday. We had had some rest, and we felt like one big happy family.

"Cris, my good man, load up the ole twenty-four with some fresh tape. Let's kick some ass on 'Strummer'! I feel so good, I think we should go for a Grammy on this album!" I blurted out to everyone. "To your instruments everyone, the Grammys await!"

Mick looked at me and nodded with that Mick grin. Then he headed over to his drums with a fresh Heineken.

Although JC had certainly riled things up at the house, whatever he had said to Mick about his personal life had helped. Mick had a much-improved outlook on life, compared to the day before. And, of course, all guys get extra happy when one of us gets a new toy.

Since we were still set up from the previous day, it didn't take long before everyone was ready to play. Lindsey rolled the customary pre-tracking joint, lit it up, and passed it around. When he was ready, he counted the new take of "Strummer" off at the top of his lungs, with his head craned to the side. "Hell, yeah! One, two, three, four!"

He started strumming. Mick, John, and Christine came in on the top of the verse, while Stevie played tambourine in the iso booth. The tempo was faster and had much more excitement than it had the night before— so much so that I took the extra EQ off the drums that we had added yesterday in our gloomy misery.

I also noticed that we were listening at half volume—only about 85 decibels—and that it sounded frickin' great! Lindsey got so excited that he started singing some of the words in front of Stevie, leaving others blank, presumably to delay an inevitable fight.

"I know, there's hmm, hm, hmm, hmm /Someone, has, hmm, hm, hmm, hmm /When, hmm, hmm, hmm / times go, hmm, / lay me down hmm, hmm . . . /let me do my stuff." Once we had the vocal melody, it didn't take Stevie long to jump on the last line and give it that magic accompaniment that was starting to become the hallmark of this new Fleetwood Mac sound. Stevie is very much a lyrics person, and wrapping her voice around Lindsey's was something that had come naturally to her for years. Their first duet had been a cover of "California Dreaming" ten years earlier when they were still in high school.

Yet Stevie's stunning ability to lift a song's vocals to new emotional heights didn't hide the fact that she was obviously aware of its lyrical content, and I could see that she felt a bit uncomfortable.

Not wanting this moment to slip away, I stepped in. "Okay, I think we're ready. Shall we do this?"

Lindsey paid no attention to Stevie across the room. He was like a racehorse anxious to get out of the gate. Richard, sensing the same awkwardness but not wanting the moment get away either, got on the talkback and told the band that this was feeling like a hit. The band, knowing that they had something special, responded with a cheer, "Yeah, Richard, yeah!"

"What take will this be?" Richard asked Cris.

"Uh, thirty-two," he said sarcastically, as only he could. This was only the third attempt at recording this song. My left hand went down to the talkback.

"My man Morris says this will be take thirty-two. Let's do it for him," I said.

Someone in the band muttered, "Thirty-two?"

But nobody cared about the damn take number. They were all ready to rock. As usual, my right hand snapped the PLAY and RECORD buttons on that beautiful 24-track, and off we went. We had a number of false starts and incomplete takes before it was just right. Finally, on take 46, it was perfect. We got it just right after only two days' worth of tries. That's what I loved about working with this group of people. We each had a job to do, and nothing could stop us. Grammy, here we come!

Everyone piled out of the studio for a break. Lindsey, Mick, and John came out to look at my Mercedes. Mick and John both collected old cars, so they were impressed; Lindsey collected classic guitars, so he wasn't as impressed as he could have been: his level of enthusiasm was just slightly above Stevie's and Christine's.

The rain began again, so we went back inside to work. We sat in the control room, and Richard started up with his comedy. He could be so funny, and his timing was just right.

"Did everyone see Ken's new car?" he asked. "I actually arrived here today with Ken nearly twenty minutes after leaving. So, I may not be in early anymore. I just hope we continue to arrive here at all. I don't think many of us had been born when Ken's car was built. I just hope that the brakes still work." Richard laughed hysterically at his own jokes, but he was cracking up the rest of us, too.

He kept on going about how I had actually pushed my foot through the floor of my poor little four-cylinder 190SL, pressing hard on its accelerator, trying to make it go faster. It didn't matter that it wasn't that funny. The fact that he was laughing so hard at his own jokes put us all on the floor.

Ginny, Stevie's dog, started barking at all of us, so we wiped our eyes and got back to the task at hand. The excitement level had changed after getting that track, but now we were all wondering whether we could make lightning strike twice in one day.

"What do we have that we need to finish?" I asked.

"'Go Your Own Way,'" Lindsey suggested.

Ugh, I thought.

"Oy, vey," Richard said, giving "Go Your Own Way" a little Jewish twist. It wasn't that we groaned because we didn't like the song, but it was complex. That drum fill was exciting, but there was a lot to get perfect—such as Mick's headphones. He drove us all crazy with those headphones. We put up the last tape we had made the previous Wednesday. We had done nine takes.

"Cris, load take nine," I said, "and let's listen to where we left off." As we listened, the boys knew what this song needed: more beef, more power in the bottom end. We were ready for the task.

"Let's do this, lads!" Mick said, taking a long hit from his beer.

Mick asked Rhino to get him a couple more Heinekens. Then he went out to the studio to get everything to sound perfect.

I asked Cris to set the tom mics closer in, so that I'd have more control of them later in the mix. We also moved the drum overhead mics farther apart for a wider drum image. Lindsey was back to playing on his modified Strat with his built-in Rick Turner Stratoblaster, boosting the output enough to make Lindsey's Marshall/Hi-Watt Rig literally smoke. We moved Lindsey out of iso 2 and back into the main studio. John was in position at his Alembic #33 bass, and Christine had decided to play both her Rhodes and her Hammond organ—the Rhodes in the verses and the Hammond in the chorus.

For the second time, the cocaine appeared. Once again Mick had given the nod to the boys, and we passed it around the room. I actually thought this little burst of energy could be just what we needed to help get the master take quickly.

Feeling the clock running now, I got on the talkback. I looked at Richard and said, "Okay, everyone, this is 'Go Your Own Way.' Clean tape is loaded. Is everybody ready to kick some *ass*?"

Cris pushed the talkback and said, "Come on, Mick, make us proud. Remember, big toms."

Mick was on his third beer, and his mouth was moving like a man without teeth, if you can imagine that. They played the song down a few times, and it definitely sounded better than it had before.

Cris loaded new tape up on the beast and armed all of its twenty-four tracks. He came from the back up to the console and pushed the talkback. "Let's not let this one get away from us, guys," he said. Everyone seemed pumped.

"Count it off," I said. "Take ten, continuing from where we left off. Lift off, into RECORD, one, two, three, four . . ."

Lindsey's guitar started, then his vocal. "Loving you . . ." The band entered on cue.

"Holy shit!" I said, looking at Richard with surprised jubilation. "This is going to be it!" We worked through take 14 with about four complete takes. We had a great first half, but the tag was still falling apart.

The band's bag of coke sat on the console. Mick asked whether someone could bring it out for a last-minute boost. This time, we all did some.

"Guys, just do a little," I warned. "We don't want to get so amped up that we change the feel of the song."

All we needed was the last half of the song. We played the whole song maybe four more times, and in take 25 we had a smoking ending. The first half was still better from take 14, so they asked me to cut the two halves together.

I played take 14 up until the tag and found a likely spot to make the edit at about 2:50 into the song. Then I cut off the front half of 14 and put it on the table, still on the front reel. I got out another take-up reel, found the same spot in take 25, and made the cut again, then I grabbed the first reel from the table, took a breath, and placed the good front half on the left reel holder and the good back half on the right reel holder. I took the two ends that I had cut and laid them down on the two-inch splicing block, making sure they touched perfectly, then I cut off a piece of splicing tape and stuck it across the spot where both ends touched and rubbed the tapes firmly down. Now I had one song again, spliced from two takes.

I threaded the tape through the tape machine, rewound it about thirty seconds before the splice, and pressed PLAY. Richard cranked up the level. The splice passed unnoticed and sounded perfect—as if it were all one take.

"Cutlass! Cutlass Caillat!" Richard said.

Lindsey laughed, "Yeah, Cutlass!" He slapped me on the back and then rubbed his hands together enthusiastically as only he could do. Now I had a nickname!

We had done it! Two songs in one day. We listened to the whole song a couple more times, and it did sound great. It would become something even better when we were done adding colors, but it was a great foundation, and we were all psyched.

"Agatha's?" I asked aloud. "It's Saturday night."

"Definitely!" Richard and Lindsey said in unison. Again, Lindsey rubbed his hands together with glee, and we were off. Lindsey and Richard rode in Lindsey's blue BMW, and Scooter and I cruised out in my new old Mercedes.

What a great day! I thought. I love it when everything goes well. Suddenly, while driving, I realized I could see my breath in the cold night air, so I zipped up my jacket and smiled.

I looked over at Scooter, who was shivering. "Oops. Sorry, buddy," I said. I reached over to turn up the heat control, but it wouldn't move. It was stuck and wouldn't budge. I pulled into Agatha's parking lot and again pushed the stubborn heater lever toward hot, but to no avail.

"I'll fix it in the morning when I can see what I'm doing, buddy. I promise." I got an old towel out of the trunk and put it over him. "I'll be back in a while." His big brown beagle eyes looked at me as he settled into the cold to wait for me in the car.

Concerned about Scooter, I stayed only a short time. Then we headed back to the warm place we called home. I wished I had known where Nina lived. I would have preferred to go there. "Scooter, want to go to Nina's?" I asked. He sat up and licked my face. "Exactly, buddy! Soon, I hope."

Back at the house, I played that day's recordings on my Revox. John, Mick, Ray, and Rhino were still up. We listened to both songs a couple of times. Things were sounding really good! Scooter and I went downstairs to bed. I noticed that Richard's bed was finally back to normal.

I chuckled and shook my head. I got into my simple double bed with Scooter on the floor next to me, comfortable on the shag rug, nestled in some of his favorite bedding. I dropped my arm down to rub Scooter's head. "This is pretty cool, huh, buddy?" I muttered. With my hand on Scooter's head, we were both out in a flash.

5

You Make Lovin' Fun

"You Make Loving Fun" was pretty basic, and Lindsey wasn't there when we started to record it. So, I had the luxury of building the song on my own.

—*Christine McVie*

On Sunday, February 8, 1976, I woke up and the sun was shining through the clouds. All right, finally a sunny day! I thought.

Ray and Rhino were already outside enjoying the sun, and I was dying to see what my 190SL looked like without its hardtop. The Mercedes had both a hardtop and a soft top; the hardtop was screwed on, and it had to be removed before the soft top could be raised.

"Hey, Ray, do you have a wrench?" I asked.

Ray was a very easygoing, likable twenty-one-year-old guy from the Midwest. He had a sarcastic sense of humor, and sometimes I couldn't tell when he was kidding. He liked working for sound companies because the bands came to them. He didn't want to work directly for a band, so working that close with Fleetwood Mac was new for him.

Rhino was young, too, but he had a harder edge—a don't-fuck-with-me edge. Rhino was there to do a job, and that's the job he did. If the band wanted something, he would try to take care of it. He made sure the equipment was ready, that it was put into the truck at night, that it got set up the next day, and that the show went well. Whatever he could do for the band, he did. His days started at eight in the morning and ended at midnight. Both Ray and Rhino did their jobs really well. They took care of the band.

Ray handed me a wrench and watched me unscrew the top. I went around to the other side of the car and took out the last of the bolts holding the hardtop down.

"All right!" I said. "I can't wait to see what this looks like off."

Rhino came up beside me. "Step aside, Caillat, let the men do it."

Ray and Rhino took the top off very carefully and set it down next to the car. Rhino had a cracked front tooth, and I remember that it showed through his smile. He was not going to let me do the work because I was the band's engineer. He wanted to let me know that they understood there was a hierarchy, and they respected it.

There she was, topless. I rubbed my hands together, feeling a little like Lindsey at that moment. I slid into the car to connect the front latches. Then I heard Ray and Rhino laughing.

"Hey, Caillat, nice top, but it's got holes in it," Rhino said.

I looked above me, and, sure enough, there were two tears about six inches long running lengthwise across the top, and the rear window was no longer transparent. The car looked great, though—silver with a black top. I duct-taped the torn areas closed from the inside so that, unless it really dumped rain, the tape should have been enough to keep Scooter and me dry.

Down the hill and to the studio I went. The usual girls weren't there because it was Sunday, and that meant no Nina, either. Damn! I wanted her to see my car with its soft top.

Christine and Stevie got to the studio around 12:30 p.m., and we went straight to work.

Since we'd arrived at the Record Plant, Christine had been playing this one riff, off and on. That day Christine said she wanted to cut a new song, and I found out that her idling riff actually had a name. "It's called 'You Make Loving Fun'," she said.

"Sounds great, Chris!" I said. "Why don't we start working it out while we wait for everyone else to arrive?"

Stevie was in a great mood. She was very positive about Christine's new song. "I'm going to play the tambourine on this track," she said enthusiastically.

Wow, I thought. She must have had a great Saturday night! I wondered whether Stevie had gotten lucky the night before. Had she met someone or did she have a secret rendezvous—or did Lindsey stop by? Whatever. I didn't have time to speculate any further. I had work to do.

Christine sat down at the Rhodes and played the keys hard, almost making the sound growl. The action on a Rhodes—being a mellow and cooler-sounding instrument—is such that you have to really attack it to get it to growl. We wanted to make it even crunchier, so we ran it through an amp, cranking it up. I grabbed my custom-boxed Rick Turner Stratoblaster, boosting the instrument's output by 15 decibels. Putting the Stratoblaster in the circuit really made the Rhodes growl.

"It almost sounds like a clav," Christine said.

"There's one in Sly's room," Cris said.

A light went off. "Good idea," I said. "We'll add one later." Christine ran the song down so that we could perfect the clav.

Mick and John arrived, and Ray got a beer for Mick and a vodka-float screwdriver for John. Ray and Rhino would put lots of ice in John's drink, then orange juice, and finally just a float of vodka on top. All John would taste was the vodka. Christine had a glass of champagne and, naturally, a cigarette.

While that was happening, Ray walked in and said to me. "John is not going to play well today."

"Why not?" I asked.

"He's already trashed." It was only one thirty on a Sunday afternoon.

"Great. Now what?" I asked no one in particular.

Sometimes John would start drinking as early as 6 a.m. He tended to come into the studio around ten to start working on his bass parts. Then he'd often disappear about two in the afternoon. He didn't stick around the studio the way Lindsey did, perpetually hunched over his guitar or chain-smoking one joint after another. Richard and I had to accept this and learn how to work around it.

I walked out to talk to John, who was sitting at his bass station, lighting up a cigarette. "Morning, John!" I said, trying to assess our chances of getting a take from him that day. "I love this song of Chris's. We should get this take in no time. Do you want to start with your Alembic bass? That should sound really strong against the keys."

"Yeah, sounds good, mate," he said dismissively.

Hmm, I thought. He's not very talkative, but he's not bad. That's just John. We just might get this one today.

After Mick got his headphones on and was settled into his drum cubicle area, surrounded by four-foot-high sound baffles to keep his sound in and other sounds out of his mics, we got started on Christine's song.

Christine began to play, and soon we were recording. The track sounded really great, but, without Lindsey, we knew that it wasn't finished. We decided to add the clavinet as an overdub to see how it sounded.

We set up the clav through the wah-wah pedal. After a couple of takes, we realized that Christine couldn't play the clav part and the wah-wah rhythm at the same time.

"Hey, Mick, can you run the wah-wah pedal for Chris while she plays?" I asked.

"If it's rhythm you want, then it's rhythm you got! There's no need to fear, cuz Mick is here!"

John rolled his eyes at his rhythm mate. "Sod off, then!" he said.

I started playing the tape. Christine was sitting in the control room playing the clav, and we were taking it directly into the console, straight through the wah-wah. Mick was standing over the pedal, sitting on the table next to Christine, actually creating a wah-wah rhythm in time with the track that Christine was playing, while pushing the pedal up and down in time with the track. I'll never forget that sight. This thin giant of a man hunched over a tiny foot pedal, about the size of a shoe, frantically pushing the pedal up and down.

The clav part took about six minutes to get right, and it gave such a great feel to the song that suddenly everyone had ideas for things they wanted to add. Stevie had laid down a tambourine track, and it sounded fine, but she wanted to lay it down again. We obliged, even though we knew that Mick would ultimately play all of the final rhythm parts. But how could I say no to Stevie?

Lindsey finally arrived at the studio late that afternoon. Christine was on a roll. She already had the electric piano and signature clav tracks. Next, she wanted to lay down an organ bed to smooth out the whole track and also add the deep rich color of a Hammond organ sound far back in the track.

Lindsey was very happy with Christine's song and her parts. I think he was really proud of her. He sat down and quietly rolled a couple of joints while she was finishing up.

By the time she was done, he already had some guitar ideas he wanted to try. Lindsey went out and just started to play along with the track while we worked on sounds. He chose to play his Gibson Les Paul for the rhythm parts. I ran his guitar sound through an amp and also the extra Leslie in iso 2. We were ready to start tracking for real this time.

After a while we took a break. Mick asked if he could get a toot. At this point, the band kept a plastic bag containing three or four ounces of cocaine in the control room, often sitting on the console, right there in plain sight. Looking back on it now, the band's bag of cocaine—that's odd because if cocaine is really a part of your life, then you always have your own on you, often in a small vial. At this point, though, Fleetwood Mac was still very green and naive about coke. They tended to leave it in one central place, as they would with their booze. With marijuana, the smokers all had their own, but not with coke. That didn't happen until later.

Someone brought the baggie out to Mick; it was usually one of the band who wanted some coke, too, and we would all look on longingly while the band partook, hoping to be offered some.

I thought this could make for the setup of a great joke. After Mick and John finished their drinks and their toots, I went to the kitchen and found a plastic baggie and some flour. I poured the flour into the baggie and rolled it closed so that the open top of the bag was in the center of the roll and the bottom of the baggie was actually the top or handle. It looked exactly like the real bag on the console.

I went back into the studio. The band was in the middle of the first take of "You Make Loving Fun." It sounded great. My new favorite song!

"More snare, more kick, more everything!" I said.

Mick made some adjustments to his headphones. During take 2, I put the phony baggie on the console and covered the real one.

"That felt amazing!" Richard said, his voice rising in the middle of a-MAY-zing.

"Let's do one more, just in case," Mick said. "One more massive toot, and I'll be ready to knock it on the head. Can someone bring it out?"

Ah, this is perfect! I thought, grinning to myself. "Richard, you do it," I said. I wanted to watch.

"Oh, no, Cutlass. It's your joke."

Ray and Rhino were already laughing. Stevie was in the control room with us, and everyone was encouraging me to go for it.

"Okay . . ." I heaved a big sigh. Having second thoughts almost immediately, I picked up the baggie from the flap at the top, pinching the bottom of the baggie closed with two fingers until I got into position. I headed out through the double doors into iso 2, and then I went straight into the studio.

"Who's first?" I held the baggie up high, releasing the roll, and it unfurled upside down, flour falling to the floor all around me. Deliberately not paying attention, I clumsily flailed around the studio, offering the bag haphazardly to anyone who was interested.

Aghast, Christine, John, and Mick were speechless for a second, eyes glued to the disaster that they thought was unfolding in front of them. Mick and John started pointing wildly, words still not available to them.

Christine spat out at me from her keyboard, "My God, you stuu-pid twit! You're spilling it!"

I spun around fast, expelling more of the flour in a circle around me, and Mick and John rose almost in unison and started toward me. Maybe the joke's on me, I suddenly thought.

I started to back away from the soundproof control room, and we could all hear muted hysterical laughter. I turned around to see Richard laughing so hard that he was bent in half. Stevie was up off the couch, pointing and laughing. Back then, Stevie had a really great sense of humor. Then I started laughing, too, as understanding dawned on Mick, Christine, and John.

"You bas-tard! You really got us good!" Mick cracked up. "It wasn't the real blow?" he asked, just to be sure.

John was already on all fours on the floor, trying to save whatever he could. "Good one," he said, relieved, with a big smile. "You bastard!" John seemed to be handling his booze reasonably well that day, despite Ray's warning. These English always could. Maybe it was due to the help of Mr. 'Caine.

Richard was already on his way out of the control room to save my hide.

Christine hugged me, instead of erupting at me. "I couldn't believe you could be so stupid," she said. "I was ready to fire you!"

"Now get us the real stuff!" Mick demanded.

I was prepared for this. I pulled out the official baggie, and we passed out a round of the real thing.

I always appreciated Christine for her honest reactions. You always knew where you stood with her. She often criticized me for my flaws but praised me for my strengths. And she defended me when she thought I was in the right.

"Ken had a dry sense of humor. I didn't think so at first, but when he fooled us with the cocaine bag joke, I got him," Christine said later.

Once they all had their next bump, and I was safely back in the control room, I breathed a sigh of relief: no one had said anything horrible to me during the joke. That would have ruined everything. To this day, people who know about this practical joke still mention it to me.

Once everyone had enjoyed a good laugh and a second helping of the Peruvian marching powder, we were amped up and ready to record "Lovin' Fun."

"Okay, if everyone is done being mad at me, how about we put this song to bed?" I asked, laughing.

"Let's do this one for Cal-lay!" Richard said, stretching the pronunciation of my name out, for fun.

"'You Make Loving Fun': Take three, count it off," I said.

Mick did his count in with his sticks: *click, click, click click click click.* On the very next beat everyone played, and it was a glorious wall of sound. Lindsey was playing electric rhythm chords and accents as only he can do, tastefully sparse with compelling musical punctuation between the drums, the bass, and the Rhodes. Again, we tracked with the Rhodes electric piano first. Stevie played tambourine in iso 1. Lindsey played a mock guitar solo, and then he played one in the tag, too, alternating between picking and a combination of strumming. The Leslie was a big part of his guitar sound.

Ordinarily, a guitar player wouldn't play his guitar through a rotating organ speaker cabinet but rather a guitar amp. We had an extra one, though, and I liked the sound. So, I sent his guitar through the Leslie cabinet. When Lindsey heard it, he liked it, too. That was probably my biggest contribution to the album, my sounds.

We finished that take, and I held up my arms, signaling for quiet at the end. As the instruments stopped resonating their final tones, Richard announced, "Fucking great, mates! Come on in and listen."

The band came into the control room, and we were all happy. Even John. Christine had told everyone that the song was about her dog, instead of about Curry, to avoid flare-ups.

I suggested that we add the clav back to this version of the song. Mick and Christine went back to their clav stations and repeated their clav dance. John said he had to go. I could see that he was running on fumes.

Christine played her organ part again. The cocaine increased her stamina, and, fortunately, the effect was very subtle and smooth—not at all jittery. It added just enough energy, like a mild coffee rush.

It was about six on Sunday evening. Richard and I begged Mick to give us the rest of the night off.

"Mick, everyone's beat. Tomorrow will be almost two weeks nonstop without a break," Richard pleaded with the stubborn Englishman.

"John has left, and you should, too," I suggested. Christine, Lindsey, and Stevie agreed with us.

"Fine, but let's get an early start tomorrow!" Mick said sternly.

"Absolutely," Richard said.

"Let's shoot for eleven thirty," I added.

Richard and I left in my car, stopping by the 7-Eleven for a giant Pine St. cookie.

John and Mick were already home when we got there, having run completely out of steam. Six songs in one week can take it out of you. Not bad for a couple of guys who almost got fired!

Monday morning, and I sure felt fine! Looking out the living room windows, I could see the bay. The day was clear, brisk, and sunny. Suddenly, I realized I hadn't called my folks since I'd started work in Sausalito. They only lived about an hour or so south in San Jose, which was only about twenty to thirty minutes from where Lindsey had grown up.

I phoned my mother to tell her that I'd survived more than a week of living and working with these musicians. "And I bought a Mercedes," I said at the end of my story.

"Honey, you have to be careful with your money," she said. "You don't know how long this job will last."

What am I, crazy? I wondered. Why did I just tell my mother, the worrier, that I was spending money as fast as I was making it? After I hung up, I wished that I could take a day off and go see my parents.

At the house, everyone was still asleep. I took a quick shower and headed off to the park near the studio with Scooter. I'll get to the studio early, I thought, and I can spend some time with Nina, showing her my car. When I wasn't thinking about music, I was usually thinking about girls. We got to the park, and I let Scooter out of the Mercedes to run around.

About six years ago, Kathy Brown, my girlfriend at the time, had found Scooter as a two-year-old stray. He had been beaten, and, apparently, he had run away to save himself. When he first saw Kathy, he ran right up to her. Like I said, he was a smart dog. He could tell good people from bad ones. Kathy brought him over to my place, and Scooter put his butt down on my carpet and, yes, scooted across my carpet using his front legs. He was so cute, and I had never seen a dog do that before. "Hey, a scooter dog," I said. That's how he got his name. Scooter Brown because he was a golden-brown beagle.

I had read a book that explained a dog could learn about 250 words, so I took him everywhere and taught him everything I could. He never wanted to leave my side, so I never had to use a leash. All I had to do was lightly snap my fingers to get his attention.

When I got to the studio on Monday, it was almost 11 a.m. I was there early to check John's bass on "You Make Loving Fun" to see if he needed to redo it, initiating his new policy of carefully scrutinizing all of his bass parts.

"John isn't coming in early," Ray said.

"Fine with me," I said.

"He figured out what Christine's song was really about," Ray said.

"I thought it was about her dog," I said.

"No, it's about Curry," he explained.

"Oh! That's not good!"

Nina and the rest of the staff were preparing for another band that was coming into studio B. I wanted to spend time with her and show her my car, but she was taking care of business. Though I was a little disappointed, I really liked this about her.

Wally would have, too. "Uh, Ken, aces!" he might have said. "Ain't she a gas?" Wally and that previous life seemed a long way away. A wave of homesickness hit me as I walked back into the studio. Cris was there.

"Hey, Cris!" I said.

Cris looked up at me. "Hey, big guy, you're here bright and early."

"Yeah, I couldn't sleep, because I got a call early this morning. My grandfather is in the hospital." I really felt down.

"Nina looks great. Did you notice the sweater she's wearing?" Cris asked, trying to wind me up.

"Yeah, it took me a while to catch my breath so I could speak to her."

"She sure has got a great pair of . . ."

"Hi, boys," Christine interrupted, walking into the control room, her dog, Duster, following her. Duster barked at Scooter—just one yip.

"Morning, Chris," Cris said.

"Did you have a good night?" I asked Christine.

"Not particularly. Duster heard noises and kept me up half the night." Christine sighed.

I don't know what kind of dog Duster was, some sort of Pomeranian, I think. But with that long straggly gray hair in disarray all the time, Duster looked like the working end of a dust mop. Despite a pleasant personality, Duster wasn't Scooter's type.

A few minutes later, Lindsey, Richard, and Stevie came into the control room together. Mick and John followed about ten minutes after that. John was noticeably quiet. He immediately asked Ray to get him a screwdriver.

We were back on our noon start time, perfect, in my opinion. This gave everyone enough personal time to run errands or get personal things done beforehand, so that when they were in the studio, they could let go and really focus.

Richard and Lindsey started to argue about the local mayoral race; Sally Stanford was the incumbent in the upcoming election. She was a former madam from San Francisco and had run one of the best-known brothels. She had come to Sausalito years earlier, changed her ways, and actually got herself elected mayor. Richard, ever the comedian, had ridden in with Lindsey and heard all of his moaning about this, and he was trying to shake it off with a joke.

Richard was going on about how Sally had been elected, on her back, and how she probably got bills passed by trading BJs. It wasn't really that funny, but with Richard—nearly crying from laughing so hard at his own jokes—it was an amusing scene. Actually, I had heard that Sally Stanford had done a very good job during her terms in office.

"A former hooker, the mayor of Sausalito." Richard's voice went up on "lito." "That's a new twist on the term *dirty tricks*, isn't it?"

Christine laughed her Dame Edna laugh. Stevie laughed, too, an easy laugh that had gotten her through seven years of living with Lindsey and then a few more years living with both Lindsey and Richard. Richard had started in the music business the same way I had—working in a small studio. Then Lindsey and Stevie had come to the studio, and one of the engineers, Keith Olsen, started recording them. They traded work around the studio for studio time.

Richard had started out cleaning toilets there. Soon he worked his way up to assistant engineer on *Buckingham Nicks*. Stevie and Lindsey were so broke that Richard had let them live at his house for free. When Stevie and Lindsey joined Fleetwood Mac, Richard was again the assistant engineer on their first album with the band, the White Album. Then, when the band went on tour, Richard started doing the live sound for Fleetwood Mac on the road and also driving the car for them. Richard was very easygoing and a great friend to them.

"I drove the baggage in the station wagon with Lindsey, and JC would drive the rest of the band in the other car because Lindsey and I would smoke pot, and no one wanted to ride with us," Richard told me. When they got to the hotel, Richard had to deliver the bags. "And, boy, did Stevie have a lot of bags."

In the studio, Mick stood up. He was just about to start one of his famous skits with Richard when John Courage came in and interrupted us to say good-bye.

"I'm off. Keep up the good work," JC said to all of us. "Remember what I told you," he said to Mick. Then he whispered loud enough for me to hear, "The show must go on. Keep it together, man." Mick patted JC on the shoulder, and JC walked out the door, heading back to L.A.

Through the open door, I could see Nina talking to the band in the studio across the hallway. Then the door closed. I turned and looked back at the band. "Hey, I have an idea," I said. "Why don't we make some rough mixes of our new tracks? That'll give us a chance to hear where we are with everything." They all agreed, and Lindsey rolled up a couple of joints to get things going. That's how we listened.

Cris put up the first song on the 24-track, "Keep Me There," and handed me the track sheet. Then he took the masking tape off the wall that contained the name of each instrument on each track. Much like the layers in a Photoshop image, there were lots of elements that we had to lay on top of the others and blend perfectly for the song to really work.

To balance the tracks, I placed the drums and the bass in the center of both speakers so that you really got the full impact of those elements. Then I added tracks from all of the instruments to the mix, mostly hard left or hard right, opposite from each other. For instance, I added acoustic guitar left, electric right, Rhodes left, and organ right.

I positioned the vocals into the empty space in the middle and added some reverb. That got the stereo mix placement. Next, I wanted to get the levels perfected. I hit PLAY on the machine and pulled all of the volume sliders or faders down. Next, I brought them all back up, one at a time, until the song was really pumping. I then added a little more kick, like a pinch of salt, until the bass and the kick were one instrument.

"Keep Me There" was a guitar song, so I turned up the guitars to about the same volume as the drums and the bass. Then I brought in the piano, the organ, and the work vocal. It was sounding pretty good, and Richard turned up the monitors, knowing that Lindsey liked to hear playbacks loud. Lindsey would tell us that we were wimps if we didn't listen at 110 decibels, which is actually about the same level of sound a jet engine makes, taking off, at 300 feet away.

Richard reached over and pushed up the vocal a little. I added some high end to the cymbals, a little midrange EQ to the guitar, and a compressor on the bass direct to keep it up in your face.

Then we listened to it a few times from top to bottom, making notes on the track sheet to figure out what we should do next. Most important, the song still needed a proper vocal. It also needed more rhythm guitars, percussion, background vocals, harmonies. It would all come in good time. First, we had to get a good vocal to really understand the song.

"Chris, do you feel like singing now, before we put a mix down on tape?" I asked.

"Not yet. Maybe later, after I've had a couple of drinks and some you-know-what." She cocked her eyebrows up and down.

Most of the singers I've worked with don't like to sing early in the day—their voices aren't ready. Late afternoon or evening is much better for them. Christine would have a few cigs, a few glasses of champagne or wine, and a bump or two. Then, she'd be ready to go. The perfect combination over the perfect amount of time was the goal. This combination consumed over too few hours and you had a disaster; over too much time, and you add another type of disaster. Between three and four hours was the right amount of time: just enough magic.

We mixed five songs that day, occasionally adding a vocal or a harmony or replacing an errant bass note or some new guitar part. We would sit together all day in our little world inside our sealed studio, listening, fixing, adding, and mixing, really enjoying what we were doing. These were the good times, and we knew we were having them!

Finally, it was almost midnight, and we were all thoroughly satisfied; no one wanted to stay and play that night. We were each fulfilled, and we went home knowing that the last ten days had been successful. My car heater was working fine; my roof tape was still holding; and Scooter was entranced by the ocean out his window.

"O-cean," I said slowly to him as he looked at the surf, teaching him another word. Hey, I realized, I never saw Nina again today! Scooter yawned.

Richard and I got to the studio early the next day so that we could check the bass on "Lovin' Fun" and redo it again if John wanted to. John showed up at the same time we did—10 a.m. sharp.

"Sorry about yesterday, guys," he said regretfully. That was the John I liked. Ten o'clock was usually a great starting time for John because it gave us about an hour, maybe an hour and a half, before his buzz kicked in and he might not be able to concentrate on his part.

After lunch, Christine wanted to do a quick lead vocal. Then Lindsey and Stevie were going to add some background vocals. I needed to consolidate some tracks to make room for the new vocal parts. I bounced the two extra ambient drum mics down to one track, and I was nearly ready for the singers.

Years earlier, when I was second engineering back at Heider's, I had worked for the great engineer-producer Bones Howe when he worked with the Fifth Dimension. Sometimes he had to erase great vocal parts, because, back then, there just weren't as many tracks to record on, so he could keep only the best ones. That made me nervous, but that was before we had 24-track recorders. Then it was only 8 or 16 tracks. For *Rumours*, I had a luxury that Bones didn't have. I recorded everything— guitar licks, riffs, and ideas that came up—and I kept them for later.

I had a knack for remembering good parts that everyone else had forgotten. I would surprise musicians with them later. Sometimes I was able to make complete solos out of pieces. Occasionally, Lindsey wouldn't even realize that he hadn't actually played a whole solo as one piece.

Often, Lindsey would play just to look for ideas. He came up with brilliant parts in passing—leads or rhythm licks. By recording all of it, I could play back the good parts, and Lindsey could make a whole track out of whatever he chose. He had some truly brilliant moments. I love his guitar playing.

Anyway, that day, Lindsey put some nice rhythm guitar parts in and some nice licks. You can hear some of them if you listen to "Lovin' Fun" at the ten-second mark, the fifteen-second mark, and again at 2:38 to 2:40 minutes. I love the three high hat hits, and then all hell breaks loose with the song!

So, in those next few hours, we had made a dramatic change in the track. At one point Stevie wanted to do something, too, and, of course, what she did best was sing. We played around with some ideas, and, eventually, Stevie and Lindsey were sitting on two high stools out in the studio, each of them in front of a microphone, working on background parts, singing, "You make lovin' fun, you make lovin' fun . . ." When I stopped the tape to rewind it, Stevie suddenly looked at Lindsey and cried out, "Fuck you, asshole! You can go to hell!"

Lindsey responded with a tirade of his own. "When we get back to L.A., I'm moving out."

"I don't want to live with you, either!" They went back and forth, screaming and yelling at each other.

I couldn't rewind the tape fast enough. When I got to the beginning of the tape, I hit RECORD. Stevie and Lindsey looked at each other. Then they turned toward their microphones and, right on cue, right in the middle of a fight, they nailed their parts!

"You make lovin' fun, you make lovin' fun . . ."

What just happened? I was flabbergasted.

Of course, Richard knew exactly what was going on. That's the first time I found out that Stevie and Lindsey were having serious problems. I mean, I'd seen Lindsey flirt with other women, and he hadn't seemed that close with Stevie in the studio, but I just thought that this was how they were. That shows you how naive I was. This back-and-forth fighting, singing, and fighting went on for about a half hour, and it was contagious. John started fighting with Christine. Soon Stevie and Christine left the room. Finally, everyone who was still in the studio walked outside to get some air.

A few friends of the band were there, and somebody had some opium. As I recall, it was a little lump that you smoked. I remember thinking, If you smoke it, how bad can it be? I think we even put the tips of our cigarettes in it and smoked it that way. Anyway, I don't remember feeling much from it.

Eventually, everyone wandered off, and I went back into the studio. I was rolling up some cables when I heard Christine playing the grand piano. I stopped what I was doing—it was so beautiful! I just stood there listening to her sing.

She had written it at the hotel the night before. Then I did something I've never done again. I went over and sat on the piano bench next to Christine. She continued playing and singing, but she looked at me as if she was thinking, Why the hell are you sitting here while I'm playing?

I snapped out of it. I got up and went over to our 2-track reference tape, and I hit RECORD. Christine played it again, and I got the whole thing down on tape. It was "Songbird."

A few months before working with Fleetwood, I had been the main engineer on Joni Mitchell's tour, and I had recorded twelve of her live concerts. "Songbird" felt to me like it should have a live sound. I tried adding some reverb to Christine's piano and vocal, but it sounded corny. One of the Joni Mitchell shows I recorded had been in a beautiful theater near the Record Plant—the Berkeley Community Theater.

About that time, everybody came back into the control room and heard Christine play "Songbird." Christine was so excited, she was shaking. I'm not sure whether the rest of the band was as excited as Christine and I were. For a studio track, the song didn't have much vibe or personality. As a comparison, imagine if the Academy Awards were presented and recorded on a small stage like the ones that Letterman and Leno use. You wouldn't have the "wow" factor that you get from a larger hall.

I showed the band what "Songbird" could sound like with live-sound-ing reverb. Then I had a brilliant idea. "Hey, let's record it live over at the Berkeley Community Theater! It's a beautiful-sounding hall. I recently recorded Joni there." Mick, Christine, and Lindsey gave me their nod of approval. "Great, I'll start to make arrangements tomorrow," I said. I made a cassette of "Songbird" for Christine to take home, and we left the studio close to midnight.

I'm not sure if I had even felt the opium, but I had invaded Christine's personal space by sitting on her piano bench. Trust me, not a great idea!

Settling into my bed, I pulled the sheets up around my neck and nestled my weary head onto my pillow, and I was fast asleep. Suddenly, someone yelled, "Fire!" They were telling me that my Mercedes was on fire! I ran outside, and everything was burning. The flames were burning so high, I was afraid that the trees above were going to catch fire.

"Scooter! Where's Scooter?" I yelled. "I don't know where Scooter is!"

"Scooter's right here, you idiot," Richard said. "What are you yelling about? We're all trying to sleep."

"Huh?" I sat up in bed. Scooter was on the floor next to me.

Richard sat up in his bed, shaking his head at me. "If it's okay with you, can we go back to sleep now?"

No more opium for me, I decided.

6

Songbird and Gold Dust Woman

When Christine played "Songbird," grown men would weep. I did every night.

—*John McVie*

"**H**appy Birthday to you, Happy Birthday to you, Happy Birthday, dear Joy, Happy Birthday to you!" I sang. It was my younger sister Joy's birthday. So, the morning started with a quick call to her before I made the arrangements for the concert hall recording that we had planned the night before.

I called down to Biff Dawes at Wally Heider's and told him that I wanted to do a remote recording as soon as possible in Berkeley. "Can you check the truck's availability?" I asked. He said that they were booked for the next month and weren't available. So I called the Berkeley Community Theater to reserve the hall, but they were also booked up for weeks in advance. They suggested Zellerbach Auditorium as an alternative. Zellerbach was a beautiful hall, too. It had hosted many terrific concerts. I made a few quick calls, and we were set to record there in three weeks. I called the Record Plant and inquired about their remote truck's availability on that date. They told me that they had one we could use.

So, I was all set. I requested that the Record Plant bring every expensive microphone they could get their hands on for the recording, and then I recommended that Mick call the label and tell them our plan. Mick got the expense cleared through the label, and the date was set for March 3, 1976. Christine was thrilled when she learned that we were going to record in this amazing hall with great acoustics—a place where many top performers had played.

When Stevie got to the studio that morning, she was anxious to do one of her songs. The word went out for all hands on deck.

Stevie had a cassette of a song called "Silver Springs" that she'd written while she and Lindsey were on the road in Maryland; she'd seen the sign "Silver Springs, Maryland," and she liked the name. She wanted the song to be her epic moment on *Rumours*.

Although "Dreams" would be a contemplation of Stevie's and Lindsey's breakup, "Silver Springs" was an out-and-out condemnation of it. Especially of Lindsey personally—of his inability to let her love him. The song was as gorgeous as its name, and it was powerful. "Silver Springs" was a masterpiece. There was only one problem: I knew the song was too long to fit on the album.

"As far away as Lindsey goes from me, he'll never get away from the sound of my voice, ever," Stevie said. "And John will never get away from Christine's voice."

We worked on "Silver Springs" for a few hours, making progress. At dinner, a guy named Jimmy Robinson came in to see us. Jimmy had been sent by Chris Stone, the owner of the Record Plant, to check in and make sure we had everything we needed and that we were happy. Jimmy was an engineer with the gift of gab. Jimmy, Lindsey, and Richard went out into the studio and smoked a joint. I was talking to Stevie about "Silver Springs." I hit the talkback to see if the other members of the band were ready to finish the song, but they were gone.

As I walked out of the studio to go find everyone, I saw the light from my favorite porthole beckoning to me. I stopped for a minute to gaze outside and wonder what the rest of the world was doing as darkness fell. Then I turned and walked down the narrow, dark, uneven hallway to the lounge. I couldn't find Lindsey or Richard anywhere.

Through the kitchen, I could see out to the front lobby where Nina was getting ready to go home. "Nina, did you see Richard and Lindsey?" I asked.

"Yeah," she answered. "They went outside for some air. They don't look so good."

About an hour later, Ray came in and told us that he had taken them home; Apparently, there had been some angel dust in the joint they had smoked with Jimmy, and it had ruined them for the rest of the day. With nothing else happening, the girls left soon afterward, and it was an early eleven-hour day.

The next morning I heard a knock on my door.

"Ken, wake up!" Cathy was shaking me awake. The Record Plant had hired Cathy to run the house for us. "Quick, come help me. Scooter and my dog are doing it again. Your damn dog is screwing my sweet dog."

"What the hell time is it?" I grunted.

"I don't know. Six-fuckin'-thirty? Now come help me get him off of her!" she demanded. I heard Richard laughing from the other bed.

"It's not funny, damn it," I blurted out blindly. "I'm comin', I'm *comin*'! I've only had four hours sleep." I threw my pants on and went outside.

I knew the drill: hit 'em with hose water, and they'd break it up. I went outside, grudgingly, and I was immediately blinded by the sun. It was freezing, and Scooter's ears were straight back, as he was having sex for the second time in his life, as far as I knew.

"Stop him! Stop him!" Cathy shouted.

"Aw, the poor little guy. He's just having fun," I groggily pleaded Scooter's case.

"She's too small to have his puppies!"

"Shit!" I said and grabbed the hose and turned it on. Scooter wasn't listening to Cathy or me. Whoosh! The cold water hit them both. Scooter looked at me for a brief second. The little dog he was humping took the opportunity to try to slip away, running down the steps and out into the garden, Scooter in tow. I hit them with more water, and Scooter finally broke loose. I opened the door so that I could go back to bed and yelled, "Damn it, Scooter, next time do it away from the house!" He gave me an angry look.

I managed to get about three more hours of sleep. When I got to the studio, I told Nina all about Scooter's adventures, explaining that I hated to stop them when he was having so much fun. Nina laughed aloud. She had a very wide smile and white teeth. Her laugh was distinctive, and I liked talking to her. I didn't want to stop. We were both laughing hard at poor Scooter's predicament when Ray and Lindsey came in and started off on the story, too.

"I just don't know how he got out," I managed to sputter between guffaws.

"That's easy," Ray said, laughing even harder. "I let him out when I got up for some water—he was sitting there by the door, just begging to go." Somehow that struck everyone as even funnier, and we all broke up into hysterics again.

"I'll get you for this, Ray!" I said, laughing.

We started the day out with piano-tuning problems, again; this was the third or fourth time in only the first few weeks. We were always having problems with the piano staying in tune. We all knew Christine had perfect pitch, and we could be right in the middle of working on a track, then Christine would stop and demand that we have the piano tuned again.

For a while, the tuners thought that this time it was the humidity, although none of them had complained about it before. Some of us in the studio thought it was just a matter of too much weed; others called it the curse of the Mac. I think, eventually, it turned out that the tape machines, which were very new technology from 3M, were not running at speeds that they were supposed to be, and it was causing problems.

We finally got the piano sorted out. That day, it took about three hours to resolve the problem. So naturally there was a lot of sitting and waiting for the members of the band, which inevitably led to more smoking and drinking. Finally, we got the go-ahead, and we got started again.

We added some more parts to "Strummer," "Oh, Daddy," and "Gold Dust Woman," mostly vocals, guitars, and bass fixes. Then we did another batch of rough mixes after that. It's extremely important to build a strong foundation for the songs; if the tempo isn't really solid, adding layers of instruments becomes impossible. That's what the Fleetwood sound is, layers and layers of colors.

The day had been a bad combination of things: a lot of sitting around and being bored, some small jokes, a little pot, maybe a bump or two, champagne, vodka, beer. It wasn't like we were partying; it was just another day at work, the seventeenth straight day without a real day off. It wasn't excessive consumption, either. Everyone could function, but we were starting to go batty. That evening, we went to Agatha's for a change of scenery. Sausalito had so many beautiful women—they were every-where. It was exactly what we needed.

On Friday the 13th we started up where we had left off on Wednesday with "Silver Springs." Nina offered Stevie the use of Sly Stone's pit when Stevie wasn't busy in the studio, so that she could have a quiet place to work on her songs.

Stevie was thrilled—there was nothing she liked to do better than play her songs on the piano. Much of the time, Stevie sat curled up on the couch behind us in the control room, with a shawl around her and Ginny at her feet. Sometimes she took baby tokes off a joint and drank tea. She could sit for hours on that couch, observing and chatting; she loved to laugh. I thought she was especially cute when she was laughing. She was so great back then, really down to earth. What a change she would go through.

We had cut "Silver Springs" with the Fender Rhodes keyboard, elec-tric guitar, bass, and drums and Stevie's work vocal on Wednesday, so that's where we started. We needed to get the basic track just right; ulti-mately, we'd use a grand piano on it, but for now the Rhodes was fine as a placeholder for the grand piano later. Laying out a song this way often meant that we'd have to use our imaginations to fill in the sounds until we added the other parts.

We got about nineteen takes, some all the way through, others just partials. Yet none of them were right, and, finally, we just ran out of steam. Perhaps relying on our imaginations just wasn't good enough. Richard and Mick did a couple of skits to break up the work. One of their favorites was reenacting a plane crash, as odd as that sounds.

Their airline was called Air Maybe or Air 50/50. The pilot and the copilot (Mick and Richard) were on final approach when they would realize, "Something has gone terribly wrong!" and they were "going in." Sitting in their studio chairs, they'd slump back until their heads touched the back of the chairs, and in their hands they held the invisible controls to the plane.

"Captain, Captain, how can you fly this plane with a saber sticking in your side?" Richard asked in a very concerned voice.

"Why, you're daft, man. There's no saber in my side," Mick said dramatically.

"There's not? Well, check again, because I can assure you there is, sir," Richard warned, then suddenly he thrust his invisible dagger into his captain's side. They would both fall forward out of their seats onto the floor. Here's another variation on this that I remember:

"Captain, Captain, did you remember to fuel the plane?" Richard asked in a concerned voice.

"Why, yes, I'm sure I did," Mick said, pausing dramatically on each word, as if trying to replay the moment in his mind.

Richard leaned forward, pretending to tap his index finger on his unhappy fuel gauge (as he'd seen in so many old war movies). He cocked his head to the side and made a twisted face. "But, Captain, there doesn't seem to be any f-u-e-l left in our tanks, at all. Captain, I think you've made a terrible mistake! I think you've killed us all, sir."

They both looked at each other with horror on their faces as their plane fell out of the sky, and they screamed like girls until their screams turned into laughter.

All of us who were forced to watch this foolishness laughed hard and wondered where these guys got this stuff. After the skit, they commented on what it would really be like if that happened, and Mick pointed out that being an English gentleman, he would always be prepared by wearing clean underwear.

Other times, Mick fantasized about what he would do if he were to commit suicide. How he'd get all of his affairs in order first, then bathe and have an enema, so as not to be rude and make a mess. He'd dress in his finest garb and find the most brilliant way to go. Would it be poison, the wrists, or a dagger to the heart? The most brilliant part of the plan was the enema—leave it to a Brit, always needing to be just so precise.

Anyway, in our little ship, together we floated, searching for the magic ingredient that would make the song fly. Sometimes we'd add parts, and we'd immediately know if they weren't right. Sometimes they were great, and other times we would change them weeks later.

We decided to try "Silver Springs" again the next day, playing to a click track (another name for a metronome). When we used a click track, we would have Mick listen to it in his headphones so that the track would remain at a consistent tempo, subliminally helping to create a hypnotic feel. We would also mic up the grand piano in iso 2 so that Christine could play live without the drums leaking into it. If they did, they would wash out both the piano sounds and the drum sound. We got everything planned for the next day so that the staff could set up the studio before we got there in the morning. Then it was Friday night, and we were off to Agatha's.

When we got in on Saturday morning, February 14, 1976, someone mentioned that it was Valentine's Day. Because Christine was English, she thought that the holiday was quite unusual, but I found out that she had invited Curry up for a romantic weekend, anyway. We were still working on "Silver Springs."

We checked out the new mics on the piano and all of the routing. Then we listened to Lindsey's guitar tracks and decided to make his guitar swirl more. So I ran it through a B3 Leslie. The B3 was actually a big wood-grained speaker cabinet with a spinning fifteen-inch woofer at the bottom of the cabinet and a spinning high-frequency horn on the top. The Hammond Company had made the box so that people could play other instruments besides the organ into its moving speakers. Both speakers could be made to spin independently, fast or slow. Microphones placed in front of each spinning speaker would let you hear the sound passing the mics as it gave a wobbly, swirling sound to the guitar.

I placed the guitar amp through my left control room monitor and the Leslie through the right monitor and the reverb in the center behind it all. It made for a dramatic sound. It was especially fitting for Stevie to be singing this song to Lindsey. Now that I was aware of what was going on between them, I wondered if we would see any outbursts that day. Suddenly, I looked up to see Curry Grant trying to come through iso 2 and sneak in to see Christine in the control room with us. I looked around. John was in the control room, sipping on his first screwdriver of the day and talking to Mick. I waved Curry off frantically, slashing across my neck with my hand to warn him that the coast wasn't clear.

Just at that moment, John stood up, deciding to go out to the studio to his station and get ready to play. He walked behind me and started to open the door to iso 2. My eyes went wide. This is going to be ugly, I thought. But somehow Curry got away without being seen, then came around the other way through iso 1 into the studio and gave Christine a big kiss. It was like a scene out of a Marx Brothers movie.

There were times when we were in the control room and we could see the vocal booths. Curry would come into one vocal booth. Coincidentally, John would be ready to get up and go get coffee and would head toward the door, but Richard or I would say, "Hey, John! Do you wanna listen to this bass part real quick?" Curry would run out the double doors.

Curry had a big beaming smile. Christine was beaming, too—they were clearly in love. He gave her a Valentine's card, then kissed her again and disappeared the way he had entered. Stevie saw the whole thing. She got up and gave Curry a hug and a kiss—it was nice that she was happy for Christine.

Lindsey was playing his Strat for us through the Leslie, and we were playing with the sounds.

"I love that guitar sound," Stevie said.

"Chris, Mick, are you ready?" I asked.

"Yes, love," Christine said to me. Wow, I thought. No sarcasm. That's the Christine I liked best. She walked out to the grand piano with her champagne and her cigarettes. Cris followed her with an ashtray so that she didn't burn the place down. She asked Ray for more champagne.

By this time Mick, who had gone out through iso 1, was already at his drum set. We heard the usual *tap, tap, tap* of his drumstick around his drums and Mick loosening or tightening each head screw slightly as he listened. He put his headphones on as Richard hit the talkback: "Okay, shall we do this?"

"Why don't we play it down a few times, and we'll adjust the headphones," I added. "Just stop if you have a problem."

Christine played a few chords. "Can I have a little reverb on my piano?" she asked, taking the last drag off her cigarette.

"How's that?" I asked, adding just the right amount from one of the knobs in front of me.

"Great, thanks, perfect," she said.

"Boy, is she in a good mood," I said to Richard. "Do you think Curry got here last night?" Richard just looked at me and smiled.

The band played the song down three times. Stevie wanted to sing the work vocal in the studio with the guys, so we gave her a very directional microphone and built her a little room made of baffles. It didn't stop the leakage from the other instruments, but it helped. We knew she was only laying down a guide vocal right then, anyway. If we got the take that day, we'd probably do a temporary lead vocal afterward.

The song had really changed by this point—much closer to the way it sounds in its final version. Playing the airy guitar part and the beautiful piano parts was inspiring to everyone, and we got it on take 8. The earlier version had had a much harder feel, more rock and roll. This later one had a more epic ballad feel.

"Guys, I love this! It sounds just like I imagined it would." Stevie was really excited. "Since we're all set up and on a roll, would you mind if we tried another take of 'Gold Dust Woman'?"

I thought "GDW" would sound great with the same instrumentation that we had just used.

"Okay, let's make some music!" Richard said, and everyone went back out to the studio.

After we ran "Gold Dust Woman" down a few times, we decided that the Rhodes might be better than the grand. Christine moved, with her bottle of champagne and cigarettes, back into the studio. At the same time, we moved Stevie back into iso 2, then we dismantled the temporary vocal booth in the studio so that Stevie could see better.

I used this opportunity to take Scooter outside for a pee, and when I came back, I stopped to talk to Nina. Scooter dashed in from outside and ran right over to Nina, and flopped down on the rug next to her. She reached down and softly rubbed his head. I walked up to Nina's desk, watching my dog get Nina's affection.

"Hey, hi," I said. "He loves that. What a lucky dog! I'm surprised you're working on a Saturday."

"Yeah," she said slowly. "I had a lot of work to catch up on."

God, she is cute, I thought. "You know, I think we're going to be ending early tonight—Valentine's Day and all. Would you like to go get some dinner later?"

"Really? Do you think you can? Um, sure!" she said, smiling brightly.

"Great!" I said.

"You know, every place is going to be busy tonight. Do you want me to try to find us a reservation before I leave?" she asked, ever the efficient manager.

"That would be great!" I said. "Maybe someplace not too loud? My ears could use a break."

"Yes, sir. I'll see what I can do!" she kidded. "I have to go now. I'll call you from home. See you later." Nina walked out the door.

"All right!" I walked back into the studio with a happy bounce in my step.

Mick had decided to play a cowbell on "Gold Dust Woman," so he had mounted it on his drum kit. This made for a completely different feel than we had on any song to date. A cowbell! Mick actually played it as one of the components of his drum kit, replacing his usual high hat with the raucous cowbell. I think this was the first time I had ever recorded a song with a predominant cowbell part.

Everyone had a different take on "Gold Dust Woman."

"It's an evil song," Lindsey said. "It's very dark, and I'm guessing that the acrimony was directed at me."

"I wrote 'Gold Dust Woman' before we started *Rumours*, and there weren't that many drugs around back then," Stevie said. "It's about groupie-type women who would stand around and give Christine and me dirty looks. But as soon as one of the guys came in the room, they were overcome with smiles." We recorded seven takes of that song and kept take 4 as the master.

Working with Lindsey and Richard could be trying. Richard would generally agree with Lindsey, but Lindsey would often see things differently from one day to the next, depending on his mood and his response to his pot. He could easily get paranoid. For instance, if I had done an unusual mix on a song, he might insist that we needed to recut it, only to later decide that he loved my mix and just wanted me to refocus it a little. Sometimes he would go from hating it to loving it and back to hating it, all in one night. We'd have to wait until the next day to listen with fresh ears, not knowing whether we had gotten it right.

The night receptionist came in and handed Cris a note. He gave it to me. It was Nina's address and directions.

Christine was packing up to leave in a hurry—her hot date with Curry, I guessed. Richard said he needed some alone time and had decided to spend the night at the studio. I think he knew I had a date.

"Cutlass, I can't go any farther. I'm going to stay right here tonight. Don't ask me why, I just gotta do it, mate," Richard said, putting a hand on my shoulder.

Richard was funny that way; he hoped for the best for me and was willing to sleep on the couch in case my Valentine's dinner went really well. He and I had been together literally 24/7 for the last three weeks, and I knew he needed a break, too. He ended up sleeping under the console that night, and I had the bedroom we shared all to myself. I headed off for my Valentine's evening with the lovely Nina.

The weather was cold and drizzly, typical Northern California crap weather. I picked up Nina from the cute little house she was renting. She was wearing a long coat and gloves, me, a baseball jersey and a ski jacket. She had made reservations at a small restaurant in Mill Valley.

I took her for a candlelight meal at a restaurant called the Roadhouse, a long-standing local favorite. It was dug into the side of the mountain, surrounded by oak trees.

We walked into the restaurant and could see the night lights of Tiburon reflecting off the cold waters of the bay. I gave the waiter my name. On the opposite wall was an old rock fireplace with a warm fire blazing. The restaurant was dark and secluded, with a single red rose on each table along with a couple of candles.

"Can I take your coat?" I asked and helped Nina. Underneath, she wore a soft clinging red dress. She looked wonderful.

We stood in front of the fire, close to each other. Her skin seemed to glow in the firelight. The maître d' came over, told us our table was ready, and took Nina's coat from me. He sat us at a table for four, but we sat next to each other. The table was made of a dark rustic wood, fitting for Mill Valley.

From our table, we could see both the fireplace and the lights on the bay. When our waiter came over, I ordered a bottle of Christine's favorite champagne. The waiter opened it and poured it into our glasses. I raised my glass and said, "If only I didn't have to work all the damn time, maybe we could go have some fun and do this more often."

She put her hand on mine. "We will," she said and gave me a broad smile.

After dinner, I ordered two glasses of cognac. As we sat and sipped our digestif, the candlelight flickered on our table and made her even more lovely. Her face was radiant. I was finally alone with this beautiful woman. I leaned over and kissed her.

"Would you like to come over to my place?" I asked. A few seconds passed. She was still smiling.

For the last week or so, Stevie had continued to go to Sly Stone's pit, spending hours there, while we added and changed parts on the songs we'd already recorded, trying to make each song better. We had six and a half songs in the can (as long as no one changed his or her mind). So, when she wasn't with us in the control room, Stevie spent time in Sly's dark room. It was like her personal writing space.

Stevie was foremost a singer-songwriter; she wasn't into the technical end of the music. So, while all of this experimentation was going on in the studio with the other members of the band, she was frustrated and pretty much bored out of her mind. Sly Stone's weird space had a four-poster bed covered in black fur and an entrance resembling two furry red lips. Stevie took Ginny with her, and they immersed themselves in the space. The quiet of Sly's pit was the escape she was looking for; she was in there for hours at a time.

Later that evening, she came into the studio and said, "Guys, you have to hear the song I just wrote!" She sat down at the Fender Rhodes in the control room and played her new three-chord song. It was instantly dubbed "Spinners" because it reminded us of a song off the Spinners' album.

We listened to one play through, and Christine said, "That's great. Play it again."

Lindsey grabbed his acoustic guitar and started playing along. The acoustic guitar really added a nice color to the song. That's how songs are; you hear it one way with one instrument, and then you add another, and the whole vibe of the song changes. That's a major reason it took us so long to make *Rumours*. We kept looking for the perfect part to complement each instrument in our songs.

After three rundowns in the control room, the band went to their instruments in the studio to work out their parts. Mick jumped on his drums, John on the bass, Christine on the Hammond B3, and they all started playing with Stevie, who had scribbled some lyrics for the first and second verses and chorus. She sang them into her mic. "Dreams" was a sad but hopeful song about her feelings for Lindsey, their breakup, and how he was taking her for granted.

We cut the track drums, bass, acoustic guitar, organ and Rhodes piano, and work vocal. Like "Gold Dust Woman" and Mick's use of the cowbell, Mick's focus on "Dreams" was the high hat, which runs hauntingly throughout the song. To make the high hat more mysterious, I ran it through a phaser, making it sound slightly swishy and swirling.

Lindsey played his acoustic in iso 2, and Stevie sang the work vocal while she played the Rhodes in the studio with everyone else. Christine sat in on the B3 organ, and we recorded ten takes before John left, calling it a night and ending the session.

During the next two weeks, we worked on more overdubs on all of the songs. On February 25, we recut "Keep Me There," beefing up the beginning to match the strength of the ending. The track sheet says that take 8 was "the final thrust," which we cut into the great original end portion of the song. On February 26, nearly one month after arriving in Sausalito, we worked on "Gold Dust Woman" a little more to see if we could get a better version. Finally, on March 2, we did five more takes of "Dreams"—I remember that we called take 24 "classy." Finished with "Dreams" for the day, we ended early because the next day was our recording of "Songbird" at Zellerbach Auditorium.

I had made special arrangements at the Zellerbach Auditorium for March 3, 1976. I wanted the orchestral shell placed onstage to project the sound of the nine-foot Steinway out into the empty hall. I had also rented eight $3,000 classic tube microphones and placed them throughout the auditorium to pick up the lovely nuances of the piano. Then, as a surprise for Christine, I had requested that a bouquet of roses be placed on her piano with three colored spotlights to illuminate them from above. I really wanted to set the mood!

An empty auditorium is a beautiful thing; sound reverberates freely without any people in it. Richard and I arrived at Zellerbach at 9 a.m. The remote truck was already there. It always got to location recordings early, in order to get the best parking. The Record Plant remote truck was a complete recording studio on wheels. It was air-conditioned with a full-size console, two 24-track tape machines, and a complete complement of microphones and mic stands. In addition, they were able to find eight expensive tube microphones (I was still going for that Grammy).

At least four 250-foot cables were rolled out and into the hall. One was a 220-volt cable to power the truck; two other cables (called snakes) carried the twenty-four individual mic cables inside; the last snake also handled audio and video communications so that we could see and talk to the stage.

This reminds me of a story: A few years earlier, when I was the guy rolling up the heavy cable on my hands and knees in downtown New Orleans after a recent rainstorm, a man and his beautiful woman were walking past me. I remember the cable was muddy and wet, and this guy was smoking a pipe and had his overcoat hanging on his shoulders, the way Italians and spoiled rich kids do. He looked down at me on the wet sidewalk in my dirty Levi's and said in a "Frasier-esque" tone, "My good man, can't you get a decent job during the day?" They kept walking, and I never saw them again. I knew he had no idea who I was or who I'd turn out to be. I had big plans, and this was the road I needed to take. (Sir, if you're reading this, please contact me. I'd love to talk to you!)

In the auditorium, everyone was counting on me for sound direction because I had the most experience in live recording. The first thing we had to do was position the big nine-foot grand piano. Then we opened its lid to the full stop to get maximum sound projection into the hall. I chose the microphones to use on the piano—four for the grand, two close, and two farther away. In the audience, I spread eight more mics throughout to capture the best ambient hall sound.

When Christine arrived, we dimmed the house lights so that all she could see were the flowers and the piano with the spotlight shining down from the heavens. She nearly broke into tears. Then she started to play.

In the truck, I listened to every pair of mics to see what I liked and what I thought needed to be changed. The piano sounded fantastic. We soon realized that Christine needed to play a consistent tempo, so we asked her to play to a click in her headphones the way Mick did. She tried it and hated the click popping in her ears.

"Ken, I can't play my lovely song with this bloody fucking clicking blasting my ears!" she said, irritated.

"Okay, I completely understand. How about if someone else listens to the click and plays an instrument in your headphones?" I asked through my talkback.

"Who would that be?" she asked.

"Well," I paused. "I could give Mick the click in his headphones, and he could play his snare drum in a room somewhere, quietly using brushes instead of drumsticks. You could play your piano listening to Mick's snare in your phones."

"Or . . . it could be Lindsey on his acoustic guitar," Richard added, finishing my thought.

Lindsey agreed, and we put him on the other side of the orchestral shell so that his guitar wouldn't be picked up in the room mics. We fed the click to Lindsey, and he counted off the intro. Christine and Lindsey started playing "Songbird" together.

It was beautiful, except for one problem: we couldn't let Christine sing while she was playing the piano because her voice would leak into the piano. Actually, there were two other problems: the next was that when the more distant piano mics picked up the sound of her voice, they would compromise the vocal quality of her actual vocal mic, and if she made a mistake on either instrument, then the take couldn't be used; and third, Lindsey was playing his guitar too loud. We could hear it in the sensitive ambience mics I'd rented. So, the fix was that Christine had to sing "Songbird" in her head, while she played the piano and listened to Lindsey's softer strumming for tempo.

Christine is a natural performer, and this was a challenge for her. I felt bad for her, but it was the only way we could get the clarity and flexibility we wanted for the recording. By this time it was already after midnight, and she was starting to get tired and cranky. It didn't help that we had to keep stopping because Lindsey would forget and play too loud. We'd hear his guitar in the ambience mics again, and we'd have to stop the take. At that point, we weren't sure we wanted a guitar in the song. We asked for everyone's patience, and about 1 a.m. we got the perfect piano take.

After singing all night in her head, Christine could finally stand onstage and sing the song aloud. She sang to the final piano take, playing in her headphones. I expected her voice to reverberate throughout the hall, creating the perfect natural reverb, but it didn't. She was singing up close and personal to our expensive microphone, so we got only minimal reverberation.

"Okay," I said. "Let's just get the vocal and worry about the reverb later."

"Thank you, Ken. I want to go home," she said.

She got the perfect vocal in less than an hour, but I still needed more of the hall's natural reverberation, and I wasn't going to stop until I got it. I thanked Christine and sent her home, planning to solve the problem after she left.

"Thank you, darling!" she said, kissing me on the cheek. She hopped into her limo and headed home.

"What do you want to do now?" Cris asked me.

I remembered that reverb chambers used to be isolated rooms, built so that they were especially reverberant, much as a large bathroom is today. Studios would put a speaker in one end of the room and a microphone at the other to get this effect. The engineer turned a knob that sent a vocal or an instrument through the speaker into the echo room, and the mic would bring it back to the engineer's console.

"Hey, do we have any speakers around here?" I called out.

"Backstage," someone answered.

"Great. Let's hook them up. I want to play the vocal through the speakers and record it."

About an hour later, we were ready. I hit PLAY and sent Christine's vocal into Zellerbach Auditorium. I stood onstage as "For you . . ." floated through the auditorium. It sounded so fucking good. There was one volume level that sounded best for the recording, so I gave the okay to re-record Christine's vocal track. Everyone was quiet in the hall. I played her final vocal performance through those stage speakers out into the hall and recorded it in all of my expensive rented microphones.

By the time we were done, it was after 4 a.m., and everyone was exhausted. They had all given their best and never complained, and the result was amazing.

"That's a wrap!" I said.

As the crew packed up all of the gear, I made a rough mix of Christine's piano part, her final vocal, and all of the piano ambience mics and vocal ambience tracks. "It's perfect!" Richard said.

"Nice one, lads!" said Mick, patting us on the backs and giving us our last toot for the road.

Christine once said, years later, when the band was talking about getting back together, "I agreed, as long as we didn't have to play 'Songbird.' John asked me why, and I said, 'Because I don't want to cry anymore.' And he said, 'You cry, too?'"

When we loaded out of Zellerbach, the sun was just coming up. We had limos waiting to take us home. As Richard and I crossed over the Bay Bridge that morning, we were feeling very proud of what we had done. As a man, I feel it's akin to giving birth to something real, something alive. Out of Richard's and my love for this music, we persevered and overcame all obstacles to make this perfect recording for the world, and it still lives on today.

7

Don't Stop

I thought I was drying up when we started recording *Rumours*. Then, one day in Sausalito, I sat at the piano, and my four-and-a-half songs on the album are a result of that.

—*Christine McVie*

As my career was just getting started, my mom and dad were just winding down theirs. Both of my parents were retiring at the same time—my mom as executive secretary at Saratoga School District and my Dad from Ames Research, a division of NASA. Friday, March 12, was a big day for them. Ames was throwing a retirement party for my dad in Redwood City, about a half hour from the studio. I was invited. So was the rest of the band, for that matter, but they weren't about to leave the safety of the studio.

Somehow I managed to get the afternoon off, and I drove down to the party. I came late, and the first thing I saw when I walked in was my mom and dad dancing together, cheek to cheek, forties style. Everybody was dressed in nice clothes, but there I was in my Levi's and brightly colored tennies. I think I wore a sports coat to accompany my long hair and beard.

As soon as I walked in the door, I felt out of place, as if I were hung over in front of all of my folks' friends. I probably was, but in the safety of the studio, I just never noticed that I felt "weird." Anyway, my folks were happy to see me, and I asked my mom to dance with me.

Meanwhile, my dad played the Fleetwood Mac card, mentioning how proud he was of his boy. Suddenly, I felt welcomed by everyone. I had a couple of drinks and immediately felt better, but I couldn't wait to get that sports coat off and get back to my weirdo friends and coworkers.

I stayed at the party until the traffic died down, then I headed out, up past San Francisco to Sausalito. On the drive home, I thought how great it was to be able to get out and see my folks and celebrate their retirement. I called Nina, and she asked me to come over to her quaint home in Mill Valley. We spent the rest of the evening sitting in front of her fireplace, drinking fine red wine, and listening to the rain outside.

At the studio on Sunday morning, we all managed to have smiles on our faces, even though we were working on another fucking Sunday! I don't know what it was about Mick, but I just couldn't convince him that we needed a day off. What was even worse, nobody else sided with me, because on most Sundays, Stevie, John, Lindsey, or Christine, or any combination of them, just wouldn't show up until much later in the day. Or John would be there early, Lindsey would come in during the afternoon, and Mick, Stevie, and Christine would take the late shift. Yet Richard and I had to be there all day long.

I was starting to go a little bit nuts. I needed some alone time; I needed some Nina time; I needed some Scooter time!

"Hey, Ken! Check out John," Richard said, laughing loudly.

I looked up from my position at the console and out at John, who was sitting on the floor next to the guitar stand that he had rigged to hold a wine bottle—upside down. He had a tube coming out of it, and the wine looked as if it was going into his arm like an IV.

Then Stevie said she wanted that day to be hers. She pulled a cassette out of her purse and played her song "Think About It (Before You Go)." This was an unusual song for Stevie. When I first heard it, I thought the

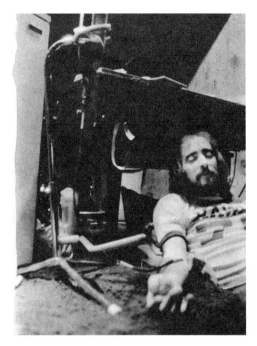

Everybody laughed at John's practical joke.

music and vocal style were very country, not her typical rock ballad. Her voice had a country "twang" that I had never noticed before. It was as if she had just gotten lazy about hiding her country accent.

Lindsey sang the duet with her, and I'll be damned if he didn't sound like he had a country twang, too! The song had a very straightforward rock track, drums, bass, electric guitar, organ, and Stevie's vocal. We put Stevie in iso 2 and everyone else in the big room.

When we ran it down, I thought, This is different. I didn't hear it fitting on the album, though. It was a simple song, no strange changes or parts; I figured we'd get it right away, and we did—in only about an hour and a half. We put down eight takes and got one we liked.

Unfortunately, I was right, and "Think About It" didn't make the album. During the next few months, we added some guitars, bass, and background vocals. Stevie decided to keep it for one of her own albums. Ultimately, it found a home on her *Bella Donna* album, released five years later, in 1981.

One of the cooks brought a plate of warm baked cookies into the control room and set it on the table behind me, in front of the couch where the girls were sitting. It was perfect timing, because we were all hungry.

"I guess we'll have to make this a backward dinner," I said, laughing. "That's where you start with dessert first."

"I'm in," Richard said.

"Me, too," Lindsey said.

The smell of the warm chocolate chip cookies was amazing. Christine took one. Stevie had one, and Mick and John did as well.

"These are delicious," Richard said.

"But there's kind of a strange aftertaste." Christine put hers down. The rest of us kept right on eating, because we thought that they were really good!

After a few minutes, I started to feel strange. A very heavy confusion came over me. "I need to get some water," I said to everyone and escaped out of the control room door toward anywhere I could find. I went outside by my car. It was still drizzling. I had an overwhelming feeling of paranoia. I went back inside to find that everyone else was feeling the same way.

"Hey, what was in those cookies?" I asked Cris, the first person I saw when I came back inside. My vision was distorted, and I couldn't see things clearly in the dark studio. I felt tense and uncomfortable, just awful.

"I heard there's almost an ounce of really good pot in these cookies," Cris said.

"I'm really stoned, Cris. I don't even want to be with people now. How are you feeling?"

"I didn't have any of the cookies," he said. "I can't eat chocolate."

"Cool, you take the session for a while," I said. "I'm going to go get some coffee to see if I can snap out of it."

I wasn't the only one who couldn't handle the pot cookies. The band had called the piano tuner, again. He came in with his girlfriend, and she started eating the cookies. They were very straight people, and she started freaking out when she felt the effects of the cookies.

"Oh, my God! What's happening to me?" she asked in a panic. "I'm going insane! I need to call the doctor! Call the police!"

Mick came in and took her out of the studio, bringing her into the conference room, where he helped calm her down.

Later, we learned that Andrea, our cook, had simmered pot with melted butter and used the mixture in our cookies.

Richard and I teamed up a little later and tried to act normal. Some of the girls from Agatha's came down to the studio, but we were too wasted to talk to them. Really! Instead, we took them into the lounge/game room where the roadies were vegetating in front of the TV, and then we disappeared, leaving them to fend for themselves. Stevie and Christine went back to their hotel, then Lindsey left with John and Mick.

That ended the session for everyone that day. I never found out exactly what made that pot so potent, but I remember that I couldn't sit down. I wasn't comfortable being with anybody, so I just kept moving. When I saw someone coming, I went the other way. We must have been a sight! Richard and I drove home together that night in silence.

By Monday, March 15, I had lost all ability to keep the band sane and sober. There were continual outbreaks of drugs, alcohol, and paranoia. We still had a month to go in Sausalito, and everyone was getting home-sick. Our start time was slipping later and later each day. As I explained earlier, the twelve-hour rule always held true. If they left the studio at 4 a.m., then they would not be back until 4 p.m. Period.

After the tracking sessions wound down and we started the overdubs, the band members each chose the best time for them to be in the studio. This meant they were rarely all there at the same time, so Richard and I had to cover the overlap with longer hours. Sometimes we'd take shifts or else one of us would bail out early and leave the other there with the crazies. Whenever we went past midnight, the Peruvian marching powder showed its ugly face. As I said, I couldn't run the board if I was drinking, but I could with a little pot or coke, so I didn't drink.

Mick was the worst influence. He always made the excuse that genius music would come out of the transcensions, but it never did. Maybe that was because the whole band was rarely there for most transcensions. Just the coked-up crazies: Mick and usually Stevie or Christine. If Mick could get either of them tooted up enough, then off the deep end we'd go. Very rarely would Lindsey fall for the late nights, and John never did.

Mick had a phrase he frequently repeated, which I later learned was a quote from Robert Frost: "The woods are lonely, dark and deep, and we have miles to go before we sleep." If that phrase was spoken to him, he would go into a trancelike state and reach into his pocket and pull out his tiny bottle of coke and share it with us. It became a game of sorts.

We were working later and later every night. At one point, we started the session at 8 p.m. and worked until 8 a.m. the next morning. We didn't usually work after the cleaning crew arrived in the morning. Inside the studio it was always dark, making it hard to tell what time it was—I think Mick wanted it that way.

Back at the house, word got out that we weren't sleeping in our beds on most nights. So, friends of the band or—very often—girls who just wanted to be close to the band would frequently sleep in our empty beds.

We didn't start one day until 2 p.m. We were tracking a new song Christine had written called "Yesterday's Gone." This was the original title, but in a few weeks, after Lindsey sang the duet with Christine, the chorus line "Don't stop . . ." developed so strongly that we all just started calling it "Don't Stop."

A lot of people think that "Don't Stop" is a Lindsey song, because he sings the first verse, but Christine wrote the song about the end of her relationship with John, after it was beginning to improve. Lindsey wanted to sing it with Christine, and they agreed to alternate verses. "'I never meant any harm to you' is the sentiment of the song," Christine explained.

The song is a shuffle, a blues term for a style of music. Basically, the high hat plays a triplet feel and the kick and the snare hit on the 1 and the 3. So the high hat is playing a faster feel, while the main drum is playing a tempo about half that of the hat. Many of the swing songs of the 1940s were shuffles.

On "Don't Stop," I could really see that everyone in the band was starting to collaborate and work together. They were always democratic when it came to expressing different ideas, but everyone had an unswerving faith in Lindsey's visionary ideas and production sense. Lindsey, in turn, knew that he could push the other members of the band to give their best—not just Stevie, but also Christine. After six years of being in a blues band, Christine felt liberated by the band's shift to a more pop sound. That better suited her songwriting style.

Drums, bass, electric guitar, and electric piano were the setup of the original tracking session, so that Christine could sing and play her electric piano. Later, she and Lindsey would re-sing the song as a duet, and Christine would replace the electric piano with an upright tack piano. Christine was really excited about this song. We got the master on take 25.

I was never happy with the drum sound, because the snare was soft, and I couldn't make it crack the way it did on "Lovin' Fun," but the song works. Even though the song's potential always eluded me, it ultimately was the second single released off *Rumours*, and it reached number three on the U.S. singles chart. In 1992, Bill Clinton chose it as the theme song for his presidency when he won. Then, in 1993, he persuaded the then disbanded Fleetwood Mac to reunite and play a live performance for his inaugural celebration. So, yes, Clinton played a pivotal role in getting the band back together for their 1997 comeback tour and concert video, *The Dance*, shot on a Warner Bros. sound stage in Burbank, California.

By the end of the night, when we were first recording "Don't Stop," Christine was really happy, and she was getting on a pretty good buzz. But we were tired from our cookie event from the night before, and nothing was helping. So Richard and I split at the first sign of John's departure. I went to see Nina, and Richard went to see Ginger at Agatha's. Lindsey ended up staying over at Christina's, who was fast becoming Lindsey's new girlfriend. I was thrilled when I got to the house to find no one sleeping in my bed that night!

The next week was tough. My step-grandfather, Pa, had surgery to remove part of his lung. We overdubbed lead vocals on "Don't Stop" and guitars and background vocals on ". . . Addy," "Strummer," and "Think

About It." Hours-wise, this week had been the worst yet; we had taken only one day off, but we'd worked until 2:30 a.m. the night before. By the time we got home that night and wound down, it was closing in on 4 a.m.

John was already awake for the next day. We all sat and stared at episodes of *Happy Days* and *The Mod Squad* to help us get to sleep. A couple of weeks earlier, about halfway through our run in Sausalito, I had decided that I needed to find a way to get to sleep quickly and more effectively than all of the booze, coffee, and cocaine allowed. I discovered that NyQuil was perfect for this. On many nights, Richard and I would take a shot or two of NyQuil on the drive home to ensure that we'd get to sleep. I started to keep a bottle in my car just for that purpose. The best alternative was brandy, but NyQuil was my go-to solution.

A few times when we got home, we found groupies sleeping in our beds, because the road guys had probably told them that it would be okay; they figured we wouldn't come home until morning. The groupies were cute enough, but sleep was vastly more important than having sex with a groupie—and working fifteen hours a day takes most of the fun out of sex. One night Richard and I came home to find two naked girls in each of our beds.

"Remember, the show must go on, mate," Richard said. I was tired, and the last thing I wanted was to stay awake any longer. I slipped into my bed with the girls as quietly as I could.

I should point out that I had seen these girls at the house several times earlier, so I sort of knew them. They would be leaving for work as I was coming home from the studio in the morning. They were flirtatious and very cute, but that was that. This particular night, though, they weren't going anywhere, and they were happy to see me. They awoke as I settled into bed.

"Good morning, ladies," I whispered. "Sorry to bother you. If you can make room for me, I'll be asleep in a second."

They weren't having any part of that. This was the seventies, after all. But, then, I was asleep ten lovely minutes later.

On the way into the studio that morning, I realized I hadn't paid my bills. My bank account was getting low. I had all of the checks that I had been tossing into my glove box these past weeks, and I had almost forgotten them. I drove into Sausalito, parked, got the envelopes out of my glove box, took the checks out of their envelopes, and carefully endorsed them. This was the most money I'd ever had at one time, and I still had three checks to come.

I walked into the Sausalito branch of Bank of America with my seven checks, approached one of the clerks, and opened a brand-new account. I remember their new policy was to ask for a six-letter secret password. I was still sort of dopey that morning from my late night of NyQuil and sleeping with the groupies, and all I could think of was "CALLAG."

A few months earlier, I had been given a gold record for my live recording of George Carlin's *Class Clown* album, and on it they had misspelled my name as Ken Callag. So CALLAG became my password for the next couple of years.

When I got to the studio, it was a little past noon. Nina met me at the door, laughing. She had this great, really happy laugh, but I couldn't spend much time talking or flirting with her because I had to get into the studio.

Lindsey wanted to work on a guitar song for a while, and he told us that it was essentially a complicated picking song with four parts and a few harmonics parts (the guitar part where you play a guitar string just so the harmonic resonates). He thought Mick would be playing brushes on his snares, a type of press roll pattern. This song became known as "Brushes," especially because it didn't have lyrics yet.

Lindsey went into iso 2 and prepared to play. It would just be him and Mick—John intended to play bass when there were more parts and a vocal to play to. We soon realized that we needed to lay down the guitar first, played to a click. Lindsey was still unsure what he wanted "Brushes" to sound like. We experimented with different tempos, finally settling on 155 beats per minute.

While Lindsey played his acoustic guitar, we could hear the click track going *pop, pop, pop* inside his headphones through his array of guitar mics. We were going for a big guitar sound because there were no other instruments. The guitar sounded great but not with the *pop, pop, pop* throughout the song. We had to be creative to get rid of this. We wrapped duct tape around Lindsey's headphones to hold them tight against his ears. Then I found a wool beanie and had him pull it down over his head and ears to seal the headphones to his head. That worked, and we forged on.

After three hours, six joints, four beers, two sets of guitar strings, and five metronome settings, we finally got a take that we liked. When Lindsey had to go to the bathroom, he had to unplug his headphones, but he didn't dare take the headphone setup off his head. He looked like a guy with serious dreadlocks and a big Jamaican pull-off cap walking around the studio. We all had a good laugh!

When we were sure we had the part, Lindsey took off his headset. Mick and John came back from lunch, and they were both a little buzzed. We were ready for Mick's brushes part. He came into the control room. We played him Lindsey's guitar track without the click. Because the song was short, only about two minutes and twenty seconds, it would be a cake-walk for Mick, even in his state. Lindsey played it a few times for Mick, and then Mick played along with the guitar. His brushes sounded good but not great. Of course, there was only the one guitar and no vocals, bass, or anything else to listen to. We recorded three versions of Mick's snare rolls. Then we asked Lindsey to add a few more parts. He played four more guitar parts, and they were beautiful and complex.

Eventually, this song became "Never Going Back Again" and, in the end, we didn't use the brushes or the bass. If you listen closely, you can still hear the click leakage in the distance. We added bottom end to it and made the click sound as if it was Lindsey tapping his foot—not because we couldn't get rid of the click, but because we grew to like the way it sounded.

By March 25, 1976, we had only two weeks left to record at the Record Plant. Fleetwood Mac had scheduled a tour to support the White Album, so they had to go immediately into rehearsals when they got back to Los Angeles.

One thing they had to decide before they got home was whether to play any of their new songs when they went out on the road. There were two schools of thought: the first was not to spoil the surprise of the new album; the second was to play the new songs on the tour, letting the music grow in front of their fans, making them hungry to buy their new record.

I was for the first plan. I thought it made more sense to save the new songs until we were finished with them. The record label, though, didn't always see things my way.

Back in the 1970s, the music business was great. We had plenty of time and money to finish an album properly. I think that's missing today. Artists are forced to finish their albums too soon, and they don't get to put the frosting and love into it that they want.

A manager of a band I once worked with asked me, "Why are you spending so much time on *that* song? The other one's the hit! By the time someone hears *that* song, we'll already have their money! Be smart, Ken!"

"Listen, I don't work that way," I said to him. "I want to make every song as good as it can be!"

Typical manager, he just rolled his eyes at me as if he had all of the answers and I knew nothing. He cut off the money from finishing the other songs properly. I would love to tell you the name of the band, but you've never heard of them because the radio stations didn't like the song he picked as the hit.

I refuse to shortcut any song before it's had as much attention as it deserves. I don't want any losers on my albums, if I can possibly avoid them.

So, there we were on Thursday: we had been adding and subtracting parts from "Don't Stop" for a while. We'd been working long, long hours for weeks, and we'd had so little down time. By then, I knew that Nina liked me, but I hadn't had enough time to pursue a relationship with her. Mick finally promised us a Sunday off. Of course, this meant we were expected to work until dawn that Saturday night.

The day before, we had decided that the tempo of "Dreams" still wasn't hypnotic enough.

"What if we try a loop?" Lindsey suggested.

"Okay," Richard and I agreed. Cris loaded our favorite take of "Dreams," and we played the track—just drums—looking for the most perfect drum section. Believe it or not, we couldn't find eight perfect bars, so we had to have Mick play about a minute of the verse to get them perfectly steady. Eight bars took about sixteen seconds to play. At fifteen inches per second, this meant that about twenty feet of tape would need to be cut out of the drum take and spliced together, front to back, to make a continuous loop. Our tape loop would be a twenty-foot-long circle.

The next step in our experiment was to play the loop on our 24-track and then record all of the tracks onto another 24-track recorder for the rest of the song, which would run about four and a half minutes. We loaded the tape onto the big 24-track, carefully threading it around the first tape guides, the tension bar, and the playback heads and through the last tape guide.

We couldn't just drop our tape in and play our big loop, because the tape machine required that the tape be held at the right tension all of the time. If it had been on reels, it would have been easy to do, but it wasn't. It was just loose tape.

"Okay," I said. "We were expecting this." Richard and I had asked for six guys to help us out in the control room. We had to create the tension without the tape being put on a reel. We had six mic stands and six two-inch empty reels brought into our room. We placed the reels around the room and used them as tape guides. Then we asked the guys to brace with their feet on the base of the stands and pull the stands and the reels apart to keep the needed tension on the tape.

The six of us—Mick, Ray, Rhino, Curry, Lindsey, and me—stood in the control room, making up the parts of a giant tape recorder.

"Ready?" I asked.

"Yes!" the others said. Cris hit RECORD on the new tape, and Richard hit PLAY on our loop machine. It was working!

"Nobody move an inch!" I said. I think each of us held our breath for the full four minutes and thirty seconds until the song finished. We played the new four-and-a-half-minute song, and it worked fantastically. It was hypnotic.

With the loop experiment accomplished, we added the keyboard. Stevie sang the lead vocal. We put on some effects from the keyboard, adding the phasing back on the high hat, and it was amazing! It was really hypnotic. Stevie had her spell-maker.

She sang the song eight or nine times, but something was off. She couldn't find the same mood she had had the first time she had sung it.

But she was a trooper and didn't give up. Lindsey played an acoustic guitar for her to sing to. Nope. She tried smoking a joint. Better. The big guns came out—Courvoisier. Interesting. She tried a magic bump. Nothing had the feel of her original vocal.

"No problem," I said. "Let's just copy the original across from the old master."

"That's sounds great, Ken," Stevie said.

"Nice one," Mick added.

"Cris, put the old master back up. Let's transfer the old vocal back to our new tape." Because we were set up to record from one machine to another, we were ready to go.

In those days, we didn't have the ability to run two machines at the same time or at the same speed. Today, this would be easy to resolve, but it wasn't back in the seventies.

We had to find starting marks on both tapes, press PLAY on each, and then move the marks until the vocal was right on it. We needed almost perfect timing to record the old vocal onto the new tape, but because the two machines ran at slightly different speeds, we knew that we'd eventually have to find new starting marks and repeat the process.

We finally got the original lead vocal transferred over at about 3 a.m. Stevie had long since fallen asleep. We left the setup until the next day so that we could listen to what we had done. Hello, NyQuil parachute!

On Friday, March 26, I was hurting from that late session the night before. We didn't get started until 3 p.m. All I was thinking about was, Off on Sunday, off on Sunday! Mick had promised us that day off.

We had to make some slight adjustments to our previous night's vocal transfer, and Lindsey put a new electric guitar part on "Spinners" through my Leslie setup. "Spinners" was beginning to sound magical. Christine had added her B3 organ part in the chorus. Then Mick had gone in and added toms and crash cymbals, and John had laid in his unforgettably hypnotic bass line. Lindsey added his acoustic.

The chorus was really shaping up. Months later, we would come back to "Dreams" and add piano, backgrounds, more tom fills, and piano licks, and we'd also attempt to improve our original work vocal at least five times—all of them unsuccessfully. The work vocal was just better than any of our later attempts. All in all, a great start to the weekend!

With all that we had accomplished under our belts, we tried some experimenting. Okay, transcending. We recorded one of Stevie's ethereal songs, "Planets of the Universe," which wasn't used on *Rumours* and was eventually recut; it appeared in 2001 on Stevie's *Trouble in Shangri-La* album. Then we did several takes of a Lindsey idea, three takes of an idea that Christine had, and another great song, a country ballad from Lindsey called "Doesn't Anything Last?" This song was never recut, and it appears on the 2004 *Rumours* remaster released by Rhino Records.

Before Mick left that Friday night, I convinced him that on Saturday we should make safeties (we call them backups today) of all of our songs, especially the new ones, in case there was an earthquake. "Hey, it could happen," I told him. In the music business, unprotected tapes are worse than unprotected sex.

The band took Saturday off, leaving Richard, Cris, the road crew, and me to straighten things up. This was important because we were getting ready to leave Sausalito. Two weeks from today! I thought.

I had to get serious with Nina. I didn't know how much I'd be able to see her in the future if our schedules remained the same. I had asked her whether she would consider living in L.A., and her answer was always, "Are you fuckin' kidding me? I made it out of New York, and I'm not about to go to La-la land! I love the Bay Area!" I should have tried harder to convince her to move to Los Angeles.

On our day off that Sunday, I slept in blissfully until about 11:30 a.m. Then I showered and jumped in the Benz with Scooter to drive down to see Pa in San Jose Hospital. I was really looking forward to the drive, and I knew it would take about an hour and a half to get there. I headed down the 101 Freeway, over the Golden Gate Bridge, and into San Francisco.

The 101 didn't go all the way through as a freeway. It turned back into surface streets after the Golden Gate. I took the picturesque San Francisco streets for a few miles before I could get back onto the 101. I passed by the Presidio and the Palace of Fine Arts and then drove through the Marina district. There were three gas stations in one block of that area, and each of them had a big sign that read, "Gas War!" I filled up my car's tank at $0.49 per gallon! Why don't they have gas wars anymore? Has the war already been fought, and we're the losers?

The 101 in San Francisco is elevated, so I could see the grand San Francisco residential architecture below, the Bay Bridge to my left, and the airplanes heading into and out of SFO to the south. In the distance, I could also see Candlestick Park. When I was young, I used to go there to watch the San Francisco Giants play. Geez, that stadium could be cold, but it had been worth it to see my favorite team play! When I was a boy, Pa had taught me how to play baseball. I loved to pitch. He had taught me how to throw my first curveball. Pa had worked for the Brooklyn Dodgers when he lived in New York, so I always thought I was learning from a pro. That's why I loved going to Candlestick to see games with him.

Ten years earlier, I had seen the Beatles play their last concert in Candlestick. Around the same time, Lindsey Buckingham was joining a folk group; guitar picking and singing were his passion. In London, Mick and John were just forming Fleetwood Mac. Christine was studying sculpture at an art college in Birmingham, with the goal of becoming an art teacher. Stevie was just graduating from Menlo Atherton High.

I say that I saw the Beatles play because I certainly couldn't hear them. The audience screamed nonstop from the time the Beatles took the stage until they finished. At the beginning of the concert, they were brought out in an armored car to the center of Candlestick Park, right to second base, where a small stage was set up. I remember thinking that it looked like the same setup they had used on *The Ed Sullivan Show*, but I wondered, How could they play all of their new complicated songs on that old set?

As it turned out, they couldn't. They played only their earlier songs, the simple ones.

I took the turn-off for the 280 Freeway to avoid all of the small cities on the 101. I drove down through the redwood trees into an area called the Golden Gate National Recreation Area. Five years earlier, I had driven the 280 from San Jose to Redwood City regularly, taking my guitar-playing partner home to his place from my apartment. We used to write songs and rehearse. In fact, we had written more than forty really lousy songs together. Through all of that, though, I had learned to tune a guitar by ear, and it helped me become a better recording engineer.

I drove by my old high school and past my old law office (where I had learned that I shouldn't become a lawyer). I drove past my dad's father's home, which was a preschool now. I went past his aunt's house, which had been the San Jose Mountain Cyclery bicycle shop in the thirties and the forties. Then I drove to San Jose Hospital, where Pa was being treated for lung cancer. My dad, my sister, and I had all been born in this same hospital.

Pa loved his Scotch and his cigars, and he was a hell of a cook. On holidays, we would go over to Nana's and Pa's. After Pa had had a few drinks, he'd break out into song: "I want to be a friend of yours, yup, and a little bit more. I want to be a friend of yours, buzzing round your door. I want to be a friend of yours, yup, and a lit-tle bit, yup, and a lit-tle bit, yup and a lit-tle bit mooorrre." This would be followed by a long and loud laugh. Pa loved to laugh.

I took the elevator up to his floor and walked into his room. My mom and dad and Nana were already there. When Pa saw me, he began to cry.

"Ken! I didn't think I was ever going to see you again." He sobbed. I bent over and hugged him as he lay in his bed.

We hugged for what seemed like ages. He said he was surprised at how much hair I had grown. Half of Pa's lung had been removed, and the doctors thought they would have to take out half of the other before he could go home. I was so happy to see all of my family that I didn't want to leave.

I stayed for an hour and a half, then kissed Pa good-bye. I told him that I'd be back soon and that he'd be all right. I didn't know whether this would be the last time I would see him, but I was sure happy that I had made the effort to come down.

Scooter and I headed back up to Sausalito. I stopped at a pay phone and called Nina. I told her I was coming back from seeing my grandfather, and it didn't look good for him. She invited me over for dinner. It took me a couple of hours to make it to her house. She gave me a hug at the door.

"Hey, you! Tell me how it went," she said with her New York accent on "you." I surprised myself by breaking into tears.

"Nina," I said, "when he saw me, he cried right there in his hospital bed." She held me tighter. "I'm such a jerk, staying up here working when he's living the last days of his life so nearby," I said, feeling really guilty.

"Come on, honey, let's sit down. Let me get you a drink." I sat down on her couch, and she kissed me on the forehead, touched my cheek, and went off to get me a drink. I settled into the couch.

"What do you want to drink?" she called from the other room.

"I don't know. What are you drinking?" I responded as she brought me back from my thoughts. "I'll have whatever you're having."

She brought back a bottle of wine and two glasses. She had the fireplace burning, and I felt warm and secure. Scooter lay near the fireplace, keeping warm.

"You sure are beautiful," I said, leaning over and kissing her briefly.

"I think it would be best for the two of you to stay here tonight. I'll make you a nice meal, and we can get to bed early," she said, with her eyes inches from mine. She kissed me back.

The rest of the night was a blur for me. Nina was smart, warm, and caring, and she knew what I needed.

The next morning, it was raining again. I pulled up the hood of my sweatshirt, and Scooter and I took off in my silver streak—my wet silver 190SL—heading back to the house to shower and change.

Later that day I was back in the studio with the band, trying to get as many overdubs done as we could before we left. By that point, there was as much going on outside our studio as there was inside. The band's last album was really taking off and so was their second single, "Rhiannon." The label wanted them to go out and promote the album. The band would do radio interviews and concerts, but the White Album was taking so long to reach its peak that Fleetwood Mac was already well into the making of their next album. So the band's agents booked some concerts and a small tour right in the middle of recording *Rumours*.

The road crew made lists of what studio stuff would go to Los Angeles for rehearsals, what would go into storage for the next sessions at Wally Heider's, and what would go out on the road.

My last night with Nina in Sausalito.

We were scheduled to leave the Record Plant on April 11. The plan was that the band would go back to L.A. and start rehearsing. A promotional film was set to be shot by Michael Collins at UC Santa Barbara's football stadium at the beginning of May. I had already booked Heider's studio, so that their mobile recording truck would be there to record the band's performance. I planned to engineer the concert with Richard mixing the front-of-house live sound. The label wanted to shoot a live film version of "Rhiannon" to promote the song, scheduled for immediate release.

We were scheduled to continue our *Rumours* recording at Heider's big studio 4 around May 15, 1976. This meant that I would have a bit of a break between when we left Sausalito and when we resumed recording at my home studio. In fact, Heider's had me scheduled back at the studio to do another band's mix-down and another live recording when I returned. To them, I was still their employee, returning to "work as usual." I didn't know it yet, but I had changed since I had left.

Christine loved to play practical jokes on people, especially on April Fool's Day. Our days had started running together, but as that day wore on, we remembered the date. For the next few hours, Christine looked for a target for her joke. This was my first April Fool's Day with her, but once, years later, I watched her call her accountant, David Bloom, at 3 a.m. to say that the band had decided to buy the *Queen Mary* and he was to meet them at the boat in one hour. On this April Fool's Day, though, she had called her attorney, Mickey Shapiro, and tell him that the band was breaking up and they would not be finishing the album.

During the day, she ran her joke scenario again and again to improve it and make it sound more hopeless; as the night wore on, she made the prank larger, saying that she and John could no longer work together, and that her attorney needed to call the president of Warner Bros. Records to let him know everything.

She picked up the phone on my console and made the call in front of all of us.

"Hello, Mickey? Hello, love, Chris here. I need you to call Warner's and tell them that John and I can no longer work together, and if you don't replace him, Fleetwood Mac is over." Christine covered the phone quickly so her attorney didn't hear her start to laugh.

"No, Chris! Are you sure you two can't work something out? You must, this is awful!" We could hear him pleading.

"We all had a talk, and it's settled. Now make the call to the label," she said sternly and hung up the phone.

She started laughing hysterically, very proud of her acting.

Although we had heard her rehearsing, we never thought that she'd hang up on him.

"Chris," I said," "you better call him back and tell him you were just kidding, before it's too late."

"One more minute. He's trying to think what to say to Mo."

A few minutes later, she called him back. "Hello, Mickey, I have one more thing to say to you." She paused for what seemed like a minute. "Do you know what day it is? April Fool's!" and she erupted into her Dame Edna laugh.

A few days later, on April 6, we decided to mix all of the songs so that we would know where we stood on everything and give everyone in the band a cassette of the album. We spent about an hour on each song, and, at the end, we had twelve completed songs.

A couple of days after that, on April 8, Ray woke me at about 8 a.m. "Ken, you have a phone call," he said.

I walked into the kitchen and picked up the phone. The house was very quiet.

"Honey, this is Nana. I have some bad news. Pa just died."

I rubbed the sleep from my eyes and paused. "Nana, I'm so sorry," I said. My voice was starting to break up, and my eyes began to water.

"He didn't suffer. He was just too weak to handle the surgery," she said. "There will be no funeral. He'll be cremated soon. He loved you very much, dear."

"Are you okay, Nana?" I asked.

"He was the love of my life. I'll miss him terribly." She started to cry, and through her tears I heard her say good-bye. I stood in the corner of the empty kitchen and cried as quietly as I could. Outside, it was foggy. Fitting, I thought.

When I got to the studio, a party had started. All of the band's friends knew that we were leaving in a few days, and they had come to visit.

Bob Welch had come up to hang out with his former bandmates. Curry was there, and so was Sandra. Lindsey's friends Tom Moncrief and Anne McClune showed up, and Lindsey's older brother and his brother's wife had come, too. Herbie Worthington, the band's photographer, was documenting their leaving Sausalito. Lindsey's old bandmate Bob Aguire was there. Cris's wife, Wendy, came for the closing ceremonies. It was exciting and sad at the same time. We had all grown so close through this amazing experience, and now we were going our separate ways. The crew of the Record Plant knew that they were a part of history now.

It would make Pa happy if he could see us all now, I thought. He must have gone through similar things in the navy at the end of the war.

Herbie had shot the cover of the White Album, which was now climbing toward number one, and he had stopped by the house to pick up my Audi. We were using it as a transportation car for the roadies since I had the Benz. Herbie had offered to drive it home for me while I drove the Mercedes.

Things were more about leaving than about working that day. We played all of the songs for everyone, and we drank, smoked, and partied into the night. There was a feeling of excitement in the air because we were all going home. I had mixed emotions, though. I was single; I had my best friend, Scooter, with me; I was working; and I had a nice would-be girlfriend in Nina. Plus, my family lived close by.

For the last five years, I had communicated with them mostly over the phone and in letters, seeing them only on holidays and birthdays. I wasn't really sold on staying in L.A. yet, but I was looking forward to going back to my house there, seeing my friends, sleeping in my own bed, and having some privacy.

I lay in bed that night and thought about all of the great memories I had of Pa. I really missed him.

The next day, Bob Welch, who had been the band's guitar player before Lindsey and Stevie joined them, came back to the studio because he wanted to play like old times. There were open beers throughout the studio, and Lindsey rolled joints neurotically, one after the other. And, yes, a few lines had been laid, throughout.

We loaded up our last roll of 24-track tape onto the big 24-track in case anything genius went down that day. It was the same setup as usual, except that we had two guitar players. Curry sat with Christine, Sandra, and Stevie. Mick was on drums, ready should any miracles of music happen.

I didn't have high hopes. For anything good to occur, I knew we would have to organize something, not just jam together. So, we spent our last day farting around. My tape log for that day shows, "Transcension with Bob Welch."

That night I took Nina to dinner at Scoma's Fish House. After dinner, we went back to her house for a romantic evening. I knew that we were going to load out of the studio the next day, but I didn't know when I would see Nina again. She was a very responsible woman, and she took her job seriously. Plus, she wasn't a big fan of Los Angeles. I didn't think she'd come down any time soon.

It was strange, actually. We both knew we'd soon be apart, but it seemed to me that her professionalism wouldn't allow her to show very much emotion. Maybe I was just another guy with a band that was leaving. Maybe it wasn't that serious, after all. I was young, what did I know? But I knew I had to finish this album, and I knew it meant everything to me.

Our last day in Sausalito was Saturday, April 10, 1976. At the house everyone was packing. I unplugged my Revox from the living room stereo, packed my suitcase, and loaded up my car. I was glad to be leaving that house. We all headed down to the studio, where it was photo day. A line of road cases waited to be loaded into the rental truck. Guitar cases were scattered everywhere. I couldn't believe how many guitars the band owned. The success of the White Album had certainly brought on a spending spree for new guitars. There weren't enough road cases for all of the new amps, keys, and guitars. More would have to be made later.

As I squeezed through the hallway between the cases, I passed by Nina's office. It was full of cases, too. I suddenly got a twinge of sadness, realizing that these had been the good times, and we had certainly been having them, despite all of the work and the demanding schedule, despite the arguments and the fights, despite the drugs and the alcohol. I was still young and alive. I had met several lovely ladies, one of whom I particularly liked. I just couldn't imagine that it could get any better. What would the next few months hold for me? Would this be a great album and the start of my career? Or would it be just another album that didn't go anywhere?

I had Cris assemble all of the masters onto two master reels. Then he carefully boxed up all of the outtake reels into boxes to be shipped to me in L.A. I had Cris make two more safeties of the two new master reels, and I carefully packed one set in my suitcase, and Richard took the other two in his.

The girls who worked in the kitchen had prepared a special going-away lunch for us, and they had cleaned out one of the holding rooms for a group photo. The Record Plant personnel were sad to see us leave—they had become family to us. The studio had truly become our home away from home.

Nina asked me when I was going back to Los Angeles, and I told her that I was going to see my grandmother, so I had to leave early in the morning. She smiled. We made plans to spend that night together. She wanted to stay home and eat in. We waved good-bye as everyone else drove away. We were the last two people to leave the studio.

"I'm glad they're gone," I said to Nina. "Let's get out of here."

I closed the door to 2200 Bridgeway for the last time. Funny, I thought. I can really be an idiot, getting sentimental over leaving!

Herbie Worthington's shot of the band and the crew on our last day in Sausalito.

Scooter and I followed Nina back to her house. That evening, over a glass of wine, I suggested that we meet in Lake Tahoe, where my parents had just bought a home. It would be a good time to get to know each other better before summer began and I had to go back to making the album. I realized that we hadn't really spent much quality time together during the last two months, and there was a lot we had yet to learn about each other. But for tonight, she was beautiful and her skin was so soft.

"I'll see you soon," I told her.

"We have some great times to look forward to. You'll see, hon," she said. We went to sleep, finally, with no wake-up time in front of us. Scooter lay on the bed between us.

Those long days at the Record Plant in Sausalito were among the best of my life.

8

Fleetwood Mac
Comes Alive!

The most memorable day I ever had was when I was twenty-nine. We played the first "Day on the Green" concert in San Francisco. The concert was a tribute to the success of *Frampton Comes Alive!* And we played before Peter.

—*Stevie Nicks*

The next morning, Sunday, April 11, Nina led me outside to my car after our night together. We kissed good-bye next to my Benz. "See you soon," I said.

"Yeah, yeah. Now go home," she said in her New York accent.

Richard had left the night before with Lindsey, who was in a hurry to get home. I was driving the 190SL back to L.A., and Herbie Worthington, the band's photographer, was driving my Audi home for me.

I pulled up to the Record Plant for the last time. I needed to pick up my copies of the master tapes. Richard had taken the safety copies with him the day before. I put the tapes safely behind my seat, close to me so that I could protect them if something happened.

I started my Mercedes for the last time in front of the Record Plant, then whistled for Scooter. "Now let's go home!" I could see the Record Plant shrinking in my rearview mirror as I drove away.

The drive took about eight hours, and I got home about midnight and went straight to sleep. It was good to be in my own bed again. I planned on going to Wally Heider's first thing in the morning.

That morning, I headed down the hill into Burbank. I made my way across the valley floor and up the hill onto the 101 into Hollywood. I got off at Cahuenga and drove the six blocks to Wally Heider Recording.

The main building was two stories; it had been built of stucco and wood in the 1920s. It sat at the corner of Cahuenga Boulevard and Selma Avenue. Directly on the corner was studio 3, and studio 1 was next door on Selma Avenue. The parking lot was opposite studios 1 and 3. The traffic office—where I had first met Wally—was right next to the studios, just north of the corner at 1604 Cahuenga.

A half block south on Cahuenga, on the opposite side of the street, was Wally's finest creation: studio 4 at 5929. Studio 4 was a freestanding building with a large control room, a large studio with three iso booths, and its own parking lot in back. In that parking lot, Wally had also built an echo chamber, complete with mics and speakers to create studio 4's own natural reverb. Today, most echo chambers have been replaced with an electronic box the size of a radio that can create any type of reverb a client desires.

It was the hustlers' job to stock each studio with blank tapes and supplies, such as leader tape, razor blades, pencils, pens, and track sheets. They also had to move the necessary complement of tape machines, microphones, and mic stands to and from the storage area behind the traffic office on the sidewalk to each of the studios, as needed, every day for each session.

The traffic office became the place to meet and hang out. It had a soda machine with twenty-five-cent beers and desks where the studio manager and his two lovely traffic girls sat, controlling the studio bookings. It also had a large couch and a few chairs. In the back were a storeroom and more chairs. When I worked there, most of the hustlers had crushes on the girls, Karen Stuart and Susan Stoll, but never really got anywhere with them. One of the maintenance engineers, Larry Comara, finally married Susan. He was the inventor of the Fat Box that was used so successfully on *Rumours.*

We had all watched the Nixon impeachment hearings in that office a few years earlier. Wally would get so mad at all of the dirty tricks. The day Nixon resigned, Wally threw a big party in the office. We were a close family. We'd have company barbecues there and at each of our houses. We all spent a lot of time together outside work.

Scooter and I pulled into the parking lot across the street. I parked, grabbed the master tapes from the backseat, crossed the street, and entered the traffic office.

Terry Stark, my friend and an ex-hustler, greeted me with his usual, "Heyyy, Kennnn!" Terry always stretched out the ending of these words. "Good to see you back. How'd it go with Fleetwood? Did you get 'any' while you were up there?"

"Hey, Terry. Yeah, it was great, really great. I had the second set of tapes shipped back here from Sausalito, and these are the masters. Please keep them safe. I also need to coordinate the upcoming Fleetwood concert at UC Santa barbara's football stadium on the first and second of next month."

Terry and I went into the back, and I drew out the stage setup and instrumentation. I chose all of the mics for the recording, including the audience mics.

Then I left Heider's and drove over to the Penguin Promotions offices about ten minutes away. Penguin Promotions was located in a group of former film studio creative offices now known as Gower Gulch, where Beachwood Drive meets Sunset Boulevard, just east of Gower Street. Inside, small bungalows lined a long covered hallway where Charlie Chaplin used to write and where Warner Bros. cartoons were penned.

Now this was the home of Seedy Management, Mick and John's management office for the band. This was where all planning and coordination for the band happened. Seedy had three employees: Gabrielle Aris,

Judy Wong, and Gabby Zinki. Judy had dedicated her life to the band, having lived with them in the studio and at some of their homes. She was of Chinese descent, and she spoke with a British accent, after growing up in England.

Gabrielle Aris was a beautiful girl from Austria. She had a long lovely face and a terrific body, but she came off as tough—a gal with brains in a man's world. I always thought she was trying too hard. She wanted to be another JC. She was a partner in Seedy Management with Mick and JC. They also had Firefall and Bob Welch as clients, but Penguin Promotions, Mick and John's company, was handled separately.

I needed to put together the set list and the instrumentation for the Santa Barbara concert. I was there to meet Michael Collins, a filmmaker who was shooting the event. Michael was a young, good-looking guy with long curly brown hair. The way he talked about the shoot, I could tell that he was a perfectionist.

Later, when I introduced him as a cameraman, he corrected me. "No, I'm a filmmaker. There's a big difference in education."

On the left is Gabrielle "Gabby" Aris, who worked for John and Mick. She was beautiful but tough. On the right is Judy "Wongie" Wong, the band's "mom" in Los Angeles.

Soon, I learned that there were many new plans in the air for Fleetwood Mac. Warner Bros. was excited about what they had heard, and they wanted to get the band back out in front of the public sooner rather than later. They wanted to simulate a live performance of "Rhiannon" in about a month. This was a few years before MTV, but it would be useful.

This was all very new to me. The last time I had been in L.A., I was just a working guy. Now, three months later, I was coming and going to Fleetwood Mac's offices, helping to plan events, meeting with filmmakers, going to the record company. The difference was huge. The girls at Penguin treated me as if I was some sort of boss, and the band allowed it.

"Let Ken handle this. Let Richard handle that," someone in the band would tell the girls. For the next week or so, the band and I had meetings with the label. I went to band rehearsals and thoroughly enjoyed my newfound success.

The label meetings were interesting. The head of Warner Records wanted the band to play a few songs off the new album for some of his department heads in the office. Mick asked Richard and me to go down and make sure it would sound good.

We each drove down to Burbank, and I brought a couple of tapes and my Revox. The Warner building at 3300 Warner Boulevard was a modest three-story building covered in dark wood siding, surrounded by trees. It didn't feel threatening at all. I had never been to a record company to have a meeting.

Richard and I parked directly in front, then walked inside and up to the front desk. Richard gave the receptionist our names and told her that we were there to set up a playback for some of the execs. The lobby had twenty-foot ceilings, the walls were lined with gold records and posters of their artists, and music was playing. This was definitely what I thought a record company should be like. It felt like home to me.

The receptionist led us up the stairs to a large conference room. The room had two big speakers on stands with wheels, and they were already set up, connected to an amp. I wasn't sure what kind of speakers they were, but the woofer was fifteen inches in diameter, so I knew they were good. I had brought my Revox two-track and my rough mixes.

The executives left Richard and me alone while we tinkered with the sound. We found the amp for the speakers and hooked up my Revox. Then I loaded up the tape and rewound it a little. I hit PLAY, and "Gold Dust Woman" filled the room. The song sounded great on this system, so I turned the amp a little louder. We were set.

Mick, John, Gabrielle, and Mickey Shapiro, the band's attorney, arrived and walked into the room. They were relieved to see us already there.

"Sounds great!" Richard said.

"It better," Mick said. "A lot is riding on this!"

Nervously, I reached down and turned up the volume a little more so that it would be good and loud when we played the tape. The room began to fill with executives; some were around my age, but most were older—the Big Bosses. Mo Austin was there and so were Lenny Waronker and Russ Thyret, the three biggest execs at Warner Bros. I didn't know who they were at the time, but I could tell that they were the guys we needed to please.

There must have been thirty people in the room, including us. Lindsey arrived, and he told us that Stevie and Christine weren't coming.

"What do you want to play first?" I asked Mick.

"'Dreams' and then 'Go Your Own Way' and that's all," he said.

Everyone sat down to listen. All eyes were on me as I walked over to the Revox. I felt the way I had in seventh grade when I had been the classroom projectionist. I was extremely nervous. It's one thing to play music in a studio that I know is acoustically perfect, but it was altogether another thing to play our precious music in an open conference room with glass and metal everywhere. I knew that it might sound horrible.

I rewound the tape to the top of "Dreams." I wanted to turn the volume up a little more, but there were so many people in the room that I couldn't get to the amp.

Here goes, I thought, and pressed PLAY. Everyone was listening intently. The "Dreams" drum fill started, then Mick's phasing high hat played the hypnotic loop we had built. Lindsey's electric guitar played through my Leslie speaker. Next came Stevie's haunting lyrics. It sounded great. Richard's head was bobbing to the beat. Home run! I thought.

"Dreams" ended, but no one said anything. They just waited for me to spin the tape to "Go Your Own Way." I wound the tape forward and quickly pressed PLAY. I had hoped for applause or some acknowledgment. Tough crowd, I thought.

As "Go Your Own Way" started, Mick's huge tom fills shook the room. These record company execs weren't easily impressed, but even they couldn't stop moving. When the solo and tag ended, they all started *applauding*. Later I found out that big-shot record execs almost never do this. They begged to hear more.

"No," Mick said. "You'll have to wait." He knew that we had blown them away, and he didn't want to risk playing anything else.

Richard and I packed up, leaving Mick, John, Mickey, and Lindsey to strategize plans for the band. The impact of the playback that day changed our lives dramatically. The label suddenly wanted new recordings, new films shot, and more time from the band. Much of this would directly involve Richard and me, but we each headed home, unaware of what was coming our way.

During our time off, Richard and I enjoyed our freedom outside the studio. Several days later, on Monday, April 26, I walked into Heider's traffic office at 11 a.m. to meet with Biff and the remote guys about the upcoming live recording of Fleetwood Mac at UC Santa Barbara the next week. I filled out my mic request list and calculated the number of mic stands, boom arms, regular-length mic cables, and hundred-footers I would need for the two-day gig. The hundred-footers were to be used for my audience mics. I believe that half of the best-quality sound of a live performance comes from well-placed hall mics. This usually meant that I would ask my remote crew to occasionally scale tall buildings to get the mics in the best positions and out of the way of the house speaker system.

I finished about lunchtime and flopped down onto the couch in the traffic office. I remember I was feeling really positive, the same way I had felt that morning several months earlier when I had first met the band. Suddenly the door opened, and this beautiful girl walked in, looking for the Biffer. Her name was Cheryl, and she was Biff's stunning ex-girlfriend. She was twenty years old, with long straight dark hair, and she wore a clinging leotard under her tight jeans, revealing her beautiful body.

I had met Cheryl a few times before, and I had recently met Biff's new girlfriend. I instantly leaped to my feet and walked up to her. "Hey, Cheryl! How are you? Wow, you look really great today! What can I do for you?" I could tell by the expressions on their faces that both of the traffic girls were somewhat amazed at my newfound confidence.

"I came by to give Biff his jacket. He left it in my car a few weeks ago."

"Come with me. He's back here." I led her to the mic room where we had just finished our meeting.

Cheryl gave Biff a quick kiss and handed him his jacket. They exchanged pleasantries, then she turned and walked out of the room. When she got back to the front door of the traffic office, she turned

Cheryl Geary became my girlfriend during the Los Angeles phase of recording *Rumours*.

to me and said, "It was great seeing you, Ken. Let's get together sometime."

"Hey, I'm free all day today. Would you like to go to lunch?" I volunteered.

"Sure," she said. "But I have my mom's car, and I need to get it back to her."

"I can follow you to her place, and you can drop off your mom's car, then we'll go to lunch."

When we dropped off the car, I met her mom, Grace. Then Cheryl and I took off in my Benz with the top down. Cheryl's long hair looked beautiful as it blew in the wind.

As we finished eating, I asked, "Would you like to come over and see my house? I need to check in on Scooter. I haven't seen him in a few days. He has a doggy door, and we keep missing each other."

"Sure," she said. "I love dogs!"

It was a beautiful day as we drove up the canyon road to my house. I went to the turnaround at the end and came back and parked across the street from my cabin.

"Wow, it really smells like the mountains up here," Cheryl said, amazed.

"That's why I moved up here."

"I could get used to this," Cheryl said.

I led her up the stairs and into my house. She loved the layout—the beam ceiling, rock wall, large fireplace, big TV and speakers.

Scooter was nowhere to be found. Punk! I thought. "I'm going to have to rein him in. He's out of control," I explained to Cheryl. I got a beer for each of us and put on some Steely Dan.

We talked and laughed for a while, sitting next to each other on the couch. She was so adorable that I couldn't help myself. I leaned over and kissed her, and she kissed me back. Great! I thought.

Cheryl wrapped her arms around my neck and kissed me again, this time longer and more intense. I put my hand on her side, under her arm, and she moved in closer. Suddenly, my beard started to itch, and I scratched at it aggressively. For the last few days I had had periodic itching episodes in the middle of the night.

"Hey, can you look at my beard?" I blurted out. "I think Scooter has given me fleas."

Cheryl was kissing my neck, just below my beard, and it seemed as if we were already close enough that I could ask her to look at my beard. She looked through my beard, and it felt very sexy, I must say!

Things were really heating up between us. Then she said, "Hey, I think you have crabs."

"I have what?" Blood rushed to my head.

"Crabs," she said, again. "They're like lice. You can get them from dirty sheets or other people."

I felt completely dejected and embarrassed. Well, that's certainly the end of this date, I thought. "I'm so sorry," I said.

"It's not a big deal," Cheryl said. "All you have to do is get this stuff called Quell from your doctor and shower with it, and then they're gone."

All I wanted was to correct this situation and my image. I called my doctor, whose office was about two miles down the hill.

"Hi, Doc," I said. "Apparently, I have something called crabs, and I need something called Quell, immediately." It was only about two in the afternoon.

"Sure, come right down," he said, chuckling.

"Cheryl, I'll be right back," I said.

"I can go with you," she said.

I was so embarrassed! I couldn't believe this was happening; a beautiful young woman was interested in me, I had asked her to look in my beard, and she had found—crabs! I felt like such an idiot.

I pulled into the parking lot at my doctor's office and jumped out of the Benz, leaving the engine running with Cheryl in the car. I dashed into the doctor's office, got the Quell, jumped back in the car, and up the hill we went again.

Out the driver's side window of my car, I saw my punk dog on the front lawn of a house on Olive Avenue. I whipped a U-turn and stopped at the curb, then leaned over and opened Cheryl's door. "Scooter, get your ass in here!" I ordered. There was nothing he liked better than going for a ride, so he leaped into the back. Cheryl pulled her door closed, and I made another U-turn, heading up the hill to my house.

I screeched up to the house, and we all went inside. I felt so dirty, and I thought about that night when those two groupies had been in my bedroom a few weeks earlier.

"Scooter, get in the house, now!" I said. We all went upstairs into my living room. I closed the front door and locked Scooter's doggy door. His long beagle ears dropped beside his face.

"You're not going anywhere for a while, mister!" I informed him.

I got some clean jeans and a shirt in the bedroom, then went into the bathroom to take a Quell shower. "I'll be out soon," I said to Cheryl.

"Make sure you shower twice, and comb your hair and beard while you're in the shower," she advised.

"Thanks," I called from the bathroom. "You're great."

"I'll see you when you're clean," she said.

"I don't need to lock this door, do I?" I called back to her, jokingly.

I scrubbed every part of my body two and a half times. Then I got out of the shower, dried off, and put on my clean clothes.

Scooter gets grounded.

When I came out to the living room, Cheryl was still sitting on the couch. "Feel better?" she asked.

"Oh, yeah!" I said, so relieved that I had killed all of the crabs. "I kept running my comb through my beard like the doc told me to, just to make sure that everything is clean."

"My turn now." Cheryl went into my bathroom, closed the door, and showered for about ten minutes.

To my delight, she came out of the bathroom wearing only a small towel wrapped around her. She sat down next to me. "All better?" I asked, my voice cracking.

She leaned forward and kissed me long and slow. "Definitely," she said. "All better." She put her arms around my neck, and we kissed again. When I put my hand on her side, I noticed that her towel had come unwrapped.

"I'll need to borrow some clean clothes from you," Cheryl said. "We need to wash ours." I was so shocked at this calm, wise, sexy woman. She was only twenty, but she was beautiful, perfect, and still so young and innocent. I didn't have a chance.

We washed our clothes in my washer, and, as it turned out, we didn't need them for the rest of that day or night.

I lit my fireplace, and the glow of it made the evening even more romantic. We made love most of the night. That was one of the most amazing nights of my life. Wow, I thought. This rock-and-roll business has its advantages!

A couple of times during the evening, I thought about Nina, but that would-be relationship seemed like a hundred years ago. Maybe if Nina and I had been able to spend more time together, we could have done this, but for now I was loving life!

The next few days were surreal in the best possible way. Cheryl worked during the day, so I would go to the park and throw a Frisbee for Scooter to catch. I went to the beach with my friends. Then, at night, I did what any other single guy does when he doesn't have to work: I hung out with my friends, then left them as soon as my new girlfriend was done with work.

I also got Scooter back under control, making him go everywhere with me.

• • •

A few days later, I got a call from Gabrielle at the Penguin office. She told me that the band had invited me to fly up to Oakland the next Saturday to watch them perform at Bill Graham's "Day on the Green" festival in the Oakland Coliseum. Gabrielle explained that the timing would be a little tricky because the following day was the daytime concert at UC Santa Barbara, and the band, Richard, and I would all need to stay together for both shows.

That's how it's usually done. When you're on tour, everyone stays together, even though the next day's event was close to home. JC couldn't risk letting any of us go home because we all had to be in Santa Barbara. So, we stayed together. This made it easier for him to herd sheep. In this case, his sheep much preferred the private-plane-and-limousine treatment to schlepping to places on their own. Who wouldn't?

On May 1, my alarm went off at 7 a.m. I rolled over and kissed Cheryl good-bye. I was already packed and ready to go to the airport. I told her to meet me in Santa Barbara that night, so that we could spend the night together and get ready for the concert the next day.

The Oakland Coliseum was both a baseball and a football stadium, home to the Oakland A's baseball team and the Oakland Raiders NFL team. The Oakland Coliseum is about four hundred miles north of Los Angeles. This meant that the band's equipment had left via truck a day earlier so that it would be there in the morning before we arrived by plane.

Richard, the band, and I had to be at the Van Nuys airport at 8 a.m. to take the band's chartered Viscount 40 propjet up to Oakland.

This was my introduction to flying with the band in a private plane. By the time Richard and I got on the plane, most of the members of the band were already there. Because it was a private airplane, all of the seats faced one another, with coffee tables in between. In the back, there was a lounge area with a big wraparound sofa.

Stevie was already settled in with a blanket covering her tiny body, and her feet were tucked up under the blanket. She had her girlfriends with her, as usual. Christine was sitting next to Judy Wong, each in one of the four leather swivel chairs positioned around a table. Christine was smoking a cigarette and enjoying a glass of champagne. Mick, John, Gabrielle, and JC were sitting near the front of the plane, drinking beer and strategizing about what they should do during the next few days.

Richard and I grabbed swivel chairs close to Lindsey. Then Linda, the stewardess, came over and asked us what we wanted to drink. Each of us ordered a beer. "Is Heineken okay?" she asked. "That's all we have stocked."

There were a lot of advantages to hiring your own plane. One was that you could order the beer that you wanted. Nice one, Mick! The Viscount 40 could hold about forty people, and because the band's entourage was still pretty small, they could invite press and photographers or friends and family.

The captain came out of the cockpit and said hello to us. Richard introduced him to me. "Chuck, this is Ken Caillat. Ken, this is Chuck, our pilot. Chuck, do you think you can keep the plane in the air this time?" Richard joked, reminding me of his skit with Mick.

Richard had traveled with the band on their plane enough times that the pilot was used to his jokes, but I realized that I wasn't. What does Richard know that I don't? I wondered.

I walked into the back lounge, passing Christine. She was laughing loudly along with Judy, who always seemed to be happy. Judy had traveled with the band for years, and she was like their mother or older sister.

I headed back toward Stevie's den. She had three other women with her.

"Ken, you might not want to go back there unless you're invited," Judy said. "It's kind of Stevie's area."

"Oh, okay, yeah," I said. "It looks a little crowded. I was just checking out the plane. Who's that sitting with Stevie?"

"Robin Snyder, Christi Alsbury, and Mary Torrey, some of her closest friends," Judy explained.

"How do you like our little plane, darling?" Christine asked me.

"It's really great, Chris. Really great!" I said.

"You better go sit down, Kenneth, they like us to stay in our seats during takeoff," Judy said.

Hmm, "Kenneth" and "darling"—two interesting names for me, I thought.

I flopped into my seat, shaking my head about the Stevie fan club. Stevie was a sweet, talented singer whose friends loved to support her. In the future, Stevie would have more and more "friends" around her. They would take control of all of her appointments, and we wouldn't be able to reach her when we needed to. Finally, we wouldn't be able to reach her at all. At this point, though, she was still the lovable, sweet Stevie.

Mary Torrey came forward from Stevie's den to talk to Richard. "Hi, Richard," she said. "I didn't see you come aboard." She bent over and kissed him on the cheek.

"Hi, Mary," he said. "How are you? It's good to see you again. This is Ken and this is Lindsey." He indicated each of us, but he didn't take his eyes off Mary.

Over the intercom, Chuck the pilot announced that we would be taxiing soon, so we needed to be seated. Mary said good-bye to us and went back to sit with Stevie.

"Who's that?" I asked Richard, knowing that Mary wasn't his sister.

"A friend I met at the Aquarius Theater a few months ago," he said, sipping his beer.

"She seems nice," I said, sipping my beer, too.

The plane started to taxi. Here we go! I thought.

It was so great to be on a private plane. We didn't have to wear our seatbelts, clear the aisles, or finish our drinks. We just sat back and drank our beers during takeoff. Linda came around a few more times with more drinks during the flight, even though the trip to Oakland took only about an hour.

It was a bright, sunny morning when we landed. Several limos were waiting for us on the tarmac. When we got to the Coliseum, I thought that it looked like a typical stadium. Then I noticed that almost all of the people were walking in with blankets and picnic baskets. The huge parking lot was quickly filling up with cars.

The limo dropped us off at the stage entrance. We went backstage, and the promoter, Bill Graham, greeted us, hugging every member of the band, but he didn't say anything to anyone else. He just looked right through the rest of us.

The concert was a tribute to the success of Peter Frampton's *Frampton Comes Alive!* album. Bill had built a giant glittering castle on top of a massive stadium stage. At this point, Lindsey and Stevie had never played in front of a large crowd, and there were seventy-five thousand people in the audience that day.

Richard and I couldn't believe what we were seeing. The enormous Oakland Coliseum was completely filled with people. Not only in the stands, but on the grass, too! It's hard to imagine what seventy-five thousand people look like when they've come to see your band until you've experienced it.

We spent the next hour or so celebrating. Now I understood what Woodstock must have been like! Everyone in the entourage drank some champagne or beer, smoked some pot, or had a little coke, but we were all so excited about the concert that we all managed to stay in control.

The backstage area was getting fairly crowded with press and friends of the band. Behind me, I noticed an older couple who looked out of place. The distinguished-looking gentleman was about Mick's height. In fact, he looked like Mick.

Just then, Mick noticed me eying these new arrivals, and he came over to me. "Kenneth, that's my mum and dad over there. I want you to meet them."

We walked over, and Mick introduced us. He explained that his father had been a wing commander in the Royal Air Force, and he had a distinguished service record as a pilot, receiving a NATO appointment.

"John Joseph Kells Fleetwood," Mick's father said, shaking my hand.

"And this is my mum, Bitty," Mick said.

"My name is Brigit, but everyone calls me Bitty," she explained.

I was struck by how regally they carried themselves. I had never seen Mick so proud of two people in my life. "My dad writes poetry, and I'm going to help him get it published," he said, beaming. Mick and his dad

We knew the band was getting huge, and the
crowd at the "Day on the Green" proved it.

were about the same height. Even though I'm 6'3", I had to look up at
both of them. Just then, two young women joined our group.

"Hello, my name is Sally, and this is Susan," one of the women said.
"We're Mick's sisters."

I was taken aback by all of the members of Mick's family. I had never
thought of Mick as having family. He always seemed so aloof and independent. Mick came around behind his sisters and put his arms around
them, giving them both kisses.

"I'm honored to meet you," I said to both of them. "So, how was it
having to put up with Mick your whole life?"

"Caillat, they were lucky to have me around to keep the stray lads at
bay," Mick said.

Lindsey and John prepare backstage for the concert.

"How's he behaving?" one of the sisters asked me.

"Mick's always a perfect gentleman," I said. Then I turned toward my boss. "That'll be five bucks, Mick."

Later, I found out that Mick had lived at Sally's house while he was learning to play drums, and he had nearly driven her crazy by practicing so much. Susan was a successful actress in British theater. Now I had a better understanding of what made Mick the way he was.

"It was a pleasure to meet all of you," I said. I still have a good relationship with Mick and his family. His father died years ago, but Bitty is still alive and well, and I've spoken with her recently, exchanging pleasantries. I also gave her a tuberose plant.

Someone came into the dressing room and announced that it was time for a brief sound check. That was over quickly, because they didn't want us to spend much time checking the band's instruments in front of their fans.

At this point, it was close to Fleetwood Mac's show time. Gary Wright had opened the show, and Fleetwood Mac was on before Peter

It's near show time, with Cris Morris (left), Christina (center), and Lindsey (right).

Frampton, the headliner, who had just had a huge hit live album. He was the biggest act in America at that time.

This was a perfect day for seventy-five thousand fans to see a concert. The stands were filled, and so was the whole inside of the football field. The grass was completely covered with people. Since I didn't have anything to do, Richard asked if I wanted to mix the show with him at the console, which was about five hundred feet away from the stage. How fun would it be for Richard and me to mix the band together live? After all, at this point, we could pretty much read each other's minds.

One of the security guards asked us whether we wanted a couple of guards to escort us out to the soundboard. Stupidly, I said no.

As Richard and I walked through the crowd, fans grabbed at our badges, trying to take them so they could get backstage. I could smell vomit as we made our way to the soundboard. Because of the crowd, it took us almost twenty minutes to get out to the console. We were standing right in the middle of seventy-five thousand people!

Mick looking Deloux. He liked to say he was
dressed "de-lukes."

Pushing through the masses of fans to the soundboard was one of the
scariest experiences in my life. People were throwing up. Others were
OD-ing. Richard and I started to panic, because the band was about to
go on and we were only about halfway to the soundboard. Luckily, we
made it there right before the band came onstage.

Then whole place began to smell like pot. Suddenly, I felt a pair of
soft hands cover my eyes.

"Well, hello, stranger! What brings you here?"

I knew that New York accent instantly. "Nina!" I exclaimed. "Hey,
good looking, how are you? Wow! It's so great to see you! Come and sit
down." Nina and I kissed.

The "Day on the Green" perspective, looking out from the stage at the tented soundboard.

After we finished hugging, Richard's big crush from Sausalito, Ginger, came up to him. She had put him off the whole time we had been in Northern California. They would talk and have a few drinks, but he could never get her to warm up to him. I think she must have had a boyfriend. Or else he wasn't her type, or she just didn't want a one-night stand.

Anyway, she seemed warm to Richard that evening, and she really looked great. She was wearing a small tube top, and her medium-length brown hair bounced up and down.

Mixing front-of-house sound is very different from studio mixing. In studio mixing, you have to get everything to sound perfect because your mix will outlive you, and many people will hear it and can compare it to every other mix in the world. You have to be diligent with every sound, prepared to do anything until it's as good as you can make it.

When you're recording live, though, everything is "gone in a second." Because of this, I tend to make my live sound as big as I can. After I've done this, I try to shape the music into a moving, momentary musical experience.

The front-of-house mixer has to be a genius. He has to be like one of those guys who can paint a picture in twenty seconds. When I mix house, I'm always riding all of the levels, adjusting the proportions of every instrument to keep every instrument up in the listeners' faces.

Richard's live sound specialty was drums. He could make them thunder! He asked me to ride guitars and keys while he rode drums, bass, and vocals. Basically, he and I jammed with each other. When I pushed the guitar up during the solo, he would slightly raise the drums and the bass.

We were having a blast playing with the music. Many of the fans were watching our antics. People were cheering. Fleetwood Mac walked offstage to wait for the audience to cheer them back for their encore.

All the way out at our mixing booth, we could hear the fans up by the stage applauding to bring the band back, but the fans who were sitting close to us had gotten distracted. I asked the sound chief if there were any audience mics up there that could pick up the applause. "No," was his answer.

The band takes the stage at the "Day on the Green."

Then I looked at the vocal mics on the front edge of the stage and reached over and pushed them way up so that the sound of the people applauding near the stage came roaring out of the speakers placed out in the stadium. Suddenly, in the speakers near me, I could hear the applause. As we turned up the volume of the house speakers, the whole stadium came to its feet around us in perfect timing with the volume coming up. Richard and I looked around, amazed. Then we looked at each other.

"Oh, my God!" I said. "Look what we did!" I looked down at my arms, and they had goose bumps. So did Richard's! I had never felt anything like that.

After the concert, we went back to the dressing rooms with Nina and Ginger in tow. Judy and Gabby came up to us and told us that they were amazed at how exciting the show had been. The thing that surprised me was how different songs such as "So Afraid" and "Rhiannon" sounded, compared to their album versions. It was as if they were on steroids. Now they were "eight-hundred-pound gorillas," to use Lindsey's phrase.

Curry Grant sauntered up to us. "Nice work, boys," he said, with a hint of a Texas accent.

"Nice lights, Curry," Richard said.

"What the hell happened during 'So Afraid' and 'Rhiannon'?" I asked. "The band just kicked ass on those songs! When did they start doing that?"

"I don't know," Curry said. "It seems like every time they play them, they get stronger."

When the band came backstage, we gave high-fives to Mick, John, and Lindsey. They were clearly aware that they were becoming huge recording artists. Their attorney's advice had been right on target, that if they made their follow-up record great, they'd be superstars.

"I was standing in the middle of the stage, thinking, 'This is the big time,'" Stevie said after the show.

This was the band's turning point. Now, they were huge. While we had been in the studio making their new album, the number of their fans was exploding. Fleetwood Mac had played three of their new songs that day, "Go Your Own Way," "Dreams," and "You Make Loving Fun," and they had blown away their fans with them.

Some of us watched Peter Frampton's show from backstage. Richard and I decided to sit out in the artists' patio under the umbrellas and talk to the girls. I was glad to see Nina again. She and I talked about meeting later in May or June when the band was touring. Richard was having a great time with Ginger as well. I didn't think about it much at the time—and I certainly didn't mention it to Nina—but I still had a date with my girlfriend, Cheryl, that night in Santa Barbara.

After the show ended, the band quickly got into their limos to beat the traffic. Frampton was having a party back at his hotel. Richard and I couldn't go because we had to go to the airport and leave for Santa Barbara to prepare for the next day's recording.

JC came up to Richard and me. "It's time to go, boys," he said. "Say good-bye to your ladies. Bill Graham has a helicopter that will take you to our plane at the airport. The band is going to stay and party with Peter. But you need to hurry because the 'copter has to come back for more guests."

JC walked us to the big helicopter. Richard and I said good-bye to Nina and Ginger, and we got in the helicopter. As the 'copter rose, I could see Nina and Ginger standing on the ground, waving up at us. I looked at Richard, and his eyes were filled with tears. He just couldn't seem to get a break with Ginger. He followed his duty to the band and left her behind, even when she finally seemed to want to be with him.

The band's equipment would be loaded out in a few more hours, and their big semis would have to drive all through the night to get to Santa Barbara by sunrise. Well, the peons got the use of the whole private airplane. It was just Curry, Richard, Herbie, Judy, Gabby, a couple of reporters, and me who flew back to Van Nuys that night.

When we landed, the limos took us directly to Santa Barbara. We checked in, and when we went to our suites, we learned that we each had a separate bungalow. The band had put us up at Santa Barbara's finest hotel, the Miramar, owned by B.B. King.

Richard and I met up at the bar and talked shop. "'Rhiannon' sounds ten times better live than the single," I said.

After the show, the band poses with Bill Graham.

"It's because of Lindsey," Richard said. "He's really growing as a guitar player, and he's gotten much more confident with his playing style. The band just reacts to that naturally. If he plays stronger, then everyone else plays stronger, too."

"Yeah," I said. "That's what happened with 'So Afraid'! That song has become a ten, but on the record it's only a six."

We continued to drink and critique the band's progress until Cheryl arrived around 10 p.m. Eventually, Curry joined us. The band showed up a little after midnight, having had a great time at Peter's party.

Stevie and her girlfriends stopped by the bar. Mary Torrey came up and put her arm around Richard's shoulders and said hello. Then Cheryl and I said goodnight to everyone and went out to our bungalow.

The news said it was going to be hot the next day. Even in Santa Barbara they were forecasting mid-80s, which is rare for Santa Barbara in May because it's on the ocean, about ninety miles north of L.A. This would be our second concert in two days, and I thought it would be a great show, especially after the one the day before.

Cheryl and I got up about eight thirty that morning. Since this was a day show, the doors at the UC Santa Barbara football stadium opened at noon. We had to get over to the venue and get everything set up before then. We had to set up not only for the concert, but also for the live recording and the filming.

When Cheryl and I walked out the front doors of the hotel, we saw that one of the crew members had a car waiting for us, ready to take people in our group over to the football stadium. We jumped in, and it was only a few miles away. Loggins and Messina were the opening act for Fleetwood Mac that day. With Lindsey's new power, I couldn't wait to see the show.

The UC Santa Barbara football stadium is just a flat football field inside a stadium. The temporary stage had a cloth tarp over it in case it rained. Heider's mobile truck was parked up alongside the stage and was already set up.

The big multitrack snake had been rolled out to stage left, and 220 volts of power had been secured. The truck's transformer was humming as it converted the 220 back to 110 volts. The maintenance engineer was aligning the two 24-track tape machines.

Onstage, the band's equipment wasn't set up yet, even though we had a sound check scheduled for around 11:30 a.m. Heider's stage crew had the mic stands out and ready. The mics I had requested were on the stands, and each stand was correctly marked as to its instrument and placement.

During those days, we would share the sound company's mics, splitting each signal into two and sending one to the house soundboard and the other to our board in the recording truck. Sound companies tended to use cheaper mics than we did, so we would often double-mic some instruments. Today, sound companies use the same mics as recording companies, so there's no need to double mic, and everything can be split. The only exception is audience mics. Sound companies don't need audience mics, so the recording truck always has to put them up some-place where they will get good audience reaction and good ambience from the hall or the stadium.

"Hey, Ken, where do you want the audience mics to go?" asked Bill Broms, the senior stage crew guy from Heider's.

"Can you put one on either side of the stage on big booms, but not too close to the front-of-house speaker stacks? Then I want the other two to go fairly deep out into the audience," I said.

"Okay. When you get a chance, can you come out and show me where you want the deep mics to go?" he asked.

"I'll meet you out there in five," I said. I wanted to go backstage and talk to JC or anyone from the band to see if anything had changed.

Backstage, Michael Collins, the filmmaker, was with his cameramen, talking about where they would position their cameras for that day's show. They wanted good stationary coverage and good roving camera-men onstage to get close to the action.

I was going to have to feed a sync pulse from the truck to one of their cameras, so that we could lock audio to picture later.

"Michael, any changes to the set today?" I asked.

"Not that I know of," he answered.

"Good," I said. "I don't like last-minute changes." I went off to find somebody who might know anything different.

Ray and Rhino were at stage right, unpacking the instruments. "Well, look who comes waltzing in after all the heavy work is done!" Rhino announced. Ray and Rhino both laughed.

"Yeah, yeah," I said. "I know the house stagehands helped you unload. Nice try. Any instrument changes that I need to know about?"

"Nah, nothing," Ray said.

Then Ray and Rhino noticed Cheryl. "Whoa! Who's that?" Rhino asked.

"My girlfriend, Cheryl," I said proudly.

"She's way too good for you, Caillat. Step aside," Rhino retorted.

"Yeah, right," I said sarcastically. "Girls love roadies." I walked away from them and went over to Cheryl.

JC approached Cheryl and me. "Mr. Caillat, I have your backstage passes. Who is this, may I ask?"

"This is Cheryl," I said.

"Hello, I'm John. Everyone calls me JC," he said to Cheryl, using his most proper British polish. "And will Cheryl be staying near you during the show?" he asked me.

"Why, yes, as a matter of fact, she will," I said, adding a little polish of my own.

JC handed each of us a laminated backstage pass to hang around our necks. "Now, don't you and Dashut fuck things up today," he said, looking back at me as he walked away.

"What do you think this is, a hobby?" I responded with a line I had learned from Richard. JC nodded with approval. And he was gone.

I grabbed Cheryl by the hand and said, "Come on, let's go out front. I need to figure out where to put the second pair of audience mics." I walked down the steps from the stage into the audience seating and pointed out toward the distance. "This should sound like shit," I explained to Cheryl. "We're in a big field. There is no ambiance here, just dirt. Oh, and the Santa Barbara airport is next to us."

The front-of-house engineer was having someone onstage talk into each of the band's mics. Cheryl covered her ears. "Test, *test*. One, two, three," he said. As the sound came out of the big house speakers, it shot out into the empty football stadium and disappeared.

"Whoa, that's not good!" I said to Cheryl. I always liked to add the hall sound, but that day people's applause would have to do. I saw Bill and pointed to the place where I wanted the deep audience mics to be hung.

"Can you get a couple mics to hang about thirty feet above right here and over there? And can you try to have the butts of the mics facing the stage so they cancel out some of the leakage from the speakers?" I asked.

"Oh, man, I knew you were going to say that," he complained. "I already have someone working on that. You're a pain in the ass. You know that, don't you, Caillat?"

"Hey, you love me, and you know I'm right," I responded.

"I didn't say you weren't right. I said you were a pain in the ass."

The funny thing was that I used to be a part of this crew, but now I was the band's engineer. I maintained good relationships with all of these guys after I left Heider's. To this day, I'm still friends with them.

Bill and I walked back to the truck. It was a little before 11 a.m., and everyone in the band would be arriving soon to prepare for the sound check.

Mick's drum kit was set up, and Rhino was adjusting the tension on the heads so that they sounded perfect. The heat had made them go a little soft. I pushed my guys to have my mics up so I could get a jump on the sounds.

Around 11:15 a.m., the band members arrived from the hotel in two limos. I introduced each of them to Cheryl. The guys liked her, but Stevie and Christine were a little standoffish. Maybe that was because Cheryl was such a looker. Or maybe because she was younger than they were. Or maybe because they were wondering, What about Nina?

We started the sound check a little before 11:30 a.m. The camera-men needed to run through every song in the show so they could learn their setup locations. The band played about one minute of each song. They were going to play "Dreams," "Lovin' Fun," and "Go Your Own Way," even though they weren't finished yet.

In the truck, I quickly dialed in the sounds of each mic. Live record-ing is always different from studio recording. In live recording, all of the mics pick up every instrument. Back then, we didn't have in-ear monitors so that we could hear everyone else. Instead, we had speak-ers pointing everywhere, vocal wedges, side fills, and back fills, so that sound was flying everywhere. We used mics that had a very narrow pat-tern of pickup, in hopes of mostly getting the instrument that each mic pointed at.

After the sound check, we rendezvoused in the band's dressing room. The film crew was doing interviews, shooting the girls having their make-up applied, and talking to Richard and me.

Meanwhile, people in the audience were taking their seats, and Loggins and Messina were playing. The stadium was filling up. About twenty minutes before show time, Richard and I left for our stations.

He went to the console dead-center in the middle of the audience, and Cheryl and I went out back to the truck.

As I walked past the stage, I noticed that the sun had moved and was now directly on the band's instruments. Earlier, the stage ceiling had been shading the instruments. Loggins and Messina were nearly finished.

It felt like it was about 90 degrees outside. I noticed that a couple of drum mic booms had "drooped" in the heat. I got on my talkback and said, "Hey, guys, are these instruments going to be okay? They're directly in the hot sun."

"What do you want us to do about it?" my stage crew answered.

I couldn't talk to the band or anyone else. I pushed the side door of the truck open and saw the camera crew wearing their headphones, while people were rushing to their seats. It was too late to do anything.

Then from the PA, I heard JC's voice announce, "Ladies and gentlemen, would you please give a warm welcome to . . . Fleet-wood Mac!"

The crowd went wild. Of course, this wasn't the first time I had heard the band, but it's always exciting when a live show starts. In live recording, we always used two tape machines, instead of just one, so that we could continuously record the whole show. Our 24-track number 1 had already been recording for about ten minutes, and number 2 would start in a few minutes. We always staggered the recording of a live event with two machines so that when one machine ran out of tape, the other would still be recording, and the tech would immediately reload and start the next tape.

I turned up the volume and said to Cheryl, "Hey, babe, uh, dig this." I scared myself by sounding a little too much like Wally then.

The band started to play. I had a closed-circuit TV so that I could see the stage directly. The first song was "Monday Morning," and, suddenly, everything was out of tune. It sounded absolutely horrible! The film cameras were rolling, and the band knew how bad it sounded.

The heat had made Lindsey's guitar go completely out of tune. So were John's bass and Mick's drums. The drums sounded as if someone was hitting on cardboard boxes. The only instruments unaffected by the heat were Christine's keys, Stevie's tambourine, and their vocals. Everybody kept playing and singing as if nothing had happened, but

Lindsey and John quickly retuned. By the second half of the song, it sounded okay.

Mick took a little extra time to fix his drums, tuning them between songs. They went on to play a fantastic set.

When I watch it now, I can see that "Go Your Own Way" didn't have the end solo that it has on the album, because it hadn't been invented yet. The same was true of the other new songs they played that day. We still had months to go in the recording process, but all in all, it was a great day. The label had footage of the band, and all was well.

That day, the band seemed as if they had healed from their recent breakups. After the show, we took a limo back to the hotel. Cheryl and I went to our bungalow, and we sat and talked about how good the show had been. We all had these cute little free-standing bungalows near the beach, connected by a walking path, and when one of the other members of our group walked by, we could see them.

Cheryl and I had left the doors of our bungalow open to enjoy the view of the ocean, so we saw Richard and Mary when they walked by.

Lindsey goes wild in the heat in Santa Barbara.

Mary, me, Cheryl, and Richard. The Fleetwood Mac version of Bob, Carol, Ted, and Alice.

"Hey, guys, come on in," I called to them.

Cheryl and Mary sat on the bed. They had talked for a few minutes the night before at the bar, so they had started to get to know each other.

Richard and I smoked a joint outside the door. "Nice work today, buddy," I said to him. We toasted each other with our beers. Curry Grant and Christine came walking by, heading to the bar. Then Sam Emerson, one of the band's friends and photographers, walked up.

I invited him in and introduced him to Cheryl and Mary. As we all talked, somehow he came up with an idea for an artsy photo. He suggested that we two couples take a picture in bed together, à la Bob, Carol, Ted, and Alice, with partners mixed. So Mary lay next to me and Cheryl lay next to Richard in bed, under the covers.

Sam had us all roll up the legs of our pants and take our shoes off. He told Richard and me to take off our shirts, and he asked Cheryl and Mary to pull their tops down so that it would look like we were all naked. Then he snapped the picture.

Later, many of my friends who saw this photo were jealous. I tried to explain, "Guys, come on! Nothing happened!"

In the morning, the limos offered all of us rides back, but I rode with Cheryl in her car to Van Nuys Airport to pick up my car. What a great couple of days!

Hearing the difference between Fleetwood Mac's old album versions and the same songs played live, I realized how much the band had grown since they had recorded their previous album. "Rhiannon" had started as a fairly tame song on the album, later turning into what I could only describe as a "monster hit" with its extended ending and Stevie's wild ad libs. Now that I had this newer, more confident Fleetwood Mac in the studio with me, I really understood that the album we were working on had the potential to be a huge hit.

9

"I Quit!"

Tell the studio you quit, Ken! Come work for us.

—*Christine McVie*

After the Santa Barbara concert, the next ten days were terrific. It was so great to relax. The band, Richard, and I hadn't realized how hard we had been working for the last few months. Having a weekend off was amazing—a whole week was even better! I had forgotten how to relax, but somehow we all forced ourselves.

I had a little money now, and Richard and I started hanging out as friends. I would go over to Richard's "Putney House" in Rancho Park. For a short time Richard and Lindsey lived together in that small house, and I often spent time with them. Sometimes we'd go to the park around the corner and enjoy springtime in L.A.

Even though Richard was relaxed, it seemed as if Lindsey could never just be comfortable. He was always uptight, which in turn made me tense, so Richard, Scooter, and I sometimes tried to take off without Lindsey and go to more open spaces.

Even though we had the chance to relax, the pressure hadn't gone away. The label was clamoring for new footage of the band playing their new songs. I thought this was strange, considering that their first album was still climbing the charts and we were already well into working on the follow-up album.

That never happens today. Normally, an album is released; it's milked to death for every single it can give; the band tours to promote the album; and then, finally, when the album drops off the charts and concert ticket sales plummet, the band goes back into the studio to start recording their next album. Fleetwood Mac had put themselves in the perfect position— they could tour while they were recording *Rumours*, allowing them to make their new songs bigger and more dramatic on tour, so that when they got back into the studio, they could make the necessary changes or additions to their song foundations.

On May 11, we were scheduled to perform a live concert and film it on Studio Instrument Rental's (SIR) main rehearsal stage just a few blocks away from Wally Heider's studio and even closer to Fleetwood Mac's offices at Penguin.

The stage was a soundproof rehearsal room in a huge building. The ceiling was about seventy-five feet high, and the building was large enough to hold a full-size stage, Heider's fifty-foot recording truck, cameras, and lights, with still enough room for about two hundred spectators. Instead of the huge crowds the band had played in front of several days earlier, that day the audience would be made up of their friends.

Michael Collins and his Rosebud crew were there to film it. Fleetwood Mac had set it up as if they were playing a big concert. They wore the same costumes, and their stage equipment included their famous backdrop, so that it would look identical to the UC Santa Barbara show we had just recorded.

I had the same Heider's mobile truck, so, essentially, I expected that this recording would sound nearly the same as the Santa Barbara show, minus the audience, the tuning problems, and the airport noise.

With no paid audience, Michael Collins and his filmmakers were free to place their cameras anywhere they needed—even onstage with the band, which would normally block people's view. The lack of a large crowd's applause at the end of each song, though, would make it apparent to the viewers that there wasn't a big audience. Michael would have to fade out or cut immediately after each song's end to hide this.

An advantage to filming without an audience was that the band could perform each song as many times as they needed until they got each one perfect. Of course, *perfect* is a pretty powerful word, but as luck would have it, history would be made that day. The band's performances had been getting better and better since their first album had been released. Warner Bros. wanted a great performance of "Rhiannon," and they got it. They also wanted a "perfect" performance of "Go Your Own Way," and they got that, too.

Finally, they wanted Michael Collins to capture the driving energy of "You Make Loving Fun" on film. And if there was still time, Warner's wanted the band to record "Dreams." In addition, Michael was supposed to shoot interviews with the band so that their fans would be able to get to know them, especially the new members. Today will be a breeze, I thought. We only have three—maybe four—songs to record.

That was less than twenty minutes of music. I figured we should be done in two to three hours, max. The way I calculated, we would finish by one or two that afternoon. In other words, we should have plenty of time to get each song perfect and have a short day.

Christine wanted to start with "You Make Loving Fun" because it wouldn't strain anyone and would get the band's blood pumping.

We had left the board set up the same way that it had been during the concerts so that everything sounded the same. The band ran down "You Make Loving Fun" about five times, adjusting the tempo slightly each time. Every time the band stopped playing, though, Michael wanted to change the camera positions, just slightly. Because they were 16-millimeter cameras, this meant that we couldn't look at the film because the cameramen were shooting footage.

Today, when we shoot live footage, we use video. Now, while we're shooting footage, I'm able to see each camera's viewpoint from the truck, which makes things much more efficient.

That day, Richard and I were in the truck, and we could communicate with the camera crew on the stage and tell them our thoughts, but we had only a stationary black-and-white TV camera to view the stage.

Heider's big truck was parked just inside the stage door, which meant that any time Richard or I wanted to make a change onstage, we would have to go down the steps of the truck and walk all the way to the stage and up the stairs. This took a couple of minutes, so, in the interest of saving time, we used our talkback or our direct-com lines to give our feedback to the onstage personnel.

"Lovin Fun" was sounding great. The tempo was perfect, the instruments were perfect, Christine's voice was perfect, and the harmonies were spot-on. We had the full Fleetwood Mac house PA system there, including the stage monitors and their monitor mixer, Kenny Delsandro.

Stevie and Lindsey made some last-minute changes to their monitor mixes. We were ready. Cris Morris had come down to Los Angeles from Sausalito, and he was on the job with us now. Cris had his hands full keeping track of take numbers and time so we could choose the right take to match the film edits. He was also responsible for the audio feed from our truck to Michael's recorders.

"Sounds great out here," Richard said through the intercom.

"Michael, are you ready?" I asked.

"Yep, ready," Michael answered.

"Fleetwood Mac, are you ready to record?" I asked the band.

"Yes, ready," Christine said from her keyboard.

My last instructions over the talkback were, "Okay, we're going to slate the song. Then the cameras will get their sync pulse, and when each of the cameras are running, the camera guys will say, 'Speed!' Then Mick or Chris will count it off, okay?"

"Okay," the band echoed. Michael gave his okay.

I put the 24-track in RECORD with one hand, while my other hand hit the talkback.

"'Lovin' Fun', take one. Waiting for speed." We all heard "speed" from each cameraman, followed by silence. Then we heard the familiar three hits on the high hat. Then the snare from Mick. Then *boom*, my favorite wall of sound hit—clav, drums, bass guitar, and the band played the intro.

Stevie played a percussion instrument called a guiro, which is a kind of shaker with ridges on it. Stevie dragged a stick over the ridges in time with the music as she sang background harmonies. Christine played her Rhodes and organ. Lindsey played his white Les Paul, and John had his Alembic bass.

They played the song down. It's funny hearing it now, because it sounds so different from the final album version. The guitar solo is different, the ending harmonies are different, and even the tag-out guitar is different. Yet that day, it sounded great.

After we recorded that first song, everyone came into the truck and listened. They thought they should do one more take to try to make it tighter. Michael agreed, because this allowed him to move the cameras slightly and get another angle for editing.

Lindsey goes wild at our SIR film shoot.

Stevie gets into the moment.

We actually did three more takes before we decided to move on to "Go Your Own Way." We didn't finish until midnight. The devil is always in the details. It's easy to do a perfunctory job, but trying to make everything sound perfect takes a lot more time. Fortunately, we had allowed plenty of time to do the job.

In a way, it felt like we were in Sausalito again, locked into our soundstage and putting things under the musical microscope. We had costume changes and discussions, we rearranged vocal parts, we reshot footage for better camera angles, and we had to deal with simple production changes.

Now that we had finished the "concert" and the shoot, the next step was for Michael to process the film, cut it together, have the band approve it, and then send a video version to me so that Richard and I could do a stereo mix, adding in the appropriate audio portions of the show.

This would take a few weeks, but, as I said, the White Album was still climbing the charts, so we knew that we had plenty of time.

Three days later was my first day back to work at Wally Heider's.

I drove down Cahuenga Boulevard, straight to 1529 Cahuenga about a half-block south from the main building, and parked behind studio 4. Then I remembered that I had to go into the main office first, so I turned left onto Selma Avenue and right into Wally's lot, parking directly opposite studio 1. I walked into the traffic office, but instead of talking to my friends, I continued walking straight through to the time clock to punch in for work.

All of the hominess I had felt a few months earlier had changed. Wally had sold a portion of his company to Filmways, and they had made some changes. They had installed corporate types in the offices and had made the recording studio traffic office feel more like a bank or the DMV. I picked up a blank time card, wrote my name on it, and punched in. This is weird, I thought. I'm an employee again.

I felt as if I were taking a step backward, and it certainly didn't feel as good as being an independent engineer. But this was the deal I had made with Wally. I had taken a leave of absence to go record Fleetwood Mac at another studio, and I had told him that I would try to bring them back to my home studio, Wally Heider Recording, for overdubs and mixing.

I had booked Heider's big studio 4 for the next three months. This meant that on that day, Fleetwood Mac would be settling into studio 4. This also meant that as staff engineer, I needed to walk down the street to studio 4 and stock it with tape, microphones, and the correct type of tape machines myself.

When Cris arrived, I would have him help, but I had the door keys and the alarm codes, so I couldn't have him do everything. When I got to the studio, all of the supplies needed to be refilled. I called down to the office and asked whether I could get some help. Gail, one of the new girls in the traffic office, told me that they didn't have any hustlers to spare and that it was my job, anyway.

Cris walked into studio 4. "Hey, buddy! Good to see you," I said. "Can you believe this? The office expects me to go get the supplies and equipment to stock the studio for our session."

"Aw, now you know how I feel, pal," he said unsympathetically.

"Yeah, but you only had to walk twenty feet, and I have to go five hundred and move not only supplies but the tape machines as well! And the band will be here soon." I continued, "Shit, never mind. Come on and give me a hand."

Cris and I went back up the street to get the supplies we needed. What a contrast to the Record Plant, where I had been treated like royalty.

We set up studio 4 the way we had set up at the Record Plant. We were in overdub mode. This meant that we wanted to be prepared for everything. We had every instrument out and set up with a mic on it, including all of Mick's percussion instruments, Christine's keyboards, John's basses, and, of course, Lindsey's guitars. In addition, I had three iso booths in which to place my effects gear.

Ray and Rhino came by later that morning to drop off the band's equipment. They set it up where I suggested, similar to the way we had set up the studio at the Record Plant. Heider's studios were much simpler and less gaudy than the ones at the Record Plant. At Heider's, the ceilings were higher and the lines were straighter. The studios were rectangular rooms with big windows so that we could see one another.

We were prepared to record the whole band if they decided they wanted to cut a new track, and I was also prepared if they wanted to do guitars, keys, or vocals. We set up the iso booths for our effects. A guitar amp was set up in the rear iso booth, and the spinning Leslie was placed in the single front iso booth to the right of the control room.

Christine and Curry were the first to arrive. She was very excited because she had just bought a home overlooking Sunset Boulevard in the Sunset Strip area of West Hollywood.

"I can see the ocean from my backyard pool," Christine said.

"Congratulations, Chris," I said. "Let me know if you ever need anyone to house-sit."

"Sure," she mused.

Christine liked the idea that her new house was nice enough that someone wanted to house-sit. Previously, she had been renting an apartment on Beachwood Drive in the Hollywood Hills with Judy Wong.

The newfound money was having its effect on all of the members of the band. John had bought a forty-one-foot boat, and he was living in Marina Del Rey. Lindsey and Richard had moved into the previously mentioned house on Putney Drive in Rancho Park. Stevie had moved out from Lindsey's, and she was buying a house near Christine's old apartment. For me, this was all a big change, compared to all of us living so close together in Sausalito. All the members of the band seemed more calm and relaxed and in control of their lives now.

Stevie called her new home "El Contento," and Tom Moncrief moved in with her. Tom had played bass with Fritz before Stevie joined Fleetwood Mac. He had taken Lindsey's place as Stevie's musical confidant after Lindsey moved on. Tom soon built a small studio where Stevie could write and record, singing to her heart's content. Mick had a new place up in Topanga Canyon.

Richard and I were making good money now. Plus, I still had those ten checks for $1,500 each from the Record Plant in my new bank account. A few days earlier, Richard had purchased an amazing black velvet sports coat that looked really good with Levi's. I followed his lead and bought the same jacket. It didn't occur to me at the time that having the same coat as Richard might lead to embarrassing moments if the two of us showed up dressed the same. Luckily, that rarely happened.

Shortly after that, Richard found a tailor who sold beautiful custom white silk shirts. Richard and I each bought three. There was an excitement in the air. Things felt good. Things were happening.

The rest of the band arrived at the studio that morning, and the first thing we had to do was settle in. I showed everybody around Heider's studio, even though there wasn't that much to see. Inside our building, we had the control room, the studio, a couple of iso booths, a storage room, and two bathrooms. Out the backdoor, we had a private parking lot, but the road crew also had to use it to set up because there wasn't a lot of space. In the back of the building was a small storeroom where people would hang out if it was too hot or rainy, instead of going outside to take

Guys gone wild in the control room of studio 4 at Heider's: me, Cris, Lindsey, and Richard.

a break. Through the front door was a very busy Cahuenga Boulevard north of Sunset.

I explained to the band that two doors down from our studio was the world-famous Martoni's Bar and Restaurant. I had often heard that some of the most important business deals in Hollywood were made in Martoni's restaurant. So, instead of privacy and seclusion as we had had in Sausalito, we now had great food and a full bar just a few steps away. When any of us took a break we could go out for a quick business meeting or a relaxing meal. Everyone in the band was happy with my choice of Heider's studio 4.

Next, we put our master tapes up on the 24-track so that we could listen to how all of our hard work sounded in this new room. We started to listen to all of our songs on Heider's speakers. They were much different from the Tom Hidley monitors we had used in Sausalito. These were Altec 604Es, a relative of the Voice of the Theater speakers used in most movie theaters.

The Altec speakers had a strong top and midrange and a good bottom end due to their fifteen-inch woofers. They were powered by Macintosh 300-watt tube amplifiers. This was right around the days of quad, so Wally had also put in rear speakers. This meant that we had two speakers in front and two behind us. Sometimes, I'd put the kick and the snare in all four speakers, and, for fun, I'd crank up the other instruments around the room. It sounded huge!

The important thing was that our tracks sounded great in studio 4. They sounded and felt more open than they had at the Record Plant. The other good news was that we were back home in L.A.! The members of the band were dating other people, and they were rebuilding their lives. I hoped that the drama of the breakups was behind us. Well, I could dream, couldn't I? Unfortunately, I was far from correct.

As we went through the songs, Christine asked for her white wine and Mick requested his Heineken. Lindsey was busy at the producer's desk to the left side of the console, rolling joints, one after another. Stevie took little tokes off Lindsey's joints, swaying back and forth to the music.

It didn't take long for the word to get out that Fleetwood Mac was recording at Heider's. During our first day in the studio, many of the band's friends came to visit. Label people stopped in, and attorneys and accountants came to see their now prosperous clients. Sandra Vigon, Herbie Worthington, and Judy Wong were all there that day. Christine asked me where the fridge was, assuming we had one just as we had had at the Record Plant.

I had Cris call down to the office to ask for a refrigerator. In the middle of the call, he told me they wanted to talk to me. I picked up the phone and was informed that if we wanted a refrigerator, we'd be charged for it. I thought this was a little petty because Fleetwood Mac was huge, and they had booked a lot of studio time. I said that the Record Plant hadn't charged the band.

Gail, one of the girls up in the office, could be a real bitch. "Well, then, why don't you go back to the Record Plant?" she said. Gail was new, and I didn't know her very well, but even some of the people I had worked with before I started with Fleetwood Mac had an attitude about my new position.

"Okay, just add it to our bill," I said to Gail. "Now, can someone bring it down?"

"No, Ken. We can't spare anyone."

"I can't leave the studio. I'm working with the band."

"You'll have to come down and sign for it," she said. "If you want it that bad, then you'll just have to make the time."

"Do you know that if I wasn't employed by Heider's and if I worked for the band, you'd provide an engineer for me, and you'd send the refrigerator down immediately?" I asked.

"Sure," she said. "But you do work for Heider's."

By this point, I could hear the band cheering me on as they listened to me yelling at Gail.

"Tell them you quit, Ken," Christine said. "Work for us." Mick and Stevie nodded their approval.

I took a deep breath, thinking about what I was going to do. Then I calmly said, "Gail, please tell Wally that I'm sorry, but I quit. I'm taking a job with the band as one of their engineers. The good news is that we'll be staying here to continue working on our album, as promised." About ten minutes later, our very own Wally Heider assistant engineer brought our refrigerator into the studio.

A few days later, Wally and I talked, and I told him I was sorry I was leaving. I don't know that he knew the reason why, because we didn't get into details, but Wally said, always magnanimous, "Ken, every bird has to, uh, leave the nest. Uh, you did good, Ken. Uh, buster's gang!"

That was Wally's way of saying that he thought I would go "gang busters" in the recording industry. He had a way with words when he finally got them out. I was a little sad to leave Wally, but I was glad I was no longer a part of what Heider's had become.

We didn't get much work done that day, but we did spread a lot of goodwill. Our confidence in this album was climbing rapidly. I played most of the band's songs at least three times for our waves of guests. Our first day of recording in L.A. was pretty great.

The band was in a decidedly better place than they had been three months earlier. Who knew that life could hand out such gifts?

On the next day, Saturday, May 16, my log records a transcension. Not surprising. The day before, we had learned that the band was going to do a few small tours in the next two months to support the still-rising White Album. During that time, they would shift gears from the studio to touring. This sounded like a lot of work to me (and I had just signed on to be their employee!).

Lindsey was anxious to get the engineers alone with the songs so that we could work on them. He suggested that the rest of the band go on vacation. They all agreed to go away, leaving Lindsey, Richard, Cris, and me to work on the songs.

Despite the workload, this sounded like heaven to me. The most fun we had with Lindsey was when we did guitar parts with him. "No girls!" Richard and I said to each other.

Mick and John decided that they could be gone for only a week or so. After all, they were the band's managers, and they wanted to work on the album, too. Christine and Stevie decided to take as much time off as they could—almost three weeks—because they had already done most of their work.

John was taking Sandra on vacation, so Christine took me up on my offer to house-sit as long as I also agreed to dog-sit Duster. Cheryl and I would be sleeping up at Christine's new house until Sandra returned from her vacation with John, then Sandra would take over for me.

The phone calls were made and the plans were booked that day. Then, after that, all of the vacationing band members were eager to play a few of their songs. I thought this would be good, because I wanted to make sure all of their gear was working and tuned up.

Stevie had a song, "Smile at You," that she had recorded with Tom Moncrief, and she wanted the band to play it that day. Mick slid into his drum space, John his bass area. Christine sat with her back to us at her keys station, and Lindsey was over to the left, on the south wall, facing Mick.

Stevie stood in the center of the studio, using a handheld microphone. Every member of the band was in transcension mode, significantly buzzed on his or her favorite substance.

I remember that two girls, Julie and a tall thin redhead, came down that day to visit, bringing badly needed supplies, sandwiches and cocaine, with them. Julie spent a long time talking to John, holding up our session. Eventually, John and Julie got married (at Christine's house, no less), and they're still married as I write this, thirty years later.

When we finally got rolling on "Smile at You," Lindsey suddenly didn't want to play the song anymore. He was annoyed when he learned that Stevie had developed it with Tom Moncrief. The more we worked on the song, the less enthusiastic Lindsey seemed to be about it. I loved the song and kept pushing him to record it.

Yet Stevie knew that Lindsey's lack of interest meant "Smile at You" was doomed as far as making it onto *Rumours*. The "Smile at You" session just fizzled out.

We continued to record various things until about two in the morning. Even though we didn't get anything usable, it was still an interesting and fun session. "Smile at You" was finally released on Fleetwood Mac's 2003 *Say You Will* album and was produced by, of all people, Lindsey Buckingham. That version, however, was much less powerful than the 1976 version we worked on that night.

Now that we were in L.A., I learned to use a tried-and-true trick of John's. When it got late and I wanted to leave, I simply went to the bathroom and left out the backdoor. Everyone was so wasted that night that all they cared about was jamming. As long as someone was there to press RECORD, they simply didn't care that I had left.

The next day the phone rang. It was Richard. "Nice one, last night, Cutlass! It was a CIA escape. I'll get you for this!" He did. During the next transcension, I was about to make my escape, but I looked around and realized that Richard was already gone. I was stuck pressing RECORD until the band was ready to quit. That's what friends do to one another.

Sunday was a day off. Hallelujah! From this point on, we started taking Sundays off pretty consistently until we finished the album. It was necessary for my sanity.

I got over to Christine's house about 2 p.m. that day to start my house-sitting duties. Christine and Sandra were packing for their trips.

Christine gave me her house key and her alarm code. She explained Duster's feeding schedule and gave me a brief tour of the house.

It was a very nice but modest single-story home in the hills overlooking Sunset Boulevard. The house had been built in the sixties, and it sat right on the street.

When I parked in front, I thought, How can a big star live here? Anyone could just walk up to her front door.

The house had a fireplace in the living room and three bedrooms. Christine had converted one into an office, and she shared the master bedroom with Curry. Sandra stayed in the third bedroom after she left John because he was still drinking too much.

The backyard was completely private. Standing there, I could look down on Tower Records and on the area where the series *77 Sunset Strip* was set. Christine and Sandra both had late-afternoon flights, so I

Me, house-sitting at Christine's. Scooter and Duster live the Beverly Hills lifestyle.

went home and packed a small bag, setting my house to vacation mode. I grabbed Scooter's dog food and his bowl. Then I called Cheryl and arranged to meet her at eight that evening at Christine's house.

That night, Cheryl and I had a firelit evening and a midnight skinny dip in Christine's pool. I was falling right into this lifestyle. While I stayed at Christine's, Richard, Lindsey, and I started to visit the popular rock clubs—the Roxy, the Rainbow on the Sunset Strip, and the Troubadour down on nearby Santa Monica Boulevard. During the midseventies, all of the clubs in the Strip area were very hip. It was a common occurrence to hear people snorting cocaine in the stalls when you went into the bathroom. You could even do it at your table, if you were discreet about it. Remember, it was the free-love era.

At that time and place, everyone seemed to exude sex, especially the women, who often dressed provocatively. Ah, those were the days to be young, single, and in the music business.

10

The Boys Are Back in Town

Lindsey punched me in the face. Then he started yelling
all this crazy stuff about how he couldn't take it, and I had
to leave.

—*Christina Conte, Lindsey's girlfriend*

With everyone else from the band on vacation, Lindsey, Richard, Cris,
and I started at noon on Monday, May 17. Rhino had brought in a
few *Playboy* magazines and spread the pictures around the room to celebrate our freedom from the women. Naturally, we weren't allowed to do
anything like this when Stevie and Christine were around.

That day we decided to begin by going through the songs, one at
a time, to check Lindsey's acoustic guitar parts and then possibly double them. To double a part means that Lindsey would play along with
the original guitar part so that it sounded bigger or fatter. Or he might
decide that he could improve the previous recording, so he would just
replay it and then double that.

The boys get to work. That's Lindsey tossing his hair.

One of my favorite things was when we added guitar accents, like a long strum just before the chorus to kick it off, such as the ones you hear in "Oh, Daddy."

Many times, we added acoustic- or electric-picking along with the strumming part for more color and movement. If we had two acoustic guitars doing nearly the same thing, we would capo up the neck of one of the guitars or switch to a different tuning on that guitar, making that part a perfect tonal color in our sonic painting.

A capo is a bar or a rod that clips onto the neck of the guitar. It pushes down across all of the strings of the guitar, similar to what your finger does while playing a bar. It's exactly what the nut of a guitar does, too, determining the length of the strings and the notes they create. Musicians can place the capo between any two frets on a guitar neck. The farther up they place it, the higher the key the guitar will play. Finally, when the key is right, the guitarist can play simple open chords that require only several fingers, allowing the rest of the strings to resonate at their natural, but now higher, key. So, whatever key the song was played in, Lindsey could place the capo on the appropriate fret and play his guitar in a higher, open tuning, giving a fresh and exciting tone to the song.

The fun of doing electric guitar overdubs with Lindsey was that he sat in the control room and developed his part with us. All that he needed was a guitar cable running out to the studio, connecting to all of his gear. He would hear exactly what we were hearing with our speakers blasting.

For the next three weeks, that's what we did. Richard, Cris, and I sat together around Lindsey and his guitar, making music together. Even if we were doing an acoustic guitar part, Lindsey usually worked with us in the control room. Then, he went out to the quiet studio to record it.

For the next few hours that day, we layered and massaged "Strummer." I can't stress enough how much different "Strummer" sounded at this point than it did from the final mix of "Second Hand News." In the final version, the snare was really bright and ringing. In the original, John had played a completely different walking bass part, and Christine had played some sort of busy Celtic organ part. For starters that day, Lindsey

Lindsey plays in the control room, while the rest of the band is on vacation.

Lindsey added unique strumming parts to "Second Hand News."

played a new, more sparse bass part because he thought the original one was all wrong for where he felt the song should go.

Next, he started experimenting with dry, stiff, aggressive strumming parts to fit into the hole that he had just opened. Finally, we added an acoustic guitar that can be heard at 0:06, 0:09, 0:21, and 0:25 in the song. Lindsey's new acoustic strumming part completely beefed up the rhythm running through the song. Then he had another idea.

"Second Hand News" had quite a few interesting textures in it. One thing a lot of people remarked on was that the snare sound was very thin and ringy—not exactly what was considered state of the art at that time. The song had kind of a retro sound, but that was cool. Another great thing about this song was that it had a percussive roll that was created by hitting the seat of a Naugahyde chair that we found in the studio.

Found sounds had always interested Lindsey. He loved it when you found something that didn't sound like music, but you could incorporate it into a recording and make something unique and interesting of it.

Lindsey was looking for a very dead percussive sound that would be the transience, or top end, of what he wanted the bass part to be. Anyhow, we found these chairs, and that worked really well.

Finding this sound from these chairs reminds me of a quick chair story. I used to engineer string and horn sessions at Heider's studio 4, which employed professional musicians. These professional string players and horn players would always fight for the padded seats during the sessions. It seems there were never enough padded chairs for everyone, so some of the musicians had to sit on steel folding chairs. Those grown-up studio musicians whined like babies, "Why can't I have a padded chair like everyone else?"

Finally, one of them would give in and say, "Okay, you can have mine. I have enough padding anyway." At the end of the session, when I was putting the chairs away, I would always find several paper bags with empty wallet-size bottles of booze under the seats. They were drinking straight booze during my sessions.

Anyway, Lindsey had this idea that we should have a rolling eighth note percussion part. Since Mick wasn't there, and Lindsey really wanted to play it anyway, we started beating on things in the studio. We tried congas, toms, and snares. All of them were way too bright. Then we tried putting tape over them, adding paper towels and blankets, but that wasn't right, either.

Finally, I hit the seat of one of the Naugahyde chairs. "Hmm," I said. "That sounds interesting."

Lindsey came over and played the pattern on the chair seat. "Yeah, let's try it."

"Mic it up, Cris," I said.

"What mic would you like to use, Professor, to win your Grammy for the best sound from the chair?" he asked me.

I paused, putting my finger to my lips. "An 87. Yes. That will be perfect."

Cris glared at me over his shoulder on his way to the mic cabinet. "An 87? Unbelievable!" I heard him mutter under his breath, à la Oliver Hardy.

"How are your headphones, Linds?" Cris asked, adjusting the knobs at the headphone mixer to the right of the console.

"Give me a lot of kick and snare," Lindsey said. "You'll probably have to punch me in a few times. I probably won't be able to play steady all the way through to the end."

"No problem," I said. "Just stop when you get tired or make a mistake."

Lindsey sat on one chair, facing another, holding one of Mick's drumsticks in each hand and using the thick end of the sticks to strike the chair.

Lindsey came in right after the count at the top of song, and—it sounded great! But the trick was to have it just loud enough to feel it. If you could actually hear it, then it was too loud.

Even though they had broken up, Lindsey still felt an obligation to improve Stevie's songs. It was strange to watch them fighting and realize

Lindsey preps to pound on a chair for the beat in
"Second Hand News."

how much coldness there was between them. Sometimes when they were together, I would see one of them get excited, briefly, when talking to the other. It was almost as if their excitement about the music made them forget that their relationship had ended.

We loaded "Gold Dust Woman" onto the tape machine and played it down a few times. Then we started experimenting with parts and sounds. Eventually, we tried the Dobro.

The Dobro looks like an acoustic guitar, but it has a steel front that acts like a resonator to make the guitar have a more guttural sound, a very mid- and bottom end-sounding guitar. This added a great vibe to an already emotional song. The Dobro plays two parts throughout the song, but it can be heard best picking at 4:07 and accenting chords at 4:14 and 4:18 of "Gold Dust Woman."

When you listen to this track, try to imagine that only a few instruments are playing. The screams, the glass breaking, the electric guitar strings were not part of the song at that point. They would be added later. We were building a foundation for a great song.

Technically, I used my ECM-50 trick, the tiny lavaliere mic. I placed a piece of masking tape on the surface of the instrument near the hole in the guitar. Then I rolled off the low frequencies and boosted the upper mid frequencies. This mic, combined with a second, more expensive mic such as an AKG C-451, made a great stereo image with enough bite to cut through all of the other layering we might use.

Lindsey was a genius. I watched him focus on the open parts of a song. Then he would find the perfect part to play and would always add just the right tempo. Of course, he played the part perfectly. Then we, the engineers, made the sound of his part the right color. Richard and I worked with Lindsey to find the right sound and effect for every part of every song. In time, I learned to do that with everyone I worked with. I have Lindsey (and many others) to thank for that.

In my most recent productions, Colbie Caillat's second album, *Breakthrough*, and her latest record, *All of You*, most of the studio time was spent on this all-important layering stage. Lindsey knew that we were supporting him so that he sounded better. Because of this, he indulged us, and we had more time to get the sound right. I believe much of the coloring or the layering we developed at Heider's shaped *Rumours* into what it ultimately became. And don't forget to listen for that chair in "Second Hand News"!

After recording the chair, Richard, Lindsey, and I decided that we had time for a dinner break at Martoni's. When we walked through the door, we were greeted by a warm "Welcome, welcome, please come in," from Sal Martoni, the owner.

Martoni's décor was honest and Italian. It was a fairly narrow restaurant, but it was deep. On the left side was a long wooden bar, and on the right side, comfortable red leather booths. Chianti bottles hung from the ceiling. Martoni's was famous for its celebrity clientele, attracted by the atmosphere, the fine food, and the strong cocktails.

That day we learned that Sal's martinis were particularly dangerous, especially since the people who carried our antidote for strong martinis—cocaine—were all on vacation. Initially, we had thought it was good that they were gone because we certainly didn't need any blow. After the first Martoni's session, however, we realized we should find some.

I called my friend Gary, but although I knew he had pot and Quaaludes, I wasn't sure that he had coke. I really hadn't done much of that before Fleetwood Mac. In fact, before Fleetwood Mac, the only time I can remember doing it had been on a very long remote recording outside of Kansas City. My chief engineer, Tom, shared some damp coke with me while we waited out a lightning storm. It was my first time, and I don't think I felt it at all.

Over the phone, Gary told me that he could get us some coke, and he'd bring it down to the studio.

When Gary arrived, I introduced him to the guys. Gary made sure that Lindsey knew that he could also get top-grade pot. Lindsey was very excited about this. Before Gary left, he promised to let us know when he had something to sample. Of course, now that we had the blow, we knew the crew would come to us for a line if they found out that we were well stocked. Because none of us liked being asked to share our coke, we agreed to hide the blow in the studio and not travel around with it.

Back at Heider's studio 4, I settled in for another day's working with music. "What do you want to work on today?" I asked.

Lindsey, Richard, and Curry check out Gary's goods.

Lindsey wanted to work on "Dreams," so we loaded it onto the 24-track and played it. He wasn't happy with his original electric part. He had played it very clean, and it almost sounded like an acoustic guitar. The part had been played very sparsely, with only about four licks to the verse. There was almost no difference between the feel of the verse and the chorus. He decided to make the chorus more of a hook.

We got his best Martin guitar and capo'd the part up so that he could play it very tight and precise, almost making it sound like a music box. The timing of the part was syncopated, giving it the effect of lifting the chorus. We had to be patient. We knew the part was right, because when we put it in place in the mix, we began to hear other parts that would work, too. That's what I love about making music. Of course, this came after a couple of hours of experimenting.

Once the chorus had been lifted, Lindsey had a better idea of what he wanted to do with the verse: he wanted to go back to the clean electric part because it was sparse but ethereal. We fired up the Leslie and fed Lindsey's electric guitar through it. I placed one side of the guitar in the left speaker, the high Leslie mic in the right speaker, and the low in the middle of both speakers.

We experimented with the amount of aggressiveness we wanted to have in this part, and we made sure that Lindsey was hearing everything in stereo, the same way we were listening to it. In those days, there were often mono headphone cue systems and dull-sounding headphones. They didn't sound as good, but they had a long life, so studio owners liked them. Many studio musicians used only one side of their headphones anyway, so they didn't need stereo headsets.

Not me, though. I believed at that time, ever since the Beatles and the Beach Boys, stereo was expected by everyone. I believed that my musicians needed to hear exactly how the record would sound in their headphones as they were playing. This meant that I asked for—and got—high-quality Sony headphones with good cups for better isolation. At the Record Plant, I had the studio overhaul the cue system so that I could send stereo effects into their headphones, or "cans," as they're often called.

I love the electric guitar tone we achieved. It has the perfect amount of growl or distortion from the guitar and Leslie tracks. Later, I would add additional reverb as needed to deepen the vibe of the part. It seemed as if we were reinventing these songs, yet again.

After a few hours of work, Lindsey, Richard, and I went to lunch at Richard and Lindsey's favorite Chinese restaurant, Kowloon, also known for its lethal cocktails. Kowloon was located about six miles southwest of the studio down on Pico Avenue. The restaurant had a large parking lot, so it was easy to come and go, and it sat next to an oversized one-story building. The restaurant had a very open feeling, yet it was still perfectly secluded and dark, thanks to the bamboo coverings on the big windows.

Kowloon had two dining areas. The waiters usually put us in one by ourselves, and they always kept several waiters standing by to serve us. Their specialty cocktails were mai tais and Scorpions, served in huge, brightly decorated bowls or tureens with eighteen-inch straws and small umbrellas. Each drink was filled to the top with a mixture of fruit juices and various types of alcohol.

Lindsey ordered a Scorpion for each of us and several appetizers. The drinks were carried out to us on a large tray. The waiter was careful to put the straws in after the drinks were in front of us; the long straws had a tendency to tip out of the sweet, potent concoctions.

We all grabbed our straws and sucked down large mouthfuls. The taste was a combination of sweet and tangy, and the drinks were perfectly chilled. They went down far too quickly. Before we knew it, we had gotten close to the bottom of our first round.

Lindsey motioned to one of our waiters for another round. It was an amazing drink, working quickly and superbly to inebriate us, while not making us feel drunk. We just got happy in this lovely place. Kowloon had very long, tall menus. While I was looking at the menu, my straw, full of liquid, tipped into the menu, which was resting in my lap, and the liquid ran down into my crotch, soaking me clean through. We all laughed. Soon after this, the same thing happened to Lindsey, and we laughed at the coincidence.

With our appetizers came the third round of drinks. Richard was careful not to let the straw drop into his lap. Lindsey was waiting for it to happen, and the next thing I knew, a wall of water came from under the table into Richard's lap. Richard jumped up, startled. I looked at Lindsey sitting across from Richard with his water glass empty. He was laughing hysterically. We began to call this getting "Kowlooned."

Eventually, there were several types of "Kowloons." There was the "CIA Kowloon"—the under-the-table attack. There was the "Waterfall Kowloon," which meant pouring water down the open menu. The "Chow Mein Kowloon" was when food was dumped into your lap. I think you get the picture.

Whenever we needed to blow off steam, we went to Kowloon. When Christine and Stevie returned, they joined us. Usually, Stevie brought some sort of plastic cover-up, which she would zip up, leaving only her face exposed. How did we get away with it? Well, we tipped very generously, and we spent a lot of money. Whenever we arrived, the staff always welcomed us with plenty of towels.

Christina, Lindsey's girlfriend from Sausalito, came down on Thursday, May 20, to visit Lindsey. Her brown curly hair was much longer than it had been when I had last seen her. As she laughed, it moved on its own. Her hair was very similar to Lindsey's Afro style.

She had rendezvoused with Lindsey in Big Sur for a long weekend right after we had left Sausalito, and, apparently, she thought a relationship was starting between them. After she flew into Burbank, she had taken a cab to studio 4 in Hollywood to spend some more time with "L," as she called him. We were in the middle of "Go Your Own Way," probably the most complete of all of the Sausalito songs, when she walked in.

We decided to stop and celebrate her arrival. We took her out for a royal Kowlooning. We left the studio early and went to the restaurant. At the end of our meal, I suggested we head up by Christine's and go to one of the clubs on the Strip. After that, we started visiting the popular music clubs on the Strip more frequently after work.

Cheryl and I were already regulars at the Rainbow, a very hip club. My velvet jacket fit in quite well on the Strip. Lots of good-looking people hung out there, and cocaine was plentiful. We were all quick learners. It was the thing to do.

Christina stayed at the Putney house with Lindsey every night after he left the studio. She really enjoyed coming down to the sessions and seeing Lindsey, and I thought they were getting along great.

One morning during her visit, I had arranged to meet Cris Morris early at the studio to figure out what to do because we were running out of tracks on some of the songs. Certain songs had many more parts than others. This didn't necessarily mean that they were more complete; sometimes it meant the opposite—that they had a lot of bad ideas we hadn't discarded yet. Or, we may have recorded background vocals separately so that three vocals could each be on a separate track—or even on six tracks, if we had doubled them.

I could have chosen to put all of the background vocal parts together on one track. Sometimes that works, and sometimes it doesn't. When you have just one track, though, it means that all of the parts have to be recorded in one pass, and everybody has to get everything right. An option I had was to free up some tracks by combining the six vocal tracks down onto two open tracks as stereo background vocal tracks, or three mono tracks of two vocals each. Finally, I could erase all of the originals, which would give us six open tracks.

Cris wanted to meet early that morning, because he thought we needed to bounce some tracks down to make room for more ideas. We went through the track sheets and made notes.

Suddenly, Lindsey barged through the front door from the street and went directly into the studio. A few minutes later, Richard and Christina came in the back door, having parked behind the studio. They both walked past Lindsey without saying a word and went directly into the control room.

Christina was white and trembling. There were no jokes coming from Richard, either. "I'll go talk to him," Richard said to Christina. He walked out of the control room and closed the door.

"What happened?" I asked Christina, who had begun to cry hysterically.

"I don't know. I think it's over. And what's worse is that Lindsey punched me in the face. Then he started yelling all this crazy stuff about how he couldn't take it, and I had to leave."

Richard came in and told Christina that Lindsey was sorry, that he didn't know what had happened, but he did want her to leave. I called a cab for Christina, and that was it. She was gone.

I really thought Christina and Lindsey had been great together. I'll never forget how she trembled after Lindsey attacked her. Her face had red marks on it where he had hit her. Lindsey always seemed to be wound a little too tight, but I hadn't expected that he would get physical with a woman. I felt sick, as if the magic had been destroyed. Little did I know that I would also experience his physical rage in the near future.

Richard was upset, too. He had been at the house at the time and had seen the whole thing. "What are you doing, Lindsey? Are you fucking crazy?" he demanded when we were alone with Lindsey. "You don't do that to people!"

"I know. You're right," Lindsey said. "I don't know why she got me that mad."

"Let's get out of here," Richard said. Lindsey and I agreed. It was Saturday, and we decided to take a break until Monday at noon.

• • •

You know how you get an impulse to do something? Well, that next Monday morning I had one. For me, it often starts in the shower, where I do my best thinking.

Anyway, I was taking my shower, and my brain started going. Maybe it was the water flowing over my body. Eventually, I ended up standing with my back to the shower, the hot water hitting the base of my skull, my arms folded, and I could see the world clearly. I knew what I had to do.

Now, in 2011, I would have jumped on my computer to put my thoughts in motion. Back in 1976, though, I had to dry off, get dressed, and head out. Cheryl had made breakfast for us in Christine's new kitchen after we had skinny-dipped in the pool, again. I told her my plan—she understood my quirks.

First, I had to drive over the hill to Burbank to pick up my mail. As I headed back toward Hollywood, I stopped at a little tech shop in North Hollywood. They had all kinds of electronic stuff there. I had built my "door mouth"—my doorbell that would play any audio I wanted—from parts I had purchased there.

I had stolen the idea from Bill Cosby. On one of his records, he imagined having a voice yell, "Somebody's at the door!" when the doorbell was pushed. So I had built one that played Bill's voice. I hid speakers on either side of the door, and there you have it. I liked to mix up the audio. Sometimes I played dogs barking, horns honking, or other sounds on the tape. I know, it sounds annoying, but I was still in my twenties.

I walked around the store, but I couldn't find what I was looking for. I went up to one of the guys behind the counter and politely said, "Hi, I'm looking for something to answer my phone and take a message for me when I'm not home."

The clerk looked at me as if I were crazy. He turned and asked another clerk if they had anything that could answer my phone.

To my surprise, the other guy broke into this big smile. "Not many people even know these exist. I don't get much call for them. In fact, you're probably the first."

The second clerk went to the back of the store and then came out with a box the size of a small microwave. He was struggling, so I could tell that it was heavy. He opened it, pulled out a big machine, and carefully set it on the glass counter.

"Check out this baby," he said. "It has two tapes so you can record as long as you want. It has knobs on the back, and you can adjust how many times the phone rings before it answers. Then, it has another knob to control the length of the caller's message. It also has plugs for both the old-style four-prong phone and for the new modular phone, so you can use it with either type of phone."

I was stunned. The answering machine also came with a small box about the size of a pack of cigarettes with a speaker built into it. This meant that I could even retrieve my calls when I was away!

That morning, in the shower, it had occurred to me that while I was house-sitting at Christine's, people were calling me at my home and I wasn't there to answer. Back in those days, if you were expecting a call, you had to stay home and wait for the phone to ring. If you were trying to reach somebody, you just had to keep on trying until you finally got hold of them. Even back in the seventies, this seemed illogical to me. My impulse that morning had been to find a machine that would solve this problem.

The clerk said he had another type of answering machine, but it didn't have all of the functions of the one he had shown me.

"How much is the good one?" I asked.

"Four hundred dollars. It was built in Canada by a very good company, and it will last for years."

I bought it and took it back to my house. I played my favorite Steely Dan song, "The Boston Rag," off *Countdown to Ecstasy* on my stereo and recorded my message over the song: "Hi. This is Ken," I said in perfect timing with the sliding intro guitar part. "Please leave a message after the beep, and I'll call you back as soon as I can." I set it to "answer" and left the house, taking the blue remote box with me. I was the first person I knew of who had an answering machine, but that changed soon. Before I knew it, everyone had one. At first, people didn't know what to say:

"Err, is this a machine?"

"Ken? Are you there?"

"Ken, call me."

A couple of my more old-fashioned friends ridiculed me. "If you're not home, why should I leave a message?" Chiggy asked.

"So that I'll know you tried to call me," I tried to explain. "That way I'll call you right back, so you don't have to keep trying me."

Soon, most people accepted it, and my outgoing messages got more elaborate.

I was going to be late to the studio that day, but it was okay. I was just going to work with the guys, and by this time, we were all pretty comfortable with one another's schedules. If one of us was running late, then the others would pick up the slack. There was always something to do in this layering stage of the album—some combining or bouncing of tracks.

When I got there, I had Cris play "Strummer." I was amazed at how different the song sounded now that we had the extra guitars in the verses and the new acoustic part in the chorus—and that amazing chair part!

I got to the studio before Lindsey and Richard that day because they had been listening to "Strummer" at the Putney house, working out ideas for it. Mick and John would be back in a couple of days, and Lindsey had decided that he wanted Mick to add a "spastic" tom fill to the chorus of "Strummer."

As I played the song through the chorus, Lindsey played an imaginary drum set, showing us what he wanted Mick's part to sound like. It was erratic and impulsive, and as he played, his hair bounced all around from his violent movements.

"Cris, can you hand me the sheet?" I made a note for a new tom part for the chorus. Then I checked out how we were doing for open tracks. "We need to bounce all the new acoustics we just recorded down to two or three tracks," I explained. "Lindsey, can we do that now?"

"Sure," he said, rolling another joint. We had recorded two new verse acoustic guitars and two doubles or accent guitars. I bounced those four tracks down to two stereo tracks.

I played the verses, sending all four tracks down to two new ones, panned hard left and right, and adjusted the levels of each part so that they were perfect. I added a little more top end to their EQ. Lindsey gave me a nod of approval, and I put the two new guitar tracks in RECORD, combining the four tracks down to two.

The chair part had been recorded on two tracks for simplicity. Now, we bounced those down to one complete track, compressing them slightly with an outboard compressor. Then we added a little upper bottom, while we bounced them onto one of the old acoustic tracks.

We erased the other acoustic tracks after we bounced the chairs. At that point, we had five more tracks we could use. That's how we had to do it back then. We had to keep bouncing tracks down, making room for more layers because we had only twenty-four tracks to work with. A few years later, we were able to add a second 24-track machine and lock it up with the first to make them play together, giving us forty-eight tracks.

Today, we don't use tape. Instead, we use a digital computer system called Pro-Tools that can give us a virtually unlimited number of tracks. Many people think this is progress, but I disagree. When we had only twenty-four tracks, we had to stop and listen to what we were recording and make intelligent choices about what to keep. Today, no one takes the time to listen to what they've recorded. Instead, they just record tracks and move on to the next part, planning to "fix it in the mix." By the time you get to mixing, though, it's too late if you realize that you haven't recorded everything you need.

We constantly listened to and massaged our music, layer by layer, building the perfect song. It takes longer to work this way, but we made better records, and they sold more copies because of what we put into them. In comparison, the Beatles had only four channels to record with, at a time when people simply recorded live onto the four tracks. The Beatles were forced to invent multitrack recording by using two four-track machines and bouncing back and forth between the two until they were finished.

After we finished the combining, I picked up the phone, placed it in speaker mode, and called my house. "Listen to this," I said to the guys.

Out of the speakerphone came the electric guitar intro (at 0:26) to Steely Dan's "The Boston Rag" with my voice, perfectly timed, running over it, instructing people to leave a message. Everyone in the room thought this was very cool, and they each took turns leaving rude messages on my machine.

"Cutlass, this is Dashut. You're finished, do you hear me, finished in this business!" he joked.

"Ken, only you would think of this insane device. You're an idiot!" Lindsey quipped into my machine.

"Caillat, fuck off," Cris said in his typical dry way.

Then I got out my little remote and rewound the messages. We all had a good laugh as I replayed their messages over the speakerphone.

"Strummer" was sounding very strong. The bass made a huge difference. John's old version was a brilliant walking bass line, which meant that it moved more and played more notes than Lindsey's. Lindsey's was very simple and sparse, playing only a single bass note in each bar of the chorus.

"Lindsey, are you going to have John replay your bass part when he returns?" I asked, knowing how sensitive John was about his bass playing and, especially, about criticism from the young Lindsey. The fact that Lindsey had not only criticized it, but had also replaced it with a much more simple, straightforward part meant that this would be a touchy subject.

"Uh, yeah. That should be interesting," Lindsey said, laughing nervously. "I want to re-sing my vocal," he added.

Now that the song was cleaner and tighter, our old lead vocal seemed too loose and sloppy. We had originally put a big washy effect on that vocal, but now that the song was shaping up, it wasn't as wild as it had been.

The guys were getting along really well at this point, but I kept thinking about what Lindsey had done to Christina a couple days before. I was fighting a battle, admiring his musical genius and being disgusted by his personal behavior. I guess I should have been prepared for his violent streak against Christina by his actions in the past, but time would reveal the real Lindsey to me soon enough.

I'd had the weekend to think about Lindsey's attack against Christina. Talking to Cheryl had helped. She felt that it was good that Christina was gone, or it probably would have gotten worse. I wondered whether Lindsey had ever physically hurt Stevie. I didn't know if he had in the past, but I would see him kick her in the butt onstage during the *Tusk* tour three years later.

Lindsey was just Lindsey, an immature, insecure, overly intelligent, extremely talented musician who couldn't control his emotions. I'd seen outbursts from him earlier with me and Stevie, so I knew this kind of behavior was always lurking below the surface. But I had a job to do, and I wasn't going to dwell on it. Maybe this dark streak was why he made such good music.

I set up Lindsey's vocal mic, a Shure 546 with a 1176 compressor. The Shure mic was dynamic, meaning that the closer you sang to it, the more bottom you would get out of the voice. This was good, because I could control it with EQ. I found that with this mic, I could place a pop filter over the end, and, with a rubber band, I could keep a set amount of distance from the singer's lips and the mic capsule. This would give me the perfect vocal sound that would cut through the song and still dominate the track beneath.

Most engineers believe that using an expensive tube mic like the ones we had used for "Songbird" was better for lead vocals. This was probably true for singers such as Barbra Streisand, who had full-range vocals with large dynamic ranges. For rock and roll, though, I needed vocal presence and power. I wanted my singers' vocals to be strong and powerful enough to cut through my rock tracks, which already had a very aggressive sound.

Lindsey spent the next couple of hours singing a much straighter vocal part, which now didn't fit with the timing of Stevie's old background harmony part that she had sung in Sausalito. Her part would have to be re-sung. I made a note of this on the track sheet.

So now we had toms, Stevie's background vocals, and the bass part that all needed to be redone. It seemed as if we were moving two steps forward and one step back with every change. Despite this, I could really hear the improvements in the songs. When the rest of the band got back, I knew they'd be happy with our work.

It was a great day already, and we were all getting hungry. I knew of a first-rate Japanese restaurant a few miles away. Cheryl and I had had dinner there a couple of weeks earlier—the Pear Garden was on La Cienega, north of Melrose, about four miles from the studio. This was one of those Teppan restaurants that served sushi and cooked fish, grilled at the table by a Japanese chef.

Cheryl and I had met one of the Teppan chefs, named Freddie Yamasaki, and he spoke pretty good English. Cheryl and I had joked that he spoke record-industry English. He knew a lot about music and musicians, so we hadn't had the usual conversation with a Japanese chef. He was very personable, and, to top it off, the restaurant made killer Scorpions that rivaled those at Kowloon. The Pear Garden was a step up from Kowloon—it was more brightly lit, cleaner, and more elegant. There was no way we could get into a food fight at this place.

Lindsey, Richard, and I drove to the restaurant, and Cheryl and Mary Torrey met us for lunch. Lindsey was impressed with Freddie and the restaurant. He loved their Scorpions—they were served in large bowls with long straws the same way they were at Kowloon.

I remember that the hostess was a beautiful Asian woman, and she was very proper. The sushi bar was to the left of the hostess stand, and the cocktail bar was just to the right. A rice-paper wall separated the front door from the Teppan cooking area. In the main dining area, there were about twenty-five Teppan grills, with a copper ventilation hood above each grill.

Our group sat around one of the Teppan tables and watched Freddie as he began to cook our orders. He juggled his cookware and tossed food in the air, then caught it behind his back. Great! There was no need for us to "Kowloon" one another while Freddie was putting on his food-tossing show.

Then we almost fell on the floor laughing when one of the straws in Richard's Scorpion fell into his lap, soaking his crotch. One thing led to another, and a few more straws tipped—on their own or with a little help. It's funny, but it always seemed as if Lindsey was the ringleader of these escapades. I could never understand how Lindsey could be wound so tightly in the studio and then be such a carefree kid when we were in a restaurant. Maybe it was the jet fuel.

As we were leaving, we all agreed that it was nice to find an alternative to Kowloon. The guys decided that we wouldn't return to the studio after lunch.

Cheryl and I met back at Christine's house. I wanted to show her how my new answering machine worked. I even played back the messages the guys had left when they called my machine from the studio. There were also a couple of messages from startled friends who had called to talk to me. "It works!" I said proudly.

On the news that night, the reporters announced that California had just won the biggest prize in a wine contest in Paris. This was the first time that a European wine had been beaten by a wine from anywhere else. In that historical contest, now called the "Judgment of Paris," nine French experts had agreed that the Californian wines they had blind-tasted were better than the French. The result turned the wine industry in France on its head—along with delivering a deep blow to French pride. Until then, it had been taken for granted that American wines were never going to be as good as French wines.

"I guess Chris will have to start drinking something other than Pouilly Fuissé," I said to Cheryl.

The next morning I stood in the shower, thinking again. I knew that I had forgotten something. "Oh, shit!" I finally blurted out.

"What's wrong?" Cheryl said. She was at the mirror, putting on her makeup.

"Today's my dad's birthday, and I didn't send him a present."

I realized, though, that I still had time to buy him something and ship it to him that day. Fortunately, Shaffer Camera was right next to the studio on Cahuenga. I had an idea of what I wanted to get my dad. He could be intellectual, and he tended to live in his own closed world. So, I decided to buy him something that would get him outside but still allow him to be analytical. I bought him a telescope, complete with a tripod, a light, and extra lenses. I asked the traffic office to ship it to my dad and gave them his address.

Now that he'd retired and moved to Lake Tahoe, I thought that he might like to go outside with my mom to look at the stars, instead of staring at the television. It seemed like a good idea.

"Okay, so look for a big box in a few days, Dad. Sorry I didn't get it there for your birthday. Love you. I'll call you this weekend. Give my love to Mom. Bye," I said, calling him from the studio. Lindsey and Richard arrived as I finished talking to my dad.

"Hey, guys, wow," I said. "That was close. I almost forgot my dad's birthday. But I think a birthday call on his birthday and telling him that I sent a present should be fine."

"It's your dad's birthday?" Lindsey asked. "It's Stevie's birthday today, too."

"What did you get her?" Ray asked Lindsey.

"I got her another bag of weed. Wanna smoke some?" he asked, laughing.

"What do you feel like working on today?" I asked.

"'Brushes,'" Lindsey said.

"Okay," I said. "Cris, load it up, please."

"Can't," he said. "We didn't record any of it that day."

"Oh, yeah," I said, remembering how that day had gone. "We shouldn't have that problem today."

When we had first played "Brushes," Lindsey had been too uncomfortable to sing the lyrics in front of Stevie. But Stevie wouldn't be home for another week. "Great," I said. "New tape, Cris. We're cutting new stuff here at Heider's."

Lindsey, Ray, Richard, and I went out to the studio. All of Lindsey's guitars were on stands in rows, the way you would see guitars in a music store. Lindsey grabbed his big box Martin guitar and started to play it.

"I'm going to start with this," Lindsey said.

"Let me put new strings on it," Ray said.

I moved Lindsey's guitar mics near to where he would be sitting, and I brought my ECM-50 lav mic over to place it on his guitar after it had been restrung.

Lindsey came into the booth to roll another joint. When Ray was finished restringing Lindsey's guitar, about twenty minutes later, he signaled to Lindsey to come out and that we were ready.

I opened up the mics, a Neuman 414, an AKG C-451, panned hard left and right, and my little Sony ECM-50, taped to the front of Lindsey's fine guitar.

I adjusted the balance and the EQ of all three mics until the guitar sounded enormous coming from those big 604-Es. This was going to be my masterpiece recording, I thought. It would be Lindsey's in layering but mine in sound recording. The song was fairly complicated to play, and Lindsey wanted it to be perfect. After about forty minutes of playing, I noticed that the new strings on Lindsey's guitar had stretched out a little. They weren't sounding as good as they had at first.

"Lindsey, the new strings really sounded fantastic," I said, "but now they sound a little worn. I'd like to get this part with new strings."

He agreed to have the strings changed every time they started to fade. So there we went, looking for perfection. It took twenty minutes to change the strings, and we got only about thirty minutes of use out of each set of new strings. The day dragged out until finally we got the first pass of the primary guitar part about four hours later. Next, Lindsey wanted to add some harmonics, and we had to follow the same routine as before, but this time it took about an hour and a half to get the part.

Lindsey kept adding parts, and it sounded so amazing—like a big music box, played by guitars. It was Lindsey at his best, adding a capo'd up harmony part, then Nashville tuning accents. It was fabulous, but it was getting late. We had been working on this song all day. We had gotten completely caught up in the recording, and we were starving.

We talked about quitting for the day and going out to eat. We certainly deserved it, because we had worked more than ten hours on this song, adding layer upon layer of perfect guitar parts.

"Before we go, can we put a work vocal on?" I asked. We had asked Lindsey to do a vocal several times that day, because having one helps put the song in perspective, but Lindsey was focused on his guitar parts, and he had wanted to finish those first.

"Let's do it tomorrow," he suggested.

"Come on," Richard coaxed. "Just a quick one before we go home so we can all hear it."

"Fine," Lindsey said. Before he could change his mind, Cris threw any mic he could find in front of Lindsey.

"Here we go," I said.

The intro started. I added a little reverb to one of the guitars. When we got to the first verse, Lindsey got as far as "She broke down . . ." and he stopped. He sounded like Alfalfa in *The Little Rascals* with his voice cracking.

"Let's try it again," he said, clearing his throat.

I rewound the tape to the top and hit PLAY and RECORD, and the song started playing from the top.

Lindsey tried it again. "She broke down and let me in . . ."

We all stared at him.

"Fuck! Fuck me!" he shouted.

"What?" I shouted back.

"The song's in the wrong key," he sheepishly admitted. "I can't sing it."

"What do we need to do?" I asked.

"We have to re-record everything, again," Lindsey said.

The rest of us just looked at one another in the control room. We were stunned. It had never occurred to any of us that Lindsey could be playing one of his own songs in the wrong key for his voice. Not Lindsey! We were all blown away. Dejected, we went to Martoni's to drown our troubles.

"How about if we just speed up or slow down the track until it's in your key?" I suggested.

"No. It's too far away," Lindsey replied. "I'll sound like Mickey Mouse."

A little later, while we were still at Martoni's, Tony Orlando came in and walked up to the bar. We were in one of the red leather booths, and he didn't see us. I remember that we snickered at him because we didn't think much of his music, compared to ours. I don't remember driving home that night (or many others, for that matter). But I do remember that I took a midnight swim with Cheryl, and then we went to bed together.

11

"You're Fired!"

When Mick and John called us into the studio, they had
serious looks on their faces. I knew that this was going to
be a pivotal moment in my life.

—*Richard Dashut*

On Thursday, May 27, Cheryl woke me up early, about ten, because
Sandra was coming back to Los Angeles, and she was going to take
over my house-sitting duties at Christine's. I threw my clothes in my bag
and fed Duster one more time. Then, as I was leaving for the studio,
I told Cheryl that I'd see her back at my house that evening.

I parked in the rear lot of studio 4, then went into the building and
straight to the control room. I asked Cris, who always arrived at the studio before I did, to put up "Brushes" from the day before. "It's already
up," he said.

I engaged the speed control on the tape machine. Then I slowed it
down about two whole keys and listened. It sounded horribly slow, and
going two keys up made it sound like music for a cartoon.

"Lindsey was right," I said. "This isn't going to work. We have to re-record it."

I could use speed control to make minor tempo changes, but I couldn't use that trick to fix a track that had been recorded several keys off the singer's range. Speeding the track up made all of the instruments sound as if they were playing faster and faster, and the pitch shifted upward along with the tempo.

Today, computer-recording systems allow for just about any kind of adjustment. I can change the pitch of an instrument or an entire track and keep the tempo the same. Or I can change the tempo of the track and keep the key of the song the same. We can even bring a bad singer in tune, using Auto Tune.

Back from their vacations, Mick and John each arrived at the studio around two that afternoon. They were excited to be back to hang with the boys. They briefly admired our *Playboy* collection scattered around the room.

John clowns for the camera with Rhino in the background.

We were excited to let them hear what we had done while they were gone. We played "Dreams" and let them absorb the new acoustic guitar part and electric guitar parts in the chorus. One thing I was particularly good at was saving exceptional guitar parts, possibly small tidbits or guitar licks that I liked and thought I could maybe use later in the song.

As I played the track down from the top for the second time, I also included my stashed parts, which really added to the energy of the song. Lindsey nodded approvingly when he heard that I had saved some of his best licks, instead of erasing them. John and Mick were also very happy with the work we had done while they were gone.

Then we loaded "Gold Dust Woman" and played them the new Dobro parts. They were edgy, and, with a slight bit of reverb added to the part, the song had an even eerier feeling than the earlier version. I could see that Mick and John were happy with what we had accomplished in their absence.

"Job well done, lads!" Mick praised.

"Bloody right," John echoed.

We decided to take a break and went over to Martoni's because John and Mick had offered to buy lunch. Richard, Lindsey, and I described how much fun it had been to focus on the music with only a few people around.

Martoni's had a completely different feeling during the day. There were a lot of executives eating and meeting, and the ambience was much more subdued than the gaiety we were used to when we'd slip over for an evening martini. Everyone in our group ordered beer, thankfully. I felt as though we were out of place in that room, as if we were wannabe rock stars in a world of professional businessmen.

Then Lindsey began to broach the difficult subject of how he had replayed Mick's and John's instruments. "I was thinking that you could add some toms to the chorus of 'Strummer' when we get back to the studio."

"Sure, I'd love to. What kind of part?" Mick asked.

Lindsey leaned forward, as excited as a kid asking if he could go outside to play. "Something raw and edgy!"

"All right," Mick said. "We can give it a go."

"And, um, John, I have an idea for you, too."

Richard and I looked at each other because we knew what was coming next. John just looked at Lindsey. He didn't say a word.

"How about a different bass part for 'Strummer'? Something straighter
with less movement than what we have now," Lindsey suggested.

"Sure, mate," John said.

When we left Martoni's, we were blinded by the afternoon sun
while walking back to studio 4 at Heider's. We were studio creatures
and weren't accustomed to sunlight. Inside studio 4, as the door closed,
I sighed with relief, content to be back inside our dark studio sanctu-
ary. I hoped that Lindsey could show Mick and John what he wanted. It
felt safer to do that in our dark cocoon.

Cris put up "Strummer" and started to play it without warning. Cris
was always pushing the envelope. There it was: the new bass part that
Lindsey had played, not the version with John's original bass part. Oh,
God, I thought. This isn't going to be pretty. John didn't say anything. He
just listened as the track played down.

Lindsey realized what was happening and rolled his chair over next
to John's, trying to defuse the situation. He mimicked the aggressiveness
of the bass part he heard for the bass part in his song. This was new for
John because, up until this point, he had always decided what bass part
was best for each song.

But now he had a new and different kind of writer in Lindsey, who
was looking for a fresh, aggressive approach to Fleetwood Mac's music.
This was one of the biggest differences between the old Fleetwood Mac
and the new.

John suggested that Mick try Lindsey's drum part first, because John
wasn't ready to be tutored by Lindsey publicly. "You go first, mate," John said
to Mick with a grin. I could tell that John wanted to watch Mick interact
with Lindsey and his new direction for the band before he got involved.

Mick went out to the studio and tuned up his drums. Cris went out
with him to set the mics.

John moved in close and asked Richard if he liked Lindsey's straight
bass part better than his own moving McVie-style bass. John was wearing his usual cut-offs and T-shirt. I could see that John was tense, being
in the unfamiliar situation of having to justify his musical choices for the

Lindsey and John consult after John returns from vacation.

first time in his long, illustrious career of working with great musicians who included John Mayall, Eric Clapton, and Peter Green.

"What do you think?" John asked Richard.

Richard was in a tough spot. He understood what Lindsey was going for, and he wanted to give Lindsey's ideas a chance, but, on the other hand, he liked John's famous bass style.

"I'm not sure, John, it's definitely different. Let see what happens when we add more instruments to the track," Richard said, ever the diplomat.

"I'll have to listen to it a few more times to get used to it," John said.

"We still have your original part," I said, trying to reassure John.

"Ray, can you bring me another beer?" John asked and then settled back to watch Lindsey work from a distance.

We're probably not going to get a new bass part from John today, I thought. If history repeats itself, John will probably want to come in fresh the next morning and try it.

Lindsey had gone out to the studio with Mick to talk him through the aggressive new tom part, which would come in during the first chorus and also in the middle of the second chorus.

Lindsey asked for an additional pair of headphones so that he could conduct Mick while sitting beside him in the studio. "Ken, play the song from the middle of the first verse," Lindsey instructed me. He was taking over, becoming everyone's boss.

I spun the tape ahead about twenty seconds and started playing from the middle of the first verse. When we got to the end, Lindsey mimed to Mick, using both his voice and his body language, what he wanted Mick to play. From the control room, it looked as if Lindsey was showing Mick how to kill a snake with his bare fists. He was screaming out the drumbeats with his voice, while his arms flailed wildly in rhythm. It was a very young and aggressive drum part, much in keeping with the bass part he wanted to get from John.

"Okay, let me try it," Mick said.

I rewound to the same spot on the tape and hit PLAY and RECORD, giving Mick two tracks for his toms. Mick was very unsure of what Lindsey wanted, and his first attempt was horrible. Mick was a very elegant drummer, and his fills were nothing less than genius.

But that was not what Lindsey was going for. He wanted spastic, punk rock–style drumming.

Mick tried five or six times. Then he finally said, "Why don't you have a go at it, Linds? Then maybe I'll get the idea."

They traded places, and I rewound the tape and played the section again. This time Lindsey played the part, and he was wildly animated, his arms flailing in the air, holding Mick's drumsticks. He wasn't elegant at all, but he played like a man driven from deep inside.

After Lindsey finished showing Mick what he wanted, Mick said, "I'm sorry, Lindsey, but I just don't think I can play it the way you want. I like what you played. Let's just use your version." Lindsey was, I believe, relieved at this outcome. It was out in the open now, and Lindsey was free to play other people's parts. We ran the song down three or four more times, and Lindsey played the tom parts throughout the song.

But Lindsey wasn't done yet. He wanted to end his fill with a thin cheap-sounding cymbal splash that Mick ultimately called the "bacon slicer." Mick decided to find the appropriate cymbal and play that part himself. We spent the next few hours playing that bacon slicer all over

Lindsey began to take over the band, playing the other members' instruments.

the song. We kept all of our cymbal ad libs. Later, we would choose which one to use.

Mick admitted that he could never get the bacon slicer the way he wanted. "My version is in very random places. They don't really make any sense. They're in time, but they're in very odd places, and they're not uniform."

That's when Lindsey first started to get his way with the recording of Fleetwood Mac's songs. The other members of the band would just let him play their parts if he couldn't communicate what he wanted from them.

This reminded me of a time a few years earlier when I was watching a session in Heider's studio 1 with Paul McCartney on the *Venus and Mars* album. Paul didn't like the part the drummer was playing, so he went out and played it himself. Then after that he didn't like the part that Denny Lane, the guitarist, had played, so he went out and showed Denny how it should go. Then suddenly he was playing all of the instruments!

On later albums, Lindsey would use this strategy to get his way, even threatening to quit if anyone pushed back. Lindsey's unyield-ing drive and his single-minded vision would give Mick, John, Stevie,

Christine, Richard, and me much anguish during the coming years, but on *Rumours*, Lindsey pushed the rest of the band to get the most from every song.

Later, I realized that that day was a crucial point in my music education as an engineer and a producer. "Strummer" was Lindsey's song. He knew it intimately, and he could hear that it had taken a wrong turn. In his mind, it just didn't feel right to him. I learned from this not to feel that I had to live with any part, and, more important, I learned to start listening to the music with my emotions. I learned that when I got a flicker in my heart, I needed to give in to it. I also learned that no track of any song was set in concrete until we were done with the entire process.

Lindsey had a brilliance, and he was crucial to the band's success. The biggest problem with Lindsey, though, was that he couldn't communicate his ideas without coming off as uptight. This tended to make everyone else in the band feel defensive. Sometimes it felt as if you could cut the tension with a knife. Lindsey just couldn't cross that bridge to constructive criticism.

You can hear Lindsey's wild tom part played at 0:38, 1:28, 1:44, 1:53, and 2:00 on "Second Hand News."

That night I got to sleep in my own bed. Cheryl and I were really happy to be back at my place, and so was Scooter. When we finally got home from work, she made dinner for us, and we listened to my favorite band, Steely Dan. My JBL-99s, hanging from my beam ceilings, sounded especially good. The album seemed to reflect off the river-rock wall behind the speakers, making the music come alive.

When we finally went to bed, Scooter slept in his usual box on the floor of my bedroom closet. I had cut the sides of the box low enough so that he could get in and out easily, and I had put old blankets inside the box. The closet itself was about nine feet long and had three sets of doors, each about eighteen inches wide. When I opened a pair of doors, I had about a three-foot opening. This was just big enough to allow Scooter's bed to fit in the long way.

Scooter had many clever tricks.

At night, when we went to bed, the closet doors to Scooter's bed were open, but when we woke up, they were closed on most mornings. I wasn't sure whether Scooter had had a friend over and wanted some privacy, or if he just didn't want to see what was going on in my part of the bedroom. Scooter had lots of other very clever habits.

When I took him shopping, I tried to park in the shade so he wouldn't get hot when I left him in the car. Sometimes, if I couldn't find any shade, I left the windows down and told him, firmly, to stay. This always seemed to work until one day I discovered that after I had left the car, Scooter had jumped out the window and was lying on a nearby patch of grass in the shade, keeping an eye out for me.

I realized that when I came out of a store, Scooter would make a stealth entrance into the back of my car, just clearing the frame of the door, trying his best not to be seen. He began to do this every time I left the windows down.

I busted him one day when I came back to my car and there was another similar-looking silver convertible parked right in front of mine. When I got up to my car, I noticed that Scooter wasn't inside. I looked around for him. There were two guys by the other Mercedes, and one of them asked, "Does this dog belong to you?"

"Yes," I said. "What's he doing in your car?"

"We were heading back to our car. Then, when you came out of the store, we saw your dog lying in the grass over there. When he saw you, he just jumped into my car! He must have got them mixed up!"

After that, I would intentionally sneak out of stores. Sure enough, I'd see Scooter lying in the shaded grass outside my car until he saw me. Then he'd leap back into the car, somehow landing curled up the way I had left him.

When I got to the studio later that morning, I told everybody about Scooter's antics. Scooter knew we were talking about him. He looked at me. Then he gave a quick snort and went over to lie under the console.

Judy Wong came by from Penguin and walked into the control room, carrying a birthday cake. The lettering on it read "Happy Birthday, Cris." I explained to Judy that Christine was still on vacation.

"No, silly. It's for Cris Morris. It's his birthday!" That's the way Judy was. She was always loving, giving, and all-knowing.

We sang a quick rendition of "Happy Birthday" to Cris.

"Happy birthday, buddy!" I said. "Now get back to work! We'll celebrate later!"

We put up "Strummer," and John played along with Lindsey's bass part. Inherently, he wanted to put more movement in the part, which was his forte. He wasn't happy with his version, and I could tell that Lindsey wasn't jumping for joy, either. Eventually, John asked Cris to make him a cassette of the track so that he could study it later, when he was alone.

The elder statesmen of the band knew that Lindsey had a genius. They wanted to take advantage of that, but they also weren't comfortable with him taking over the band. They did want to listen to his ideas and incorporate them into their parts. It was a precarious balancing act at this point. With future records, it would get even more difficult.

So we left "Strummer" as it was that day, deciding to go back to "Brushes" and record it in the correct key. I put up some more blank tape, and Lindsey went out to the studio and started playing his Ovation Acoustic guitar in the right key.

"I think I want to use this guitar," Lindsey said. "I also want to make this part a lot simpler this time. Let's go with these strings."

Remembering how much time we'd put into changing strings, I didn't argue. "Great. They still sound pretty good."

I didn't have the energy to go through all of that again, knowing that we'd likely just change it later. "And just like the other day, we're going to send you a click in your headphones to help you play your first guitar part. But we don't want the click track to bleed into your guitar mics, so we'll keep it as low as possible in your can's mix. Let us know if you want it turned up more, but try to keep your headphones on tight."

Then I turned to Cris and said, "Let's record the click, too." I knew that having a "click track" might be useful later.

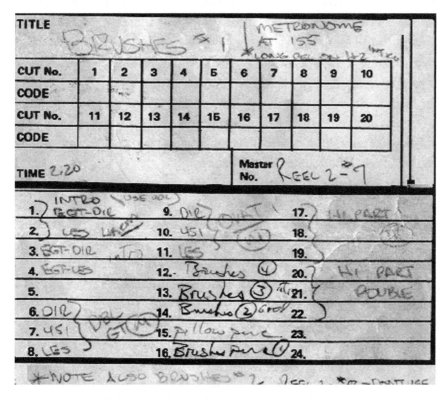

This is the track sheet for "Never Going Back Again."

We recorded the whole track in about an hour and a half. Lindsey got the main guitar track, then he played a second part. When we combined them, they almost sounded like one big guitar. As we recorded that day, Lindsey sang the vocal so that we all knew it was correct. Finally, Mick played the brushes part four times so that we had options.

Lindsey also experimented with some electric guitar parts and a staccato guitar solo. I thought we had covered our bases, no matter which way Lindsey would choose to go. When we were finished, we took Cris and his wife, Wendy, out for dinner at the Pear Garden.

Scooter waited in the car with the windows up. That way I could keep my roving bachelor in check.

The next day, Saturday, May 29, was the start of the three-day Memorial Day weekend, which signals the beginning of summer for most people in the States. For us, though, it was the day that Lindsey came in and announced that he had had a change of heart on "Brushes" and wanted to try it again. Ugh! This was our fourth try on this song, but Lindsey was a perfectionist, so we set up for another version.

This time, we tried it live with Mick and Lindsey playing together. Mick was listening to the click and playing his full drum kit with brushes. Lindsey was in the iso booth, playing his acoustic guitar. We spent most of the day doing variations on the drum parts and the tempos.

Ultimately, we completed twenty more takes of "Brushes." Amazingly, I still wasn't sick of the song, but I think Lindsey was. We called it an early night so that we could enjoy our two-day weekend.

Cheryl and I were up at eight on Sunday so we could get to her parents' house by nine and then be at Lake Casitas by ten. Lake Casitas was the smallest lake in the area that allowed powerboats. It was also known for its yellow jackets.

I had met Cheryl's mother, Grace, several times before that day, and I liked her very much. She seemed to like me, too. Grace worked for AT&T at a time when many men believed that women were supposed to stay at home. Apparently, Grace had had a hand in developing the Princess phone.

Cheryl's dad, Garney, was retired. Unlike his wife, though, he hadn't seemed very fond of me from the outset. He was a big guy—not tall so much as just big. His skin had a red glow that made me wonder whether he was always a little sunburned or if he had high blood pressure. I didn't think he was very healthy, but otherwise, he seemed like a pretty happy guy. He clearly adored his wife and daughter.

Cheryl's stepbrother, Darrel, was an L.A. cop, and he was sixteen years older than her. He had also come along for a day of fun in the sun. I felt as if the men in her family were judging me from the outset.

"So, do you work, Ken?" Garney asked in his gruff voice. I knew he wanted his daughter to have a boyfriend who was worthy of her. I also knew that I needed to give the right answers to his questions without appearing nervous. To make matters worse, I sat between Garney, who drove the car, and Darrel as we made the hourlong drive up to the lake so that we could "get to know each other."

I felt very uncomfortable during the drive. I was a little hung over, and I hoped the smell of pot wasn't still in my beard.

Scooter sat in the backseat with Cheryl and her mom, getting love and affection while I got the Spanish Inquisition.

"So, you work for a rock band," Garney said. "Generally, they're pretty wild, aren't they?"

"Do they use drugs?" Darrel quickly inserted.

I was excited about the album I was making, and I said enthusiastically, "I believe we're making history with an album that could be a huge hit. I've been preparing for this opportunity for five years."

I wanted to explain all of the genius things that we were doing, but all I could think to say was, "The members of the band are very articulate and intelligent people. Come to think about it, actually, I've never seen them with any sort of drugs. In fact, I don't even think they drink."

"Really?" Garney said. "Good for them." He thought for a moment. "Not even beer? I could really go for a beer right now."

My eye caught Cheryl's in the rearview mirror, and she just gave me a little smile.

Garney liked to eat, and he liked to drink a beer or two. Grace had packed accordingly. It was a bright spring day at the lake. Garney kept his boat there. When the food came out, so did the bees.

Naturally, I got stung by a yellow jacket, and Scooter snapped at one and got stung in the mouth. Cheryl held a cold beer on my wound and comforted me. We cruised the lake all day long.

Eventually, Darrel even laughed at one of my jokes. What made being around Darrel more difficult for me was that when I was younger, growing up in San Jose, there was a period of about six months during which I had had a friend/acquaintance who was a cop. He would drop by unannounced late in the evenings and take my roommate and me, when we were completely stoned, to his cop friends' parties. One time it was a police ball, and all of the cops were in uniform! He never seemed to catch on that we were high; he just liked us and wanted us to go to his parties. There were no other agendas—or were there? I never knew whether he was just screwing with us or simply naive. Anyway, Darrel didn't mean any harm; he was just looking out for his little sister.

I was never so glad to get home. Cheryl and I managed to make it through that day in one piece. Even though I was relieved to get away from Cheryl's family, I really liked Garney. Darrel even gave me one of those "get-out-of-jail-free" cards, signed by him. I figured that one day I'd get a really fast car, and Darrel's card would come in handy.

The Memorial Day break was just what I had needed. I got a little "me time" and had successfully recharged my batteries. Mick spent the weekend trying to put things back together with Jenny. Lindsey had smoked pot and played his guitar. Stevie and Christine had another week before they returned from their Hawaii vacations.

Richard and I were feeling pretty good about our engineering work with the band. In fact, we were doing more than engineering; we were helping to produce. Since we had been told to "wake up" and start helping the band produce the record back in Sausalito, Richard and I had started making notes on tempos, bass parts, keyboard parts, good guitar riffs, and killer drum fills. We could give the band feedback on almost any question they asked.

Sometimes musicians have brilliant moments, but other times they just have regular moments. Our job was to save the brilliant ones when they happened, so we recorded everything. Often, we'd have to play back the part we liked and remind the band of what they had done. Then they could make it into something really special. This was especially true during those weeks at Heider's.

We had got the band's upcoming schedule the day before. The next few months looked chaotic. The band had a mid-album tour planned to support their previous album. The tour schedule was spotty at best. This meant that they would start rehearsals for the tour during our days in the studio. Then the tour jumped around a bit. The band had to play one show in L.A. in mid-June. A few days later, they would travel to the Midwest and continue east during June, finishing around the end of July.

It was clear that we wouldn't be focusing on the album for the next two months as much as we had been up to this point. The band was as concerned as I was about taking off too much time from recording the album, so we decided to take advantage of a small break in their tour schedule. We booked some studio sessions right after the Fourth of July in Miami, where they had a window of six days off. The biggest studio in Miami was Criteria Studios, most famous for recording the Bee Gees, the Eagles, Bob Marley, and Eric Clapton.

Criteria Studios had been built in 1958 by Mack Emerman, a jazz musician and a location recording engineer. Like Wally Heider, Mack used to follow Woody Herman around in his station wagon, carrying recording gear to capture the band's concerts. In 1958, Emerman opened Criteria Recording Studios in a building on 149th Street in North Miami, and it quickly became a recording center for the exploding rock music industry.

Then Tom Dowd, a staff producer for Atlantic Records in New York, moved to Miami, and the multiroom complex became a major hub of recording activity. We were all excited to work at Criteria, with all of its history.

When I called Criteria Studios to check its availability, the staff told me they would make time for Fleetwood Mac. I booked a week there, starting right after the nation's Bicentennial celebration.

We thought the tour would give the band time to play a few of their new songs live. Then, at Criteria, we could try to capture some of the live energy from the tour and put it into our record. I hung up the phone. We were all excited about this new adventure in front of us.

In the studio, Cris rewound our 24-track master reel one. I listened to the tape as it rewound from the end through each paper leader to the song we were planning to work on. As the leader went past the heads, it would make a hissing sound, like sandpaper on wood. I started to think about how many times each of our copies of two-inch, 24-track master tapes had been played. It was nonstop music in our studio. We were always listening to something, working on something. I had never run any tapes as much as I had run these.

"Cris, I want you to start cleaning the heads on the tape machine twice a day, yourself," I said.

Normally, the studio's maintenance engineer would clean and align the machine each morning so that Cris wouldn't have to, but I wanted Cris and the rest of us to have firsthand knowledge of the tapes' condition on a daily basis. If a problem were developing, it would first appear on the heads that the tapes moved across.

"Why?" Cris asked. "Is there a problem?"

"No," I said. "I just think it's a good idea to start monitoring our tapes. Let me know if anything changes. We're playing these tapes a lot."

I had never experienced any tape problems before, but we had put so much work into these tapes already that I couldn't bear the thought of anything happening to them. When I got thoughts like this, I wanted to make backup copies. "And let's schedule another set of safeties, ASAP," I added.

"Sure," Cris said.

At some point during the day, Mick, John, and Lindsey were out in the studio while Richard and I were working in the control room. Ray came in and said that they wanted to talk to both of us right then.

"We'll be out in a minute," I said to Ray.

"No. They mean right now!" he said.

Richard and I looked out into the studio. Mick and John were just standing there staring at us with very serious looks on their faces. Richard and I walked out, wondering what the hell was up.

"Come over here," Mick said sternly.

We stood in front of Mick and John as if we'd been called to the principal's office, There was a long pause. Then Mick said, "Caillat, Dashut, you're both fired!"

My mind whirled. What's going on? I wondered. I was motionless, in a daze. No one said anything for the longest time.

Richard and I just stood there looking at each other, then back at Mick and John, then back at each other. Then, simultaneously, Richard and I both burst into laughter. We knew we had been working far too hard to be fired.

Finally, John and Mick couldn't keep their straight faces any longer, either, and they both started laughing, too.

Mick said, "Really, fellows, you've been doing such a great job that we're making you coproducers of *Rumours*."

"Congratulations, mates. Job well done," John added.

After John and Mick left us alone, Richard looked at me and said, "Ken, do you realize what this means?"

"What?" I asked, not sure what he was driving at.

"It means we're going to be *rich*!"

Lindsey, who had been pretending to adjust his guitar, came over to us and said, "They had you guys going, huh?" He gave his guttural laugh.

"Thanks, Linds," I said.

"You guys really deserve this," Lindsey added. "You've stuck by my side through this whole process." Lindsey hugged both of us at the same time.

We hugged one another. Then Mick and John came back, and Mick pulled two I Ching coins out of his vest pocket and gave one to Richard and one to me. "For good luck," he said. I still have mine to this day.

On Thursday, June 3, record coproducers Ken Caillat and Richard Dashut arrived at the studio with no extra fanfare. There was no special parking, no champagne. Yet Cheryl, who had never slept with a record producer before, had made it clear to me that she was very impressed by giving me an extra special gift. After Mick and John's announcement, I called to tell her the good news, and when I got home she met me at the front door wearing nothing but one of my long-sleeved shirts, unbuttoned, and holding a glass of champagne.

"Come with me," she said, taking me into the bedroom. "Let me show you how proud I am of you." She pushed me onto the bed.

"Wow, honey, is it my birthday already?" I gasped.

I drove into work the next day, smiling the whole way. I had a lot to smile about. My girlfriend loved me; my friends liked me; and I had just earned the biggest promotion of my career.

I didn't really know what to make of the new title that Mick had given to Richard and me. Mick told us that we'd talk about the details after the record was finished. That was good enough for Richard and me, but at that moment, it didn't mean more salary; it didn't bring a bonus. Just a feeling of "job well done" and a supreme sense of satisfaction. Of course, I understand that this was because Mick had no idea how successful the record would be. He wanted to wait before he promised anybody anything concrete.

I thought that later, it would probably mean that Richard and I would receive producer's points on the sales of the album. If we were lucky and the record did well, then we could possibly, just maybe, make a little extra money. For example, if the album went gold, maybe I'd make a few thousand dollars.

We still had a long way to go in the process, though. The important thing was to keep trying to perfect everything on our record. I felt as if I had become more than the producer of the record. I felt as if I was its father, and it was my child.

Stevie and Christine were due back from their vacations that day, and we expected them to stop by the studio. I told Ray to stash the *Playboys* so that they wouldn't cause an issue when the women returned. The guys decided to pull up "Silver Springs" and work on it to prep for their return.

Cris loaded the master reel of "Silver Springs" onto our 24-track machine. We hadn't heard it in more than a month. We played it down from the top, and it sounded so empty, so unfinished. The electric guitar that we thought had such a great vibe when we'd listened to it in Sausalito sounded dry and thin, in comparison to the sounds we had been getting at Heider's. "Let's go for a new guitar part," I said to Lindsey.

Lindsey decided to play the part with a volume pedal so that he could control and create swells with his guitar. As he was playing along with the track, I experimented with different combinations of sounds coming from his guitar.

Ultimately, I began to use tape delay to create a more ethereal sound. "Tape delay" is when you use a mono or stereo tape machine to record a signal sent to it from the console's effect send knobs. A professional tape machine has three heads: an erase head, a record head, and a playback head, arranged in that order. First, the tape passes the erase head, then the record head, and finally the playback head.

When we listened off the playback head to what we were recording, the speed of the tape determined how much of a delay would be heard from the time the original sound traveled over the playback head. We could control both the tape speed and the timing of the delay. All of this technical stuff may be confusing, but suffice it to say that this is an important audio tool at our disposal. I had used this technique to delay the piano and vocal playback into the Zellerbach Auditorium to make the hall reverberation last longer and sound more dramatic.

That day, I used it to send Lindsey's new guitar part into reverb, delaying it to make that part play longer and sound fuller. Lindsey's new guitar part had several components. One of these was the little lavalier mic, recording just the sound of Lindsey's pick on the metal guitar strings of his solid-body electric guitar. Some of you know that a Strat, with its solid body, makes almost no sound acoustically. My little lav mic was picking up the very high frequencies of the vibrating metal strings, giving off a delicate, glasslike, music box–type sound.

When I first put the lav on his Strat, I could almost hear everyone thinking, Eh, Ken, you're slipping. Did you forget that the Strat doesn't make any sound?

But earlier, while Lindsey was working the part out, he was sitting in the control room with us, and I noticed and instantly fell in love with the little metal "pluck" sound of his strings that preceded his pushing down the volume pedal. The next sounds to arrive were those from his guitar and volume pedal to his guitar amp in the rear iso booth and to the slow-spinning Leslie in the front iso booth simultaneously.

So, at the console, I had eight inputs from Lindsey's one guitar part: the tiny noise of his plastic guitar pick or his fingernails striking the strings, the dry direct guitar sound coming through my Fat Box, two mics on his electric guitar amplifier, two more mics on the rotating Leslie, and the reverb return from the delay machine rejoining all of the sounds about a quarter second late. I could put all of these sounds together in any combination, using the left, right, and center panning positions.

Richard and I moved and shaped Lindsey's new guitar part until it sounded amazing. It was deep and rich and full, but it still allowed for a lot of space for other things. Lindsey's part was played by plucking the proper chord, then opening the volume pedal. Then a sound wave was released into the amp, the Leslie, and the tape delay machine, going directly into the live reverb chamber. The lav mic gave an accent to the pluck, but the pedal held back the sound until Lindsey pushed the pedal down. Originally, the part he intended to play was twice as fast and not as spectacular, but the delay reverb forced him to change his part to fit in with the timing of the song. Changing the sound of the guitar part really transformed the song as a whole. A good engineer can have a dramatic effect on a production. Lindsey loved the sound and the part that he had created.

He was so inspired that he wanted to add a harmonic acoustic guitar part. It was pure frosting on the cake. We used one of the newly restrung Martins to play the part and somehow got the idea to double the part.

So, take a listen to "Silver Springs," if you can find it. It's available on Stevie Nicks's *Crystal Visions* album. Listen to that incredible combination of the volume pedal and the electric guitar recorded in Hollywood on June 3, 1976, and the stereo-doubled acoustic Martin playing harmonics!

When John heard all of this, he immediately wanted to play a new bass part. His original bass part was still sparse, but as we added intensity and depth to the song with more instruments, John felt that his bass could be more powerful. The new volume pedal electrics added warmth and color and called to John. Left to his own creativity, John was a genius. His inspiration for his bass part on Stevie's masterpiece was brilliant. It reminded me of his "whale calls" in "Oh, Daddy." An hour later, John had played a new bass part on his Fretless. It surpassed anything Lindsey could have imagined for the bass part on this magical rock ballad. It was spectacular and all John's own.

John kept his part sparse, and I felt that there was still room for another part, something simple in the high end to offset the bass at the low end. "Lindsey, maybe you could add some harmonic plucks on your acoustic guitar—kind of like *pluck, pluck, pluck pluck pluck*," I said. Richard added the last two plucks in unison with me.

"Yeah, I could try something like that," Lindsey answered. "Good idea."

Just then, Stevie walked in the front door of studio 4, the afternoon sun penetrating deep into the dark studio. She had a glowing Maui tan, and her white teeth made her smile even more beautiful. "Hi, everyone. I'm back! Did you miss me?" She laughed lightheartedly.

Stevie was with her best friends, Christi and Robin. Both girls were carrying bags full of fresh leis, which Stevie took from them, handing one to each of us.

"Here you go, Ken," she said to me. "You couldn't go to Maui, so I brought Maui to you, Mr. Producer! I hear you and Richard are doing a wonderful job." She kissed me on the cheek and turned to Richard, hugged him, and also gave him a kiss along with his lei.

Then she turned and gave John and Mick their leis, pausing a little longer in front of Mick but not really saying anything, just looking. I could see only the back of her head, but I figured the extra time with Mick was due to Mick's importance to the band.

I didn't know it at the time, but later a rumor would surface that Mick and Stevie had hooked up in Maui. It was indisputable that they had run into each other when they were in Maui, but to this day, I don't know if it's true that anything more had happened. Neither of them confided in Richard about this incident. Later, though, they did have an affair.

Finally, Stevie gave Cris, who was standing in the back of the room by the 24-track, his lei. Robin Snyder went out to the studio to give Lindsey and the rest of the crew their leis.

Cris put his lei over his head and thanked Stevie. "You're going to really like what the boys have done with 'Silver Springs,'" he added.

Lindsey came into the room, and he and Stevie politely said their hellos to each other. "Nice tan," Lindsey said. It wasn't clear to me whether this was a compliment or a dig at Stevie. I just hoped that the broken couples in the band were going to be able to get past their personal issues.

Cris pressed PLAY. As "Silver Springs" started to fill the room, Stevie picked up one of the partially smoked joints in the ashtray and put it to her mouth. Richard reached over and relit it for her as she listened to our handiwork.

"Oh, that's so beautiful!" she said, smoke coming out of her mouth along with her words. "Can I sing my lead now? My voice is in great shape."

"Sure!" I said. I went out to the studio to set up her vocal mic.

Stevie had such a terrific voice, but sometimes I thought it was a little twangy or midrange-y. To fix this, I used my rubber band trick again, placing the foam pop filter so that I could keep Stevie's lovely lips at exactly the right distance from the microphone's capsule, resulting in a strengthening of the bottom part of her vocal. This is called the proximity effect.

The rubber band keeps the pop filter about a half-inch from the front of the microphone. I would simply remind Stevie to make sure that her lips were always delicately touching the foam pop filter as she sang. This would give me an even, smooth, stronger vocal that fit much better with the aggressive sounds of the track.

We all knew this song was a winner. Of all of the songs we had recorded for the album, I was most proud of the sounds on "Silver Springs." I always regretted that it didn't make it onto the album, for reasons that I'll explain later.

The next day, with all of the members of the band back in town, they started rehearsals in Hollywood for their upcoming tour. They were rehearsing at SIR near Heider's. I went down to hang with Richard while he mixed front-of-house.

Judy Wong and Gabrielle Aris were there that day. We had planned on working on the album for a few days in the studio while the band rehearsed, but they got caught up in perfecting their show. Stevie had ordered a load of new Stevie Nicks wardrobe items on the band's

dime for her to twirl in when she was onstage, to delight her fans.
Everyone was fine with this. Lindsey had his guitars, the Brits had their
expensive booze, and Stevie had her twirling wardrobe.

The band was scheduled to play the Universal Amphitheater on
June 15. That was only a little more than a week away, and the band had
much to do to make sure that they were prepared.

We managed to get into the studio on Wednesday, June 9, and we
worked on "Go Your Own Way" a little more. Most notably, we added
some excellent guitar licks and an organ part from Christine.

I was working closely with the band on the live front because they
wanted me to start recording some of their upcoming live shows. I didn't
know it yet, but during the next four years, I would record more than a
hundred live concerts all over the world with them.

Cheryl and I went to the June 15 Fleetwood Mac concert at the
Universal Amphitheater. It's always a big deal when a band plays in L.A.
because all of the celebrities and the big shots come out to the show.
Joni Mitchell was there, David Crosby came, and even Steve Martin
showed up.

In the seventies, I loved to go to the Amphitheater. Universal Studios
had built it at the back end of their lot, just above where the back-lot tour
took place. The amphitheater was built in 1972 as an outdoor venue but
was remodeled ten years after that as an indoor venue. As an outdoor
theater, it was amazing. I had recorded Joni Mitchell there a few years
earlier. I was thrilled to be there and see all of my band friends performing onstage in L.A. I was excited to see how the L.A. crowd would receive
our new songs.

Cheryl and I arrived right after the load-in and before the sound
check. My tickets were at will-call, and I picked up an envelope containing my new stage passes that I would use for the rest of the tour.

Backstage in their dressing room, the band was putting the finishing
touches on their wardrobe and makeup. Lindsey was visiting with his
previous bandmate Tom Moncrief; Stevie was sitting quietly with her
best friends, Robin and Christi; and Christine was getting her hair done,
with Judy next to her, chatting her up. Christine had her usual glass of
wine and a cigarette. Mick and John had their beers. JC, Gabrielle Aris,

and Mickey Shapiro were all, of course, backstage with the band. Curry was talking to Richard.

"Hey, guys, what's up? This is very exciting!" I said.

"Darling, you made it," Christine said to me.

Cheryl went over to talk to the girls, and I approached Richard.

"Is everything cool?" I asked him.

"Yes, Caillat," Richard said. "While you were sleeping, we got everything working."

"Oh, Dashut, you're so full of shit!" Curry said. Then he turned to me. "He just got here fifteen minutes before you did. You don't think Dashut's going to do any hard work, do you?" Curry laughed, poking Richard in the side.

"Grant, I'll get you for this insubordination!" Richard fired back.

Just then JC yelled across the room, "Curry! Dashut! Get to your posts. Sound check's in ten."

I grabbed two cold beers from the dressing room's well-stocked bar. I handed one to Cheryl and took her by the hand, then headed out to watch the sound check. Cheryl and I picked the best empty seats in the first row and waited for the band. A few minutes later, they all came onstage. Mick wore his usual tight pants with wooden balls hanging from his belt, swinging between his legs. His bare chest was exposed under his open vest, and he wore a beret. John wore cut-offs and a Hawaii '76 T-shirt. Christine had on a peasant blouse and skirt. Stevie was in her black leotard with a top hat and a black cape. Lindsey appeared in a pair of high-waisted pants and a long-sleeved white silk shirt with ruffles. Clearly, they didn't coordinate their outfits. I liked that.

I felt a real rush of amazement when I saw them, the same people I'd been hanging out with in the studio, up there on this big stage about to play a concert for Los Angeles.

"Pretty amazing," I said to Cheryl. "I hang out with these people every day, and now they're going to be playing some of their songs with my ideas in them."

"Don't get all big-headed on me, Caillat," she kidded. "Or I'll have to put you in your place."

"I may like that place," I said.

"What are you smilin' about?" She leaned her head back to get a good look at me.

"I'll show you later," I said confidently.

The band got to their instruments and made sure everything was okay. It was a typical June day in L.A., and we had our June gloom, that damn layer of marine fog. The last time the band had played live outdoors, the sun had changed the tuning on all of the instruments, but today everything was perfect, except for their nerves. Bands usually get very nervous playing at high-profile venues. That's why every band starts their tour in some out-of-the-way venue, allowing them to work out the jitters and kinks before they play in big cities. I'm pretty sure Mick was already on his third beer, and the show hadn't even started.

They played about thirty seconds of each song so that Richard could get his levels set on his mixing console. Then they returned to their dressing room to wait out the four hours until show time. That's the worst. Talk about dressed up and no place to go! The minutes slowly passed. The band spent the time doing interviews with various reporters. Finally, it was time for them to go onstage.

"Ladies and gentlemen, please give a warm welcome to . . . Fleetwood Mac!" JC's customary announcement came over the large speakers, and the crowd roared and came to their feet. The sound of the applause was deafening. Mick raised his hands over his head and began hitting his drumsticks together, while his right foot stomped on his kick drum, *boom, boom, boom, boom.*

Richard shoved up the volume so that the whole theater shook with the sound of Mick's big twenty-six-inch kick drum. Mick finished his drum intro with three rounds of his toms. The audience was ready for the show. Immediately after Mick stopped, Christine started to play her famous intro to "Say You Love Me" on her Fender Rhodes electric piano. The crowd jumped to their feet again! The "Say You Love Me" single had just been released a few days before this concert, the third one from the White Album. The crowd went crazy.

Cheryl and I sat next to Richard at the mixing board, dead center in the middle of the audience. Richard leaned over to me, yelling above the noise, "This is crazy. This never happened last year on their tour!"

"This is very good, Mr. Producer!" I said, nudging Richard. There you have it, they were on their way to superstardom, my band! Yeah, baby!

On the console was the set list of the songs they were going to play for this tour. Depending on their mood at each concert, they would play all of them or just some of them. As we finished a song in the studio, they would add it to their set list.

"Say You Love Me"
"Monday Morning"
"Dreams"
"Rhiannon"
"Oh, Well"
"Oh, Daddy"
"Landslide"
"Go Your Own Way"
"Over My Head"
"You Make Loving Fun"
"I'm So Afraid"
"World Turning"
"Second Hand News"
"Blue Letter"
"Songbird"

The show ended with the band getting a standing O at the amphitheater! Wow, I was so happy.

Backstage, after the show and amid all of the excitement and the press and the celebrities, I said my good-byes to the band. They were going on a U.S. tour to promote the White Album that would last until the end of August. There was no rest for the weary. They'd spend their summer playing all sorts of venues, while I would be making love to my hot twenty-year-old girlfriend everywhere I could. As Cheryl lay in bed in my little hill house that night, I kept thinking about the show.

I continued to be amazed by how good the band sounded live and how different their songs were now that Lindsey had joined the band. Even their old standards, such as "Oh, Well," were powerhouses. I knew that when we went back into the studio to record, I would get some more amazing guitar solos from Lindsey for the album, such as those on "So Afraid."

The band went out on their tour, and I was glad I wasn't with them yet. I could never handle the drinking and partying all day and night that went on during tours. It was far worse than when we were in the studio, where I could resist. But I couldn't do that when we were out on the road.

This was the band's schedule, starting the day after their performance at the Universal Amphitheater:

6/18 Kauffman Stadium, Kansas City, Missouri

6/19 Omaha, Nebraska, Omaha Arena

6/20 Iowa State Fairgrounds

6/21–22 Pine Knob Music Theatre, Clarkston, Michigan

6/24 Mecca Arena, Milwaukee, Wisconsin

6/29 Busch Stadium, St. Louis, Missouri

6/30 Riverfront Stadium, Cincinnati, Ohio

7/2 Winston-Salem Entertainment Sports Complex, Winston-Salem, North Carolina

7/3 The Omni, Atlanta, Georgia

7/4 Tampa Stadium, Tampa, Florida

7/5–11 Record with me at Criteria Studios in Miami, Florida

7/12 The Spectrum, Philadelphia, Pennsylvania

7/13 Veterans War Memorial Coliseum, Syracuse, New York

7/14 Colt Park, Hartford, Connecticut

7/16 Brown County Arena, Green Bay, Wisconsin

7/17 Dane County Coliseum, Madison, Wisconsin

7/18 Mile High Stadium, Denver, Colorado

7/24 Three Rivers Stadium, Pittsburgh, Pennsylvania

7/27 Capital Centre, Landover, Maryland

8/1–8/22 Back to Heider's to record with me!

While Cris and I had time off, Richard and the band had to play nearly every day, perfecting their new songs and experimenting with different endings and other musical ideas. I knew when I saw them in the studio in Miami that they would have some positive additions to make to our songs.

I spent the Fourth of July Bicentennial with Cheryl at Lake Tahoe. Then, the next morning, I flew out of Tahoe Regional Airport into LAX and then on to Miami International Airport. I checked into my hotel room about eight that night, and I received an envelope that had been left by JC, giving me everyone else's room numbers.

First, I called Criteria, the studio in Miami, to make sure that our master tapes had arrived. They had, so I told them I was looking forward to seeing them in the morning.

Next, I called Richard's room, but nobody answered. Of course, I realized. He's down in the bar.

I didn't recognize most of the names on the room list. The new names included Sarah Bar-here, Pat Pending, and Kay De Longpre. Later, I learned that most rock stars don't keep hotel rooms under their own names, for safety's sake. So, those rooms belonged to Christine (for a bar joke), Lindsey, and Stevie (for the street she used to live on in Hollywood).

When I walked into the bar, sure enough, all of the road crew guys were there, having come in from Tampa that morning. Because they'd had the whole day off, they were already pretty trashed.

"Caillat! You dog!" Richard called out. "You finally decided to join us, did you?"

All of the guys were there—Ray, Rhino, Richard, Curry, Lindsey, John, JC, and a couple of new faces, including Leo Rossi, who would become my business partner in my record company, twenty years later. In Miami, Leo was working with both the sound and the lighting crews.

Then there were the other road guys. They reminded me of pirates. There were usually about six to eight guys who hung lights, built the stage, hung the speakers, pulled hundreds of feet of cables, drove the trucks, set the mics, and generally got everything ready for the band, Richard, and Curry. They were tough, irreverent, hard-drinking, and loud.

I hoped the roadies didn't notice that they intimidated me. I put on my loud voice, "Hey, isn't this bar a little too good for you guys? I'm surprised you weren't thrown out hours ago!"

This set all of them off in some sort of response to me. I sat down and melted into the boozing crowd. Soon, the little vials appeared and were passed around. Of course! Miami was the heart of the cocaine scene. We all went to bed drunk, stoned, and wired at about twelve thirty.

The next morning, I woke up feeling a little heavy in the head. I immediately ordered room service, which arrived just in time for me to gulp down some coffee and toast and get a ride to Criteria a few blocks away. When Richard and I walked in a few minutes after ten, Mack Emerman was waiting for us, as any good studio owner would do. The studio was in a white three-story office building.

The receptionists were young, good-looking, friendly girls. Almost every studio back in the seventies had a good-looking girl to greet you when you walked in the door.

Mac took us on a quick tour. He had a whole complex that included four studios, mic lockers, and rehearsal rooms. Everything looked pretty worn—not old, just well used. Mac had been a remote recording guy, and, initially, he had had his consoles hand-built by a friend. Then he had made friends with the people at MCI consoles, and he had become an exclusive MCI house.

I wasn't a big fan of MCI tape machines, and I wasn't familiar with MCI consoles. But I knew that plenty of hits had come out of here, so I would go with the flow. I remembered that one of the consoles had rounded faders, not flat like most, but arched in the center. I thought this was very cool, very European.

Bob Marley had just left the studios. We were all sure we could still smell his potent ganja in the studios!

Cris Morris arrived soon after our studio tour, having driven in from visiting his family in Atlantic City. We settled into our studio, and, after aligning the tape machine to our tones, we started playing "Silver Springs" to listen to the speakers and get accustomed to the room.

One by one, the band members arrived at the studio, and, strangely, so did most of the road crew. Many of these guys had never been to a big-time recording studio, and they all had six days off. They thought they might as well hang out with us, get stoned, drink beer, and listen to good music.

I looked around the small control room. There were people everywhere. The roadies were sitting on the floor and at the producer's desk. Eventually, I suggested that maybe they could take turns between sitting in the lounge and watching the session. Everyone thought this was a good idea.

While I was showing off the great sounds we had on "Silver Springs," John heard the new stereo acoustic guitar parts that we had recorded after he had left Heider's that day. He had a new idea, and he volunteered to do the first overdub at Criteria.

We set up his Alembic bass into a direct box, then into his amp. I generally didn't like to use bass amps as part of my bass sound, because I felt that they had less punch than the direct signal. After all, why send the bass direct signal to a speaker in an amp when I could just as well send it to the listener's speaker directly?

When John finished, everyone was still a little hung over, and John felt that was enough work for the day. He had himself a cocktail. Lindsey had sounded great playing his lead guitars during the fifteen shows they had just finished, so we pulled up "Go Your Own Way" and started playing it. Something was still bothering Lindsey about the acoustic guitar part, so we decided to focus on the end tag.

Lindsey recorded four lead guitar tracks, each one a little different and a little more aggressive than the one before. I made a mental note of where the good licks were. While he was playing, he was searching for the magic in his guitar part. Musicians rarely strike gold right off the bat. Good musicians play an idea over and over and over, making slight improvements until they hopefully come across the one magic lick that becomes the theme from which they can build that one-in-a-million guitar solo. For Lindsey, that solo would have to wait a few more months, and, ultimately, he would have to get some help from his friends to finish it.

That evening, the hotel bar was going strong when I walked in. The crew had gotten bored at the studio, and they had come back early to drink and smoke.

Ouch! The next morning I felt as if I was on one of those wheels that mice run on, always running but going nowhere. I had another terrible hangover and only forty minutes to order breakfast, eat, and shower. Fortunately, I could see the studio from my hotel, so I wasn't worried about being late, only about being effective. This was starting to feel a little like Sausalito, only with even more cocaine!

As usual, John was there first thing and was ready to go on another bass part. "Let's do 'Lovin' Fun,'" he said.

"Okay," I said, holding my head and taking a hit off my beer. Even in Sausalito, it had been pretty rare for me to have a beer in the morning to try to recover. We laughed at how Miami already felt like one nonstop party.

All of the roadies arrived at nearly the same time. John, especially, didn't like an audience, so JC asked the road crew to leave. By noon, we had another great bass part from John, and Lindsey was getting ready to go for the tag solo on "Lovin' Fun."

Ray helped Lindsey find a really aggressive lead guitar tone, similar to the one he had played the day before on "Go Your Own Way." Lead guitars are always fun to record. Lindsey would have to be in an aggressive place to play lead solos, but little did I know *how* aggressive he would get that day.

As the day proceeded, Lindsey got some potential parts he liked, but on every pass, he would have an idea for a new solo. Eventually, the three or four tracks were filled, and he wanted to play more. So, we started recording over our least favorite tracks. Things got hot and heavy as he got into his guitar solo. He didn't want to wait for anything.

"I can do better than that," he said after one take. "I can do better. Tape over that last one!"

He was asking me to record over what I thought was a really nice take. "Are you sure?" I asked. "That was really great."

Frustrated, he shouted, "No! Go over it!"

"Lindsey, are you *sure*?"

He stared at me through the studio glass. Then, firmly, "Yes!"

I looked at Richard. He nodded agreement. I said, "Okay," and I recorded over that previous guitar solo.

Lindsey played one more and then asked, "Play me that one from before. I think I liked it better."

Richard and I looked at each other, and I replied, "We just went over that one. Remember, you told me to?"

"You did what?" Lindsey demanded. His face turned bright red, and the veins in his neck began to throb.

Then he put his guitar down and charged into the control room, approaching me from the front while I was in my control booth seat. Lindsey placed both of his hands around my neck.

"You're an idiot!" Lindsey screamed at me, his hands tightening around my throat.

I was in an engineer's chair that swivels and tilts back. Lindsey had pushed me all the way back in my seat, and his hands could have crushed my windpipe. At that moment, time slowed down for me. I didn't feel fear or anger. I just thought that Lindsey was being really stupid, and I felt so regretful that he could so quickly cross this line with me, after all that we'd been through.

I don't remember how much pressure I felt from his hands while he was throttling me. I didn't think that I was in any danger. But before I could do anything, everybody in the room was yelling at Lindsey.

Christine was the first to call out. "Lindsey, stop it! You told him to go over it!"

"Jesus, Lindsey, you're crazy!" Richard yelled. "You told him to erase it. Don't you remember?"

Finally, Lindsey just let go of my throat and stood upright. His hands dropped to his sides. "Sorry," he said. He sat down in another chair and asked if he could hear what we had on tape. Cris took over, and I just sat there, wondering if I should quit or what.

Christine came over to me, put her arms around me, and said, "Lindsey, that was no way to treat Ken. He was just doing his job!"

"Lindsey, I think you owe him a better apology," Mick said.

Lindsey came over to me and held out his hand. We shook. "I'm really sorry, man! Can you forgive me?" he asked.

"Yeah, forget it," I said, angrily shrugging it off. I was still shaking.

"Great guitar sounds!" Lindsey added. "Can I get you a beer?"

"Sure," I said, and Lindsey left the room to go get one for me. Of course, Lindsey could have sent one of the road crew, but he wanted to get out of the studio, and I was happy to see him leave.

When Lindsey came back, we listened to his solo.

Eventually, we built a great solo out of his parts.

I didn't really believe that Lindsey was sorry that he had tried to choke me. Maybe he was sorry that he had done it in front of other people, but, somehow, I think he thought he had the right to mistreat people. After all, he had already hit Christina; now he had attacked me, and, later, his future girlfriend Carol Harris would document Lindsey's abuse of her in her book.

On Thursday, July 8, it was time for us to work on Stevie's songs. We pulled out "Dreams," and she loved the new acoustics we had added back at Heider's. We spent the day doing more vibe-y electric guitar parts. Again, we used the Leslie, but this time I sent it straight from Lindsey's guitar amp with very little volume pedal.

We made three separate passes, and each time Lindsey played something different. We made a stereo bounce of the best of the three tracks onto one stereo master track. The track came out terrific and remains on the album today as part of the final mix.

Stevie said, "I love this track, and I want to try some background parts."

With Stevie, it was only a matter of time before she wanted to play an instrument, but her best instrument is her voice. Typically, Stevie would go out and just sing different harmonies to her songs. Listen to both of the pre-choruses in "Dreams." She re-sang these parts with Lindsey and Christine after we got back home, but the song was definitely taking shape in Miami.

So far, we'd had a productive week. We had new bass parts, some great electric guitar licks, and several acoustics. I knew that the band was charged up from their recent tour performances.

On Sunday, the band packed up their gear and left for their next show, in Philadelphia, that night. Cris and I stayed behind and made new safeties of the songs we had worked on in Miami.

I'm always happy to get my ass in my seat and head home. I just couldn't seem to control myself when I was on the road. Our last night in Miami was no different. At the hotel bar, Cris and I enjoyed the relative calm of the hotel with the band gone. We stayed up late and drank way too much, as usual. My head was hurting again the next morning, but I was flying home in first class. Despite the incident with Lindsey, the band always took good care of me.

12

Fleetwood Mac Explodes

I wasn't about to be a session player and just go along with
Lindsey's commands.

—John McVie

A few days later, Nina called me. "Hey, stranger! How are you?" she
asked. "I heard Fleetwood is on tour now, so I thought maybe you'd
have some down time."

"Yeah," I said. "It's been great to have a break."

"Why don't we meet at Lake Tahoe and catch up?" she said. "I'm
ready for a vacation, but I can come up for a day." I knew that she wanted
to see me, and I sure wanted to see her.

I have to go and do this, I thought. If I have a chance with Nina, then
I have to find out how we feel about each other, I rationalized. I told
Cheryl that my folks needed my help at Tahoe, and I had to go up for
the weekend.

Nina looked great, as usual. We sat by the lake and talked all day. Finally,
I said, "So, you're still not interested in living in Southern California?"

Nina laughed. "No *fucking* way," she said with her tough New York accent.

"Well, at least we have today," I said, taking another sip of beer.

"I'm sorry that I can't stay longer. I'm so proud of you being promoted to producer." She gave me a nice kiss.

After all of the months of frustrations, and even when we'd spent the night together, it never felt like we really fully resolved our relationship. Finally, away from work, we were able to do that at Lake Tahoe.

The subject of a relationship between the two of us never came up again. We had had a great time with each other out on the lake in the sun. As she drove away, I had a feeling that this was our good-bye. I was really happy that we had finally had a chance to have some time together, but it felt like a chapter in my life was ending. I felt as if I had explored an important—potentially life-changing—possibility. Then, when I understood it wouldn't work, I was happy to return to Cheryl.

Back in Los Angeles a few days later, Judy Wong called me and asked if I wanted to go see the Dodgers play the San Diego Padres the next day. She said, "The seats are amazing."

The band's perks continued to come to me. Somehow, the band had gotten close to someone high up in the Dodgers organization, and they could get tickets whenever they wanted.

Judy also said that Richard had called from his hotel in Chicago, and he wanted me to call him in an hour. "He told me there's a problem," Judy added.

I called Richard as soon as I could, and, luckily, he was in his hotel room. "Hey, Dash, what's up? How's it going out there on the road? Anyone getting lucky?" I joked.

"Cutlass! Glad you called," Richard said. "I'm having some problems with the sound. It keeps changing every show. Nothing has any punch, and I can't seem to fix it. Can you come out here and help me?"

"Sure, when's your next gig?" I asked.

"In two days," he said. "On Saturday, in Pittsburgh."

"I'm going to see the Dodgers tomorrow," I said, "but I'll fly out after the game and see you Saturday."

"Great! Thanks, Cutlass. Oh, and have a Dodger Dog for me!" He laughed.

I arrived in Pittsburgh a couple of days later. I took a cab to Three Rivers Stadium, where the band was playing later that night. Richard was already there, joking with the crew.

"Hey, buddy, what's up?" I asked.

"Cutlass, you made it! The band should be here in an hour, then you'll see what I'm talking about."

As promised, the band started to show up. Mick and John were first, and they greeted me like an old friend.

"Nice tan," John said.

"You guys must be having a blast!" I said.

"It's a job, mate," John said.

JC came up to us. "Caillat, glad you could make it. We want to know if Dashut has lost his touch."

"Or his ears!" Mick added.

"Why don't you go play something?" I suggested.

Mick and John went up on stage.

"Hey, Ray," I said. "Can you play some acoustic guitar while Mick and John play so I can hear what's going on?"

"Sure, Ken, anything for you," Ray answered in his usual sarcastic tone. I knew, though, that Ray loved any opportunity to play with the band.

Mick and John started playing their stage riff, with Ray accompanying them. I stood next to Richard.

"So far, so good," I said.

Christine came onstage and started playing her keys. I went onto the stage to listen from that vantage point.

"Hi, Chris," I said,

"Hello, luv. So you decided to take a break from your vacation and come see us?" she prodded.

"You got it," I said. "What do you think the problem is, Chris?"

"Everything sounds like shit!" she said.

"That's not good. Can you play something?" I asked.

"Sure, luv. Guys, let's play 'Lovin' Fun'!"

Christine gave the count in to the song. Mick, John, and Ray began the song with her. Ray was a proficient guitarist, and he played the extra parts offstage.

I walked around the stage, and my ears started to bother me. I continued walking back and forth. I raised my hands and asked everyone to stop playing. The stage had big speakers so that all of the band members could hear themselves or, in some cases, everyone else. You probably wonder why they would need this. The answer was simple. When Mick plays, his drums are so loud that he often can't hear the keys, the bass, or the guitars, and especially the vocals. It works the same for each of the other band members—they hear their own instruments much louder than anything else. Back in the seventies, the solution was to put stage monitors all around the stage, pointing at each musician. Then, if the musicians needed more volume from some other instrument, they could ask for it to be put in their monitor mix, and they could hear it properly.

Today, artists don't use stage monitors. They use wireless earpieces. In Pittsburgh, the stage monitors were turned up pretty loud, and I could hear the hiss coming out of each speaker. As I walked around, the hiss shifted with my movement. That's not right, I thought.

"Something's wrong," I said. I grabbed one of the front vocal mics and started talking into it. "One, two, three, testing. One, two, three," I said, moving back and forth between speakers.

My voice kept shifting around, but I could never get it to sound as if it was full. I was beginning to think that the speakers were out of phase. I walked to each side of the stage, and the same thing happened both times.

"This is crazy!" I said. "This is a professional sound company, and their speakers should all be in phase. Guys, let's take a break, and I'll look at the speakers." The band began to leave the stage. "Can somebody bring my suitcase up here?" I asked.

Curry Grant was closest to it, and he brought it to me. I had decided to bring something that Wally Heider always required his engineers to take with us when we went on remote recordings—a phase checker box. I had stopped by the studio to borrow one on my way to the airport. The phase checker had a little handheld speaker and a box with a microphone in it. This box had a red and a green light on it.

I put the box in front of one of the stage monitors, walked over to a vocal mic, and pulled the trigger on the speaker, which emitted a loud *pop* sound into all of the speakers. The green light came on in the box. "Good," I said.

I walked over to the next mic and popped it again. Red this time! "I knew it. Out of phase!" I said. I walked around to each microphone and each stage monitor, and to my surprise, about half of the speakers and the microphone cables were out of phase.

"No wonder things sound so bad. Everything is canceling out everything else, washing all the sound out," I said to the members of the band who were onstage.

Lindsey was watching me from the side of the stage and was getting more pissed off. Not at me this time but about the situation. "JC, come over here," he demanded. "You have to see this!"

I explained to JC what was going on.

"Nice one, Cutlass!" JC said, glad the problem had been identified.

"We've been playing our asses off all this time, and they've been supplying us with shitty equipment!"

For those of you who are unfamiliar with out-of-phase speakers, I'll explain briefly. You probably know that all speakers have two terminals that are labeled + and −, and your amp has terminals labeled the same way. In stereo listening, you're supposed to make sure that the wires you run from your stereo to the speaker are hooked up so that the plus on the amp goes to the plus on your speaker. That way, when each speaker cone moves to create sound, the two of them don't cancel each other out. If you hook them up backward, however, then one speaker will move out, while the other will pull in, thus canceling out a portion of the sound. That's what was happening to the band. The PA company had somehow improperly wired its cables. So, depending on that concert's setup, as many as half of the speakers were canceling out the sounds from the instruments.

We spent the next few hours going through all of the speaker company's cables to make sure they were all wired the same. Then we did our sound check. I stood next to Richard, and his head was bobbing.

"It sounds fucking great!" I yelled to Richard.

"Nice one, mate!" he said.

It may sound like an obvious problem to solve, but it was much harder than it seems. No one had expected that the speaker company would set up its own equipment the wrong way (especially show after show). It's not something that the band's crew and engineers are responsible for. I was just lucky that Wally had taught me so thoroughly that I knew how to look for problems that were caused by technical glitches beyond the scope of what we were expected to look for.

A few shows later, the band replaced the sound company with one I recommended, because I had worked with them and knew that they were always fantastic during our live recordings for Heider's.

I watched the whole show in Pittsburgh. The band was getting better with every show. After the concert, they all packed up their stuff and headed to their next gig. One of the band's limos took me to the airport to fly home.

As I sat back in my seat in first class, I ordered a bourbon and seven. Sleep soon found me, and I slept with a big smile on my face, knowing that I had helped the band and earned more respect from them.

The next Tuesday, August 4, I was back at Heider's studio 4. Lindsey and Richard arrived just after noon. They had stopped on the way to the studio for breakfast, which was why they were a little late, but they were ready to work. Fortunately, I had also stopped to eat, so I was ready to go. I had had a late breakfast at a hamburger stand called Ken's Fine Chili, which was about half a block from Heider's traffic office.

This other Ken was a tall round black man who took pride in making the best greasy food around. He and his wife, Mae, ran the stand, which was literally a small wooden shack. The burger stand had a counter and plastic-covered stools sitting in front. At night, Ken would pull the stools inside and drop the sides. And that was that.

The guys from Heider's often met there for breakfast. Ken knew all of our names and our favorite orders. Mine was scrambled eggs on a large hamburger patty, smothered with chili and onions. I don't know how I managed to stay so thin. Oh, yeah, maybe the coke helped. What great times I had back then!

That reminds me of a story from the earlier days at Heider's. About two years after I had started there, I was working with a big-time producer, Bill Halverson, who produced Crosby, Stills, and Nash. At that time, he was producing the album *Déjà Vu* for Crosby, Stills, Nash, and Young. One day I noticed that *Déjà Vu* was still in Wally's vault.

One of the songs on *Déjà Vu* was Neil Young's "Country Girl." I was an aspiring mixer with nothing to mix, so I asked Bill whether I could do a practice mix of "Country Girl." I knew that he wouldn't let me use his master multitrack, so I asked him if I could take his master tape, make one copy of the song, and immediately put it back in the vault. That way, I would be risking this multimillion-dollar tape only one time when I played the master.

I called Bill at home. "Okay, but I can get myself fired for this," he said. He sounded a little drunk at the time. He probably never would have agreed to this otherwise.

I got two 16-track machines and hooked them up so that I could make the transfer and copy the original to blank tape. Then I got the precious *Déjà Vu* master tape out of the vault. I carefully rewound it and made a perfect copy for myself. If I had snapped the tape or somehow damaged it, I would have been finished at Heider's—and maybe in the industry.

But I was driven! I spent the next two nights in the empty studio, making my ultimate mix of "Country Girl."

I was home the next evening, blasting my mix, when the phone rang. It was Wally, calling to tell me that he heard what I had done. "Uh, Ken, you're pushing too hard. You're pushing too hard!"

"I took every precaution, Wally," I explained. "I made a copy of the master in one pass so I wasn't risking the client's tape, and Bill gave me the okay!"

"I don't care," Wally said. "Back off! Engineers don't mess around with clients' tapes." The funny thing is, Wally never mentioned it again. I think he liked the fact that I wanted it so much.

Around the same time, I was working with another big-time producer, Bones Howe, who had produced the Fifth Dimension and Brazil 66. He was one of the cleanest, politest producers I had ever worked with. He dressed impeccably and usually came straight from the tennis court, where he played every day. He was in amazing physical shape and always wore sparkling clean white shoes, white pants, and an immaculate shirt with a sweater over his shoulders. He had the most enviable work ethic. He based his schedule around the union's schedule, and he usually worked short, clean hours from 12 to 3 or 2 to 5.

George Martin, the Beatles' producer, also wore a suit to work every day. In contrast, I was a long-haired hippie freak, producing Fleetwood Mac. I came in every day with my boisterous beagle, and I wore Levi's. Apparently, the times were a-changing.

Bones would pull up in front of Heider's in his charcoal Mercedes convertible with its tan top, walk in with his leather bag over his shoulder, and produce his session. He hired vocal, string, and horn arrangers to assist him in making the perfect album. He was my idol. The only thing I didn't like about his work was that he never seemed to take any chances, swear, or blast the speakers. He was so regimented that he routinely filtered out all of the bottom end below 70 cycles so that he would never have any surprises coming from his mixes.

Back in the studio later that morning, Lindsey still wasn't happy with his acoustic guitar part on "Go Your Own Way," and I had to agree with him. From the start, the acoustic sound never seemed to fit this hard-rocking song. But Lindsey was the best. He could really play the guitar.

I would really love to use Lindsey as a guitarist on the albums I'm working on today, but he's just such a difficult, unhappy person so much of the time that it's too much work to deal with him. Lindsey and I never discussed his trying to strangle me back in Miami, even though I often thought about it when he walked into the studio, especially in the days and weeks after it happened.

"I've taken 'So Afraid' to a whole new level," he said. The song was on the White Album but was much mellower, with more of a folk rock vibe. After Fleetwood Mac recorded the songs for *Rumours* and then went on tour, "So Afraid" had become a much faster, hard-edged song. This was the only way Lindsey and I really connected as human beings—by talking about the songs we were working on.

"Great," I said. "Last time I heard you play it, I thought it was heading in that direction."

We mic'd up his Martin and went out to the studio. He put on his headphones and experimented with playing the acoustic while using different timings. Then, on one of the takes, he played this really unusual guitar part with accented timing.

"Hey, what did you just play?" I asked him.

"That was really cool!" Richard added.

Lindsey knew it, too. "Yeah! Roll tape. Roll the tape!" We did, and he got that part in only two passes. Check it out; this unique strumming starts playing at 0:03 into the song.

Lindsey was so happy after he played it that he grabbed Richard and me and hugged us together. Better than being choked, I thought.

It's a great feeling when you make a breakthrough like we'd had that day. It's hard to say who should get the credit. Well, naturally, Lindsey should get most of it for playing the part. But sometimes things just come out of a musician's brain, and the musician may not realize how special they are. I'm pretty sure that's what happened with that guitar part; it became important because Richard and I immediately noticed how unique it was.

So that's how we completed the lead solo in "Go Your Own Way." That's why I always recommend recording everything that's played. When I'm producing, I often go back and find something golden. Then, when I play it back to the musician, such as Lindsey, he can hear what I heard. Sometimes it's an interaction with another instrument that becomes a new part altogether.

So, those of you in the control room, pay attention and keep listening. Talented musicians such as Lindsey need your ears, because they often play so much great stuff that it can get lost after a few passes.

Before I left the studio that day, I got a call from Gabrielle Aris. She told me that Michael Collins needed a rough mix of the show we had recorded at Studio Instrument Rentals so that he could edit his concert film together.

The next day, we brought the various audio reels from the show into the control room. Michael had already chosen his favorite takes of the footage. He wanted us to watch and listen to them to make sure we agreed with his choices. We mixed the takes that he liked, agreeing that for the most part, he had made the best choices.

We had to fix a couple of pitchy notes of Christine's and Stevie's, but I thought that they could improve some of their parts by re-singing them. So, before we mixed the tracks for the film, I had Stevie and Christine go out and punch in their vocals.

In those days, we didn't think it was right to re-sing everything— I just liked to fix the weakest spots. I believed, and still believe, that it's important that live recordings have their own unique quality, instead of sounding just like the radio or album version.

Today, and during the recording of *The Dance*, Fleetwood Mac's album of their tour from 1997, the band re-sang or replayed almost everything, just as the Eagles did for their "live" DVD. Everything was replaced, repaired, or retuned using Pro Tools. Just for the record, Richard and I weren't involved in recording *The Dance*. Lindsey wanted the latest and greatest producers brought in to record it. So much for loyalty. I don't want you to think there are any sour grapes about that, though. I was busy at the time, but Richard was going through a dry spell, and his career could have used the reunion. No one in the band, though, asked either of us to work with them.

The same thing happened to the band's photographer, Herbie Worthington. He shot their biggest album covers, but when it came time to pick the photographer for *The Dance*, he was passed over for whoever was the most popular photographer of that moment.

As I said, it's not sour grapes, but some artists, including Neil Young and Paul McCartney, continue to work with the teams that they've been with for decades. Their musicians and other members know their artists inside and out and do everything they can to support them.

In 1976, though, we didn't re-record everything. We could have, but we didn't, because we wanted live recordings to have a different sound so that the fans could feel as if they were at the concert, experiencing something unique, instead of feeling as if they were watching a music video. Maybe videos had changed Fleetwood Mac's ideas about what their live recordings should sound like.

In 1976, the band had different standards. At that time, they didn't allow their music to be used in commercials or films. They wouldn't be caught dead hearing their music in elevators. Lindsey scoffed at bands that sold out. In fact, he thought the Eagles sold out during the next few years when they nearly duplicated the sounds of *Hotel California* on their next two albums. That's why Fleetwood Mac departed so much from *Rumours* when we recorded the band's next two studio albums, *Tusk* and *Mirage*.

The next day we played back the vocal mixes for the film so that Stevie and Christine could hear them. They had left the studio the day before, after they had finished their vocal repairs. Of course, the engineers had had to stay into the night to mix the vocals.

The phone rang, and Cris answered it. He handed it to me. It was Cheryl. "Oh, my God, Ken! My dad just had a heart attack, and an ambulance is here to take him to the hospital." She started sobbing. In the background, I could hear Grace calmly telling the paramedics what had happened to Garney and that she'd follow them to the hospital. "Can you meet us there?" Cheryl asked. "It's right down the street from our house."

"Sure, hon. I'll be right there," I said. I looked up at Mick, and he knew something was wrong. "Cheryl's dad just had a heart attack, and he's on the way to the hospital. I gotta go."

"Go, just go," Mick said.

"Give her our love," Christine added.

Scooter and I jumped into my Benz and headed to the hospital. It took me about twenty minutes to get there. I parked and ran in. "I'm looking for two women, Cheryl and Grace," I said to the receptionist at the front desk. "The father had a heart attack, and the ambulance just brought him in."

"They're down that hall." The receptionist pointed the way.

I ran in that direction. Then I heard this awful scream from Grace that I'll never forget, "Oh, no! God, no!" The scream went on for several seconds. As I came around the corner, Grace and Cheryl were coming out from behind a curtain. They were both crying hysterically. They both put their arms around me.

"He's dead," Cheryl said. "My daddy is dead!"

I didn't have much experience with comforting others in their time of grief, and I just felt awful. Eventually, I went back to their house and helped Grace make the necessary arrangements. I tried to be of some comfort to them, but, honestly, I wasn't much good at that. The next day some of their relatives arrived, and I left, allowing them to grieve together.

When I got back to the studio, I had a knot in my stomach. The band was completely supportive. Mick asked Judy to send dozens of flowers over to Grace's house, and that was the end of our session that day.

Garney's funeral was on Sunday, August 8, in the afternoon. I hadn't seen Cheryl much for the last few days.

On the morning before the funeral, I met John in the studio to make one more attempt at replacing Lindsey's bass part on "Second Hand News" with one played by John. I had given John a cassette so he could study Lindsey's version. I knew John didn't like playing his bass to some-one else's instructions, but I was sure that after he heard the song in its current form—and how well all of Lindsey's parts fit together—John would understand that the bass part needed to be a lot different from the one he had originally played so that it would work with Lindsey's overdubs. I was pretty confident that there wouldn't be a lot of head-butting that day.

When Lindsey arrived at the studio that morning, he was very up and positive about John replaying his bass part. I remember Lindsey rubbing his hands together eagerly, as if John was going to give him an early Christmas present.

John took out his Fender, and he set up in the control room with us. We ran a cable out to his amp in the studio, taking his bass direct, using Larry Comara's Fat Box. John played the bass part straight this time, avoiding the walking bass he had played in Sausalito, but he changed Lindsey's part ever so slightly, making it his own.

Of course, John had much more to play with that day than he had had six months earlier when "Strummer" was in its infancy. In fact, by this point, I think that most of us had stopped referring to the song as "Strummer," and we were now calling it by its actual name, "Second

Hand News." Still, we had yet to fill out all of the vocal harmonies in the song. That would happen soon.

I got out of the studio just in time to head into the Valley, where Garney's funeral was being held. When I arrived, Cheryl was there with her brother and his wife and Grace's sister.

It was a hot summer L.A. day. After I greeted everyone, I noticed that they were having an open-casket ceremony. An hour earlier, I had been recording a bass part on a rock-and-roll song, and now I was at my girlfriend's dad's funeral, about to view his dead body. How weird was that? This was the first time I had ever seen a body in an open casket, and it was very surreal. I had only met her dad twice, and now I was saying good-bye. It was just horrible. That night Cheryl left her mom with her relatives and came over to my little home on Country Club Drive. I comforted her as best I could.

The day after the funeral, all of the members of the band were in the studio. We listened to our songs, again. Then we worked on "Think About It" a little before moving on to one of Christine's, "Don't Stop." None of us were very excited about "Think About It," and Stevie could tell.

"Maybe I'll save it for my solo album," Stevie said, a little dismayed, even though she, more or less, agreed with us. Every artist dreams about having a solo album one day. Artists are artists because they have a creativity inside them that needs to come out. Almost all of them have a "look at me" attitude. Yet some, such as my daughter, just love to sing. Colbie would be happy singing to herself.

Stevie and Lindsey both had that desire to stand on stage and be seen. Stevie knew that regardless of whether she was performing her songs with Fleetwood Mac or on her own, she would certainly be expanding herself as a famous artist. "It's fine with me if the band doesn't want my songs. I'll just do them by myself!"

Stevie seemed to believe that she was going to become the biggest solo artist from the band, even though, at this point, she was considered by the rest of us to be a limited musician. She was a true vocal performer, amazing onstage, but she didn't add much instrumentally to the album.

She had terrific vocal ideas, but the vocal process only took about 10 percent of our focus and time.

You have to understand that the producers, the engineers, and the rest of the members of the band were working every day in the studio, while Stevie was often out writing songs. From our perspective, she wasn't working as hard as the rest of us. I think everyone in our group who had this impression in 1976 has come to recognize Stevie's unique talent and ability. Stevie is a performing superstar. Although a lot of the other band members have their own stage charisma, they may have valued performance in the studio over performance onstage. Both are critical to a band's success, though, and Stevie was instrumental—interesting word choice—in helping Fleetwood Mac become superstars because of her songwriting, unique vocals, and dynamic stage presence.

I wasn't that happy with "Don't Stop" because, unlike "Lovin' Fun," which had so much attack in all of its instruments, the snare in "Don't Stop" was too soft. It had a very busy bass and a piano that had a lot of loud and soft spots. I tried to add some midrange to Christine's piano to make it jump out more.

"Instead of brightening it up, why don't we just bring in a tack piano?" Richard suggested.

"I was just thinking that," I said. "What do you think, Chris?"

She gave me a "yes" nod while she sipped her champagne.

I called Studio Instrument Rentals and asked whether they could deliver a tack piano for the next day's session. When I arrived that morning, it was already there. A tack piano is exactly what it sounds like—a cheap, old, upright piano with metal thumb tacks in each of the hammers. It sounds like the pianos from old-time movies or player pianos in Western saloons.

The metal tacks strike the metal strings, creating a bright metal note. We set up the tack piano so that Christine could play it, mic'ing it in stereo. We tracked it, adding it to the intro, the chorus, and the tag.

The tack piano did the trick. It really made the song bounce along. When I brightened the snares a little more, the track started to feel really good. After the intro part ended, it was clear that we needed something bright moving in the verses.

Lindsey went out and added an up-strumming, syncopated electric guitar part, along with some lead licks. Layering a song is all about being patient and finding the next building block and putting it in the right place. The tack piano in the intro and the chorus exposed the need for something bright and lively in the verses.

On the second pass, Lindsey had determined the correct direction and sound for his new guitar part. After we finished that, Christine and Lindsey decided to go out and double their vocal parts. With two voices singing each line, the verses got much stronger, which meant that Richard and I could crank up the backing instruments to support the new vocals. The new guitar parts could also be raised, giving the song a new range of dynamic energy. Sometimes that's all that's needed to unlock a song's potential and wake up the imagination of the people in the control room.

Speaking of imagination, Mick and Richard were performing again that day. Richard had stopped on the way into the studio and picked up a rubber monster mask. During the day while Lindsey and Christine were sorting out what to do with the vocals on her song, Richard and Mick were kidding around.

Soon the mask came out, and Mick put it on. At his height, Mick looked like some kind of monster. Richard pretended to stab Mick, using a drumstick as a knife. Richard would plunge the drumstick into Mick's side, and Mick would slightly move his elbow so the drumstick would go between his arm and his chest. They both had it down. Then Mick would stagger around the control room like a dazed seven-foot monster, taking long swipes at us with his arm as he pretended to die.

It was funny but quite disruptive to our session. Lindsey tried to stay focused on what he was working on. He sat with us in the control room, playing his guitar, but this show was difficult to ignore. Finally, Lindsey gave in, laughing loudly with spaces between each *ha, ha, ha.*

Christine added her Dame Edna laugh. Whenever Christine started to laugh with her deep, loud laugh, Lindsey would turn and look at her, and he would start laughing even harder. It was kind of like they were laughing at each other's laughs.

I had my camera in my car, so I went out to get it and took a picture of Mick "the Monster."

Mick performs his monster skit of death.

Then Richard said, "Let's go outside and see what real people are doing." We went out to Cahuenga, and I took a picture of Lindsey and Mick outside studio 4, a place where we generally spent little time.

A little while later, after the distractions from our comedians, we got back to work on "Don't Stop." It's very exciting to have a breakthrough on a song that makes it so much better. Our inspiration on "Don't Stop" was like the realization I had had about "Songbird" when I came up with the idea to record it in a big hall. The tack piano on "Don't Stop" was a similar inspiration. The song went from wiener to winner in just a couple of hours.

On Thursday, August 12, I turned thirty. Because I had been born in the summer, this was one of the few times I had ever had to work on my birthday. By this time, in the eighth month of recording the album, we had all become like family. When I got to the studio that morning, Cris

Lindsey plays guitar, while Mick finishes his "monster" skit. We were curious how people on the street would respond to our antics.

Morris handed me a present—a bottle of booze. Richard had bought me a nicer watch than the one I had. I was into calculator watches—the latest in seventies technology. Richard gave me one with all kinds of buttons that my current watch didn't have.

Judy Wong brought down flowers and a card signed by all of the members of the band. Gabrielle Aris also came to the studio to wish me a happy birthday. She gave me a Fleetwood Mac tour T-shirt. Mick and John had gotten together to buy me a silver penguin lapel pin to go on my velvet jacket. The penguin was their good luck sign. John told me he loved the look of those creatures. He was fascinated by them. He used to go to the zoo and photograph them. He even got a tattoo of one on his arm. One of the band's earlier albums was titled *Penguin*, and it was also part of the name of Mick and John's management company, Penguin Promotions.

Mickey Shapiro and his business partner, Steven Steinberg, came to the studio to discuss the band's progress and to hear more of our songs. Steven was twenty years younger than Mickey, in his late twenties. Mickey was already starting to have that comb-over look. Even though Mickey was a little older, though, he had a huge amount of passion for the band, and he believed in them 110 percent.

Mickey said he had received a call from California governor Jerry Brown, and the governor wanted to come to the studio to meet the band later that day. Jerry came to the studio a few times, and he really liked to chat with Christine.

Mickey took note of this. "I think the governor has a little crush on Christine. 'Is she with someone?' he asked me."

Jerry was dating Linda Ronstadt at that time, so it was interesting that he expressed interest in Christine. Linda was one of the biggest recording artists in the world at that point. She was another artist who was part of the Southern California sound, which was really starting to explode. It surprised me that Jerry was "shopping" for another rock-star girlfriend. Although Christine's profile had definitely been raised, Linda was a much bigger star, especially considering that she was a solo artist and Christine was a member of a band.

We played "Don't Stop," "Dreams," "Lovin' Fun," "Silver Springs," and "Go Your Own Way" for Jerry. The governor was a typical groupie. He bopped and danced (badly) to the music. What a hoot to watch! Now he's the governor again, thirty-five years later.

A few days later, Jerry came back to our studio, but this time he brought Linda with him. Her album *Hasten Down the Wind* had just been released, and it included the song "Someone to Lay Down Beside Me." She had also had a hand in discovering the Eagles. Surprisingly, John made a beeline for Linda, and he actually started flirting with her! John usually seemed reserved and shy, but he was right there when an attractive, single superstar female appeared in front of him.

After the governor and his famous girlfriend left, everyone in the room was still awestruck. We all felt very proud of the work we'd done. I was starting to realize that we were really on the right track, and I had a velvet jacket with a silver rock-and-roll penguin pin to prove it. Everything seemed like such a whirlwind. There was no time to think, only to react. It seemed that, every day, something amazing happened.

When Jerry left after that first solo visit, the band took me out for my birthday dinner to an incredible Italian restaurant, Valentino's, a few miles from Heider's. All of the members of the band were there.

In addition, so were Judy, Gabrielle, Richard, and Cheryl. It was a fun night, particularly because the band members kept goading one another to spend more money.

"Waiter, what is your most expensive bottle of wine?" Mick asked.

"Château Lafite Rothschild 1971, sir," the waiter said.

"And how much does that run?" Christine asked.

"Eighteen hundred dollars, ma'am."

They didn't want to go that expensive, so they settled on two $500 bottles of wine for the table instead. The waiter poured wine into each of our glasses.

Of course, this celebration became more about the band than about me. It was just convenient that it was my birthday. But—don't misunderstand me—that was as it should be. The minions at the table were happy that "our parents" were taking us out to dinner. We were just as pleased that we didn't have to pick up the tab. We were simply glad that they didn't make us sit at our own "children's table."

Eventually, the band members worked themselves up to the $1,800 dollar bottle of wine. I got a couple of sips of the expensive bottle, and it was spectacular. The mood that night was that we had achieved success, and we deserved to celebrate.

Later that week Larry Comara, who was one of my friends, told me about a new studio in Los Angeles called Davlin that had recently opened. Davlin was in North Hollywood, and it had a famous $40,000 Bösendorfer nine-foot grand piano. I didn't know a lot about pianos, but I was pretty sure that this was the top of the line for grand pianos.

I told Christine about the piano, and, immediately, she wanted to play it. So I booked the next week at Davlin. We talked about playing the Bösendorfer grand piano on "Oh, Daddy," "Don't Stop," and "Lovin' Fun." When we finally tried the Bösendorfer in the studio, it sounded fantastic.

When we actually put mics on it and played it with our tracks, though, we realized that the piano had great action but also had a dark quality. For it to fit in with the aggressive sounds of our album, I would need to add quite a bit of EQ to the sounds coming from the mics.

We cranked up the top end on both tube U-47 mics, and the piano sounded really good. We put up "Oh, Daddy," and, after experimenting with various parts in the song, we decided to record a dramatic whole-note sustained chord on each of the 1 beats in the verses. Christine held down the sustain petal and then played the single chord, just letting it reverberate as the verse continued. To help it sustain even longer, I increased the sensitivity of the mics very gradually so that the chord rang for twenty to thirty seconds.

When Lindsey heard this, it gave him an idea. He decided to play sparse harmonic parts on his acoustic guitar, similar to the piano accents we had just recorded. One thing led to another, and we added two acoustic strumming parts to the song that gave the track a lilting feel around John's "whales fucking" bass part.

The new acoustic parts particularly strengthened the intro and chorus's electric guitars, which were already there. Davlin had a fine collection of tube microphones. We also recorded some excellent background vocals on "Dreams."

The owner of Davlin, Len, was great, and he knew a guy who could get us pharmaceutically pure cocaine. Of course, this worked for us and against us. I remember that Len had a fantastically beautiful wife with long blond hair. She worked at the studio, but she didn't act like a typical studio girl. She seemed more like a wife who had agreed to come to work to help her husband.

We put "Oh, Daddy" aside, deciding to revisit it another time when we were ready.

Davlin actually turned out to be a great studio for background vocals. We got on a roll and recorded many of these for the album at Davlin.

But that would be the end of our productive time. The band had to go out on the next leg of their tour. They were playing San Bernardino on August 24, San Diego on August 26, and then two shows at Universal Amphitheater, on August 30 and 31.

I waved good-bye as the band left town, but Cheryl and I went to both of the Universal shows. The band introduced some of the new vocal harmonies they had developed at Davlin.

It was already the first of September. We had had a lot of distractions in the summer, but they were behind us. It was time to knuckle down for the final sprint to the finish line. The longer we took with the album, the more often the label called to ask how much longer it would take us to finish. Actually, it shouldn't have made that much difference to them how long it was taking us (except for the cost). That's because the White Album was still moving up the charts!

In December 1975, the White Album had only reached number 44 on the charts. In February 1976, it peaked at number 3. Soon after that, it dropped, then it began to rise again with the release of "Rhiannon" in late spring. It stayed in the top ten throughout the summer. Finally, on September 1, 1976, the White Album hit number 1 on the Billboard album chart. That's really unusual by today's standards. Most number one albums reach the top of the chart on their week of release or right after that, not several months later.

The bad news was that the label executives wanted to come down and hear our progress on *Rumours*. We didn't want their input, though. We preferred to get our album done on our time line and play it for them when we were ready.

Of course, now that Fleetwood Mac's previous album was at number one, there was only one direction that this album could go—down. So, even though reaching number one was great news for the band, we knew that the album would soon start to fall (which it did the next week). This meant the record company became really nervous about when the band would be ready to release their next album. Interestingly, the White Album stayed on the charts into 1978.

We had spent much of August playing the tapes over and over, trying to figure out which songs were nearly finished and which ones needed work. We still had a couple of problem songs, especially "Think About It" and "Keep Me There," but we had had breakthroughs with "Don't Stop," "Oh, Daddy," "Lovin' Fun," "Silver Springs," "Dreams," "Go Your Own Way," "Never Going Back Again," and "Second Hand News."

"Songbird" was essentially done. We had experimented with some acoustic guitar parts, a solo, and a bass part, but every rough mix we did always came out the same—just Christine and her piano. Last, there was "Gold Dust Woman," and we knew it was coming along. Yet we knew that we still needed to devote a few days to it so that it could come together. We would get to that soon enough.

• • •

Sunday, September 5, was Sunday Break II at Steiner Ranch in Austin, Texas. This concert was intended to be like a small Woodstock on a farm in the middle of Texas near Lake Austin, which was fed from Mansfield Dam on Lake Travis. More than sixty thousand fans were attending the event, and other bands in the lineup included the Band, Chicago, the Steve Miller Band, and England Dan & John Ford Coley.

We flew into Austin in the band's chartered plane the day before the concert. We landed in the afternoon, and the first thing I noticed was how frickin' hot it was. It was Labor Day weekend, and it had to be about 115 degrees. "If it's this hot tomorrow, it's going to be miserable out there in the sun," I said to Cheryl.

We all went to our hotel rooms and eventually met up in the bar to drink and hang out. The limos would take us to the gig at about 10 a.m. the next day, so we'd need to be in the lobby by 9:45.

Cheryl, Richard, and I met in the lobby that day. We were told that so many people were attending the concert that we would have to be flown in and out of the show by helicopter because it was too crowded to get there by limo.

"Aw, that's too bad," I said. "Maybe I can get the pilot to give us a wild ride."

"Caillat! I'll get you, if you do that," Richard said. He was terrified of flying, but I always tried to get our pilots to give us some extra fun.

We got to the concert and did our sound check. The band's equipment had arrived the night before, so that it could be set up early that morning. It was already in place when we landed.

Mick's ex-wife, Jenny, had come to see the show and had brought their girls, Amy, five, and Lucy, three. Mick and Jenny's divorce had been finalized a few months earlier, but they had reconciled since Mick had returned from Sausalito, and he had managed to charm Jenny into coming back to him. They would remarry in just a month, on October 1.

About a year later, while Mick was still with Jenny, he and Stevie had an affair. This was in addition to whatever happened between them in Maui, which certainly adds credibility to the likelihood of that escapade. While Mick was having his affair with Stevie, he bought Jenny and their girls a place in Bel Air. They divorced again in 1978, and Mick moved in with Sara Recor, who was still married to Jim Recor at that time.

Jim Recor had been Loggins and Messina's manager, and the duo had been Fleetwood Mac's opening act on the tour before the band had started to record *Rumours*. Stevie had also had a hit single with Kenny Loggins around that time, "Whenever I Call You Friend." Sara Recor and Mick finally married in 1988, and they divorced in 1992. The relationships in the music industry in the seventies were complicated.

The concert in Austin was an all-day event, and Fleetwood Mac was the closing act, coming on near sunset. Just before show time for them, it was still sweltering hot, and all that we had was beer and water to keep us cool as the band prepared to go onstage.

Lindsey made a rare appearance without his shirt because it was so hot. The crowd was rowdy. There was nudity and drinking, and drunk fans were lighting fires.

Cheryl and I sat at the mixing board with Richard while the band played. Toward the end of the show, during "Rhiannon," it began to thunder and lightning.

"I knew it!" Cheryl said. "She's a witch!"

"Well, I can't argue with you there," I said. "I think there's a part of her that does believe that."

The show ended just as it was starting to get dark. The sunset was gorgeous because of the late-afternoon thunderstorm.

JC called us on Richard's communication headphones to tell us that we needed to hurry backstage because the helicopter wanted to take us right away. When Richard, Cheryl, and I finally made it backstage, we went to the helipad. Mick, John, and Lindsey were riding with us. Christine and Stevie had already gone in the previous trip. Our group was told that the helicopter would be back for us in about twenty minutes.

When our turn came, I sat in the seat right behind the pilot. "Can you make this thing do any stunts?" I asked. The pilot had a Southern accent and an air of confidence that made me ask this question.

"Sure," he said. "I used to fly one of these in 'Nam."

"We're in good hands," I said to everyone else in the helicopter. "This is going to be good!"

"No way, Caillat!" Mick pleaded more than he was ordering. He could also tell that this guy was a pro. That wasn't a plus for him, but it was for me.

Just before we were going to take off, a man ran up to the helicopter. "There's a sick girl, and we can't get her out. Can you take her to the ambulance?"

The pilot looked to us, and we all agreed. The girl was loaded into the helicopter. The pilot lifted off into the warm night sky with orange streaks peeking out from behind the storm clouds on the horizon. The helicopter's flashing lights blinked at the throngs of people below, still partying. When I looked down, with darkness approaching, I could see headlights pointing in every direction in the desert. Then I saw the red beacon from the top of an ambulance below.

Our pilot was already on the radio with the driver, and we descended into a wide ravine where the ambulance was waiting next to the river. They helped the sick girl out of our chopper.

Then our pilot turned around to the rest of us still on board and said, "Since you've been so accommodating, I'm gonna give you all a great ride."

"Oh, no. That's quite all right," Mick whimpered. "You don't have to."

"No, you deserve it," the pilot said. "You folks have been patient with your time. Now make sure your seatbelts are fastened low and tight around your waists. Here we go!"

He wound up the jet engine until it had a high whine. He pulled a lever on his left side, and we popped up about twenty feet into the air. We remained motionless for a moment, then he quickly tilted the nose down, and we were flying forward, only twenty feet above ground through the middle of the ravine. Looking up, I could see that cars were still parked on top of the ravine, their headlights shining, trying to get out of the venue.

We must have been doing more than 70 mph, even though we were only about fifty feet off the ground. When we reached the river, the pilot pulled the chopper up and to the left. At that point, I couldn't tell which direction was up. I looked out the window to my right and could see the moon reflecting on the river. We made a perfect hard left and followed the river for about ten minutes.

After we landed, we all laughed at the rush our pilot had given us. Even Mick laughed, long and deep. "Caillat, I'll get you for this," Richard told me, but he frequently said that because I kept pulling pranks on him, pushing his buttons.

We got into our waiting limos and headed back to our hotel in the hot muggy September night. When we got back to the hotel, I learned that Christine and Stevie wanted to stay in Texas a little longer. This meant that if we wanted to go home the next morning as planned, we would have to take a commercial flight.

John, his date, Richard, Cheryl, and I all took commercial flights back in the morning. On the way to the airport, Cheryl told me that she had a head cold and that her ears were clogged. I told her that she shouldn't fly with clogged ears, but she said she thought they were improving.

I told her to try to yawn to open her ears, but she didn't have any luck. It probably didn't help her sinuses that we'd snorted coke the evening before. "We'll stop and get some nasal spray. That will help open up your sinus," I assured her.

Of course, we were running late for the plane and didn't have time to stop for decongestant. When we got into the Austin airport, I bought some gum for Cheryl. John, who was a scuba diver, happened to have eardrops in his bag. He told Cheryl that they might help her.

Cheryl took the small bottle that John had given her and ran into the bathroom. When she came out, she was blowing her nose, saying she felt better. We got on the plane and took our seats. When we took off, her ears immediately started hurting. I called the stewardess over and told her what was happening.

The stewardess brought her a hot pack and told her to place it on her ears. Then she gave Cheryl some hot bourbon to drink. As the plane ascended, the pain in her ears continued to increase. She was in such agony that she was pounding her fists on her legs. I didn't know what to do to help her. I considered trying to knock her out, but I didn't know how to do that.

Eventually, one of her eardrums burst, and she was no longer in pain. That's a horrible story, but it's a lesson well learned. If you can't clear your ears, then don't fly!

"I told John that I snorted the medicine up my nostrils, but he looked very disturbed," Cheryl told me later.

"Why did you do that?" John asked. "They're eardrops."

"I explained that I had followed the directions, and I pointed them out to him." Cheryl said that John looked very sheepish after she did this.

"No wonder they never worked for me," he said.

It was mid-September, and we had new acoustics and volume pedal electrics in "Silver Springs." We still had a lot of work to do. One of my biggest concerns was that "Silver Springs" was still more than eight minutes long. On the record, it would take up the space of two songs.

In those days, a vinyl record could hold only twenty-two minutes of music per side. You see, when a record is cut, the volume is derived by the width of its groove. Back then, we eventually ran out of real estate if we wanted to keep the volume up. If we wanted to put more than twenty-two minutes of music on a side of vinyl, then the volume of the record would have to be reduced by two or three decibels. This was not good because, back then, being the loudest song on the radio or on your stereo was important. Reducing the volume of an album by even one or two decibels would make the entire record sound softer. We didn't want that!

If we couldn't edit "Silver Spring" down, then it would have to come off the record—and a shorter song would have to replace it. To resolve this problem, I sat with Stevie, trying to cut out repetitive verses in "Silver Springs." While we worked, tears ran down her face.

"These lyrics mean so much to me," she said. "They're part of the story, and we can't cut them." She sobbed.

"'If we don't shorten the song, then it may not fit on the album," I reasoned. "It's my job to try to save your song."

"It might not make the album?" Stevie asked.

"That's right," I said.

"Then cut the lyrics." She straightened up like a proud soldier.

We worked for several hours, and I could see that poor Stevie was devastated by the process.

"It's so unfair that my beautiful song has to be mutilated," she said at one point.

"I agree," I said. As I've already mentioned, I thought "Silver Springs" was one of the strongest songs we'd recorded, and I really wanted to save it. "But if you want to keep a longer version of 'Silver Springs,' then the only option is to take one of your other songs off the album. It wouldn't be fair to the other writers for you to have such a long song unless you cut another one of yours."

Stevie understood that if we took one of her songs off the record, then she would receive less money from publishing royalties on record sales. As soon as she realized this, it was as if a miracle had occurred. Suddenly, the tears went away, and she stopped resisting most of my edits to "Silver Springs." She was a business woman! Ultimately, we were able to cut "Silver Springs" down to its final run time of 4:33.

In the end, it didn't make the album but was ultimately released as the B-side of *Rumours'* first single, "Go Your Own Way."

"Silver Springs" certainly deserved to be on the album, based on its quality, but we were concerned about how it would flow with the rest of the songs. It was like a great scene from a film that gets left on the editing room floor. That happens—it's just part of the process. On a musical level, it was beautifully put together. Some of the best guitar work that we recorded for the album was on that song. I was able to contribute a lot of layering from the volume pedal work and acoustic picking textures. "Silver Springs" has a great rhythm-section track. It's got an amazing tag and a real dynamic to it. Despite this, we had to cut it from the album.

Rumours was my first big album, and it provided me with another lesson about the music business: sometimes you have to make tough choices. Thirty years later, I recorded a song for my daughter, Colbie, called "Bulletproof Vest," but it had to be cut from her second album because it was too different from the rest of the songs on the album. It featured a four-minute violin solo that had a triumphant finish. It's beautiful. Maybe someday you'll hear it.

Richard and I added up the running times of all of the other songs. No matter what we did, it still looked as if we were going to run over twenty-two minutes per side. Our only other option was to start making cuts to other songs, too, if we wanted to squeeze "Silver Springs" onto the album. As coproducers, we had to figure out what to do.

The day after Stevie and I trimmed "Silver Springs" was a typical September day in Hollywood. During August and September in Los Angeles, the temperature climbs steadily during the day, often starting in the mid-80s and ultimately reaching 100 degrees late in the afternoon.

Keep in mind that outdoors in Hollywood, it is almost all pavement, except for a few trees that line the busy streets. We were all happy to be in an air-conditioned studio during the hot days at the end of summer.

Everyone was in the studio that day except Stevie. Her "people" had called to tell us that she wouldn't be coming in. While she was absent, someone in the control room suggested that maybe we should take "Silver Springs" off the record. This meant that we might need to record another of Stevie's songs to replace it. Lindsey said he knew the perfect song, one that he and Stevie had performed as Buckingham Nicks, titled "I Don't Want to Know."

"Why don't we put it down and see what we've got?" Lindsey suggested.

"Okay," I said.

We set up for live-tracking with the rest of the band. I was charged, excited. "I Don't Want to Know" was an easy song: drums, bass, guitar, electric piano, and, ultimately, a duet with Stevie and Lindsey.

So, recording that day was only a matter of getting the tempo right. Lindsey sang it in the control room so that we could make sure that we had the right beat on the click machine. As soon as we got the tempo on the click, we were ready to play it for Mick and the rest of the band in their headphones. All of the band members who were there that day took their places, for what I assumed would be the last track we were going to record for this album.

Lindsey started, off the click in his headphones. After one round of the intro, John entered, playing along with Lindsey's part. The guitar and the bass played the second round. Then Mick came in with a double-hit accent on his drum set.

Christine was playing electric piano to fill out the track. I think it only took us about an hour and a half to cut the track. The drum track was really sharp and crisp, and the song started off in a way that sounded similar to "You Make Loving Fun," in that, when the drums entered, they were in your face from the outset.

The final version of this song starts with double acoustic guitars. Then the bass enters; then the drums come in, followed immediately by the vocals of Stevie and Lindsey.

"I Don't Want to Know" is also fast paced. This was good because we were worried that we had too many slow songs. We were concerned that when we finally agreed to the running order, the album would have an overall slow feel to it. We tracked the basic version with electric guitar, so that we could avoid leakage issues. We got the master on take 9, which meant that we probably played only four or five full takes before nailing it.

As soon as we got the master take, we went back and added the acoustic parts, which hook you immediately.

I love it when a song starts out at sixty miles per hour and just keeps going until the end. "I Don't Want to Know" was 3:16 of high-impact energy. After we got the new acoustic parts, Lindsey went out and sang the lead vocal. He knew the part well enough that he was able to sing it without Stevie. So, in about an hour and a half, we got the basic track. Then, in the next hour and a half, we got the acoustics, and in another two hours, we had Lindsey's lead vocals.

All we needed now was to get Stevie to agree to sing vocals for this track to, essentially, replace "Silver Springs." We hoped that she would like what we had done because, in one day, we had a new up-tempo track that felt nearly complete. At this point in recording the album, we all knew what direction the album needed to go because more than half of the songs were so close to being completed.

When we got to the studio the next day, we were still excited about our new song. To this day, I always get excited and nervous just before I'm about to cut a new track. Recently, I was asked to produce a new song with Colbie for the Special Olympics Christmas CD series. She knew which song she wanted to record, "Have Yourself a Merry Little Christmas."

But Colbie was on tour, and the song had to be recorded right away. She had a one-day break, so I had to have the rest of the track ready so that she could sing the vocal part in a three-hour window. I asked her to get together with her guitar player on the road and record a rough vocal and send it to me. I wasn't thrilled about cutting a track without the artist in the room with me because it's expensive, and I have to be sure to get the tempo and the key correct and make sure everything is right for her to sing her lead vocal.

I hired the same studio musicians I had used on her record six months earlier. I planned on using drums, bass, keyboard, electric guitar, and acoustic guitar. Then I wanted to add strings after Colbie had recorded her vocals.

I was nervous and tense on the day of the tracking session. Even though my daughter had sent me a rough track of her singing to an acoustic guitar, I had other decisions to make regarding drum feel, bass part, and guitar type and part.

We started the session and got all of the sounds ready. Then I played Colbie's rough track, and we got the tempo and the key. As we started to play, I suggested we go to a fretless bass, brushes on the drums, and muted eighth notes on the electric guitar. The keyboardist played a bell-sounding piano.

We cut the track in about an hour and a half.

Colbie came in the next day and loved the work that we had done. Then she sang the vocals and added a harmony. I added strings the next day and mixed it the day after that.

My point is that once you cut a track, it's a new entity, and it lives and breathes with a personality of its own. That's why cutting a track is so special to most of us.

When Stevie came to the studio the day after we had worked on "I Don't Want to Know," we told her that we had gotten the urge to cut a new up-tempo track, and it was one of hers. She was surprised and excited, but she knew this meant she would have more songs on the album than anyone else.

The rest of us had had a meeting before Stevie came in that day. "Someone has to settle this, once and for all," I said.

Lindsey had told Mick that because his situation with Stevie was already fragile, he thought that Mick, as band leader, should be the one to tell Stevie.

"All right, lads, the buck stops here, as they say." Mick stood up and straightened his jacket. "I'll handle this. I'll let her know that we've all tried, but there's just no other way to make this record perfect. She'll just have to trust us." He took Stevie out to the parking lot and told her that "Silver Springs" was probably coming off the album, despite the cuts, because it was still just too long.

"They recorded another song of mine when I was out of the studio, but they didn't even ask me," Stevie said later. "That was a drag. Not only did they take 'Silver Springs' off the album, a song that I had dedicated to my mother, but they had recorded another one of my songs that Lindsey knew because—of course—he knew all my songs."

Stevie wasn't happy when she came back into the studio, but she composed herself and agreed to go out and sing the lead vocal to her new possible addition to the album. She always loved singing, and we encouraged her to try it, telling her that we could decide what we were going to do later, especially since her other song, "Think About It," wasn't working, either.

Stevie sang her lead vocal duet with Lindsey's existing vocal part, and we had it in two or three passes. Stevie's and Lindsey's voices sound so strong together on this pop track.

So, we had solved one problem, even though Stevie wasn't thrilled, but we had other issues to consider in determining which songs would make it onto the album.

Then John told us about a brainstorm he had recently had. "With all the rumors flying around about this album, why don't we call the album *Rumours*? But let's spell it the English way, "rumours.""

I fell in love with this idea immediately. I always hated when a band named their album after one of the songs on it. "Yeah! John, I love that!" I said.

It was always hard to come up with a name for an album, and now we had a good idea in front of us months before we were going to release the album!

"Nice one, John!" Mick agreed.

Everyone loved the idea. We all high-fived and congratulated John on his inspiration.

"Brilliant," Christine said. "Nice one, John!" She toasted John with her champagne.

So, whatever rumors you've heard about how *Rumours* got its title, that's the inside story.

13

The Chain: Keep
Us Together

"The Chain" is really my song. We split [the royalties] five
ways, but the fact is that I wrote most of those words and
most of that melody!

—*Stevie Nicks*

Monday, September 27, was the day that *Rumours* almost died. I was
playing the tapes for the band, and I asked Cris, "Is it me or does
everything sound dull?"

We usually listened to the tapes so loudly that we couldn't tell
whether there was anything wrong or if our ears were just shutting down.
Lindsey was the worst; if the volume knob would only go to 10, he would
still want us to crank it to 11. He'd get mad if we didn't have the volume
as loud as possible. He would act as if I was an asshole because I didn't
want to listen full blast all of the time. My idea was that we should listen

at moderate levels most of the time and then occasionally hype ourselves up with maximum volume.

That day I began to suspect that the tapes were starting to suffer high-end loss. I just hoped my ears weren't suffering the same fate. I knew that if we had a problem with the tape, then it would be partially masked by the fact that the console had EQ knobs on each channel. Because of this, we would routinely adjust the EQ on tracks as parts got added or mixes were adjusted.

At that time, no band had ever spent a year producing an album. We hadn't given a thought to the fact that we were wearing out the tape, degrading it to the point that the lush textures of the sound were starting to fade away.

We had been playing these tapes now for more than nine months, twelve hours a day. "How are the head cleanings going?" I asked Cris.

"They've been fine," Cris said. "Sometimes there's a little oxide on the heads."

We'd been running the tapes for about three hours at this point, so I suggested that we stop to clean the heads and see if there was any oxide on the Q-Tips. After we stopped, I lifted the tape away from the head block and wiped a couple of Q-Tips soaked in cleaning solvent over the heads. They were black with tape oxide!

"They haven't been doing that," Cris said, and I believed him.

Apparently, we had reached a point where our tapes were starting to die. I put the tape back on the heads, loaded the machine, and rewound the tape to the top of the song, "Lovin' Fun," that we had been working on. I played the four-minute song another time and then checked the heads again. More black oxide had come off the tape. Not as much as before, but it was a lot for just one pass. I wanted to do one more test. I rewound the tape again, patched the kick drum and snare tracks up to two unmarked faders, and muted both. I asked Lindsey to tell me which was which. He switched between the two tracks, and they sounded the same. They both just sounded weak: "*Pah, pah.*" All of the character was gone. When the fog suddenly cleared from my brain, I realized that we were in real trouble. Everyone was looking at me.

"What does this mean?" Mick asked. "What are we going to do?"

"Are we fucked, Ken?" Christine echoed.

"No, no," I said. "We always have the safeties." But those were all a generation older, and they didn't contain some of our most recent, really great additions.

My brain was racing. Then I remembered that back in Sausalito, when Richard and I had been trying to get our act together, Nina had told me that with two 24-track machines in each room, their usual procedure was to run tape on both and record simultaneous basic tracks. So I had told her to go ahead and do it. Thank you, Miss Nina!

We had another simultaneous first-generation master in our storeroom at Wally Heider's, and I hadn't even thought about it. The good news was that the basic instruments we had cut for each song—particularly all of the drums, the bass, the guitars, and the keyboards—were pristine and perfect on those tapes. The bad news was that none of our overdubs were on them.

I called Heider's maintenance engineer, Billy Youdelman, and asked him to come down to the studio. When he arrived, I showed him the dirty Q-Tips. Then I took him to the back room where the other first-generation masters were.

"Is it possible to get the overdubs from our worn-out tape onto these unused masters?" I asked him.

"Maybe," he said. "But you'll have to sync-up two machines by hand and control the speed of one machine so it stays in sync with the other. That's never been done before, and it won't be easy."

"Who cares about easy?" I said. "I knew it could be done. Can we do it here, now?"

"We could," Bill said. "But I know this engineer over at ABC Dunhill Records who has some machines that are very accurate and can be controlled more easily."

I walked back to the control room where the band was waiting with bated breath. "The good news is that there's a solution, guys," I said. "I think we can transfer all the overdubs back to the clean master tape and use the new drums."

"You can do that?" Mick asked.

"I think so."

"Well, let's do it!" Christine said. She got up and hugged me.

Back then, we didn't have time codes on our tapes the way we do on tracks today. So we didn't have an obvious way to sync the two tape machines together.

Two tape machines never run at the same speed—one eventually gets ahead of the other. To keep the tapes in sync, we would need to start the two machines at the exact same time and spot in the song. Then, somehow, we needed to monitor the sounds. When one machine would start to creep ahead of the other one, we would need to gently adjust its speed to keep all of the instruments playing together. Billy called his buddy at Dunhill and set up a transfer session for us at noon the next day.

We arrived at ABC Dunhill Studios the following day, carrying all of our worn two-inch master tapes and our unused master tapes. The ABC Dunhill building was a record company on the upper floors, and it had a recording studio on the lowest floor. The name of the engineer who helped us perform this miracle has been forgotten, but I want to say it was Pete.

We put up the tapes at Dunhill, and we manually transferred them, side by side, using two identical 24-track machines, one for playback and the other to record the newer overdubs onto the clean drum tracks. If Pete let the machines run out of sync for even a fraction of a second, the tracks would sound out of time, and they would be unusable.

Pete put on a pair of headphones. He put the high hat and the snare from the original tape in his left ear, and the high hat and the snare from the unused master in his right ear. Then we marked both tapes and hit the START button on both machines at the same time.

Pete used the built-in VSO (vari-speed oscillator) on one of the machines, carefully adjusting the speed slightly, basically playing the VSO like an instrument, and keeping the two high hats and snare drums in the center of his head. As one machine began to move faster than the other, the image in his head would move toward the faster machine, and he would adjust the VSO in the other direction, basically, as if he were steering a boat.

We had to do this song by song. First, we had to find the same spot on every song on both tapes. That sounds easier than it was, because we had to sync the songs before they started to play—so that we wouldn't cut off the beginning. Then we'd press PLAY on both machines and pray that they would start playing at the exact same time. This was repeated over and over, adjusting the mark on one tape until both versions were perfectly synced together.

Because one machine always ran slightly faster than the other, though, Pete would have to monitor the instrument in his headphones, constantly adjusting the knob on the VSO for the entire length of the song. It's harder than it sounds. I tried that a couple of times, and it nearly scrambled my brain. "Don't worry," Pete said. "I'll take it from here."

We worked all night and finished up at 5 a.m.—*and* we saved our album. *Rumours* would have been just about dead if the only master tape had been degraded. Thank you, Pete! Please contact me. I'll put your proper name in the next printing and buy you dinner and drinks.

Of course, we still could have used the most recent safeties that we had made in Miami, if this hadn't worked. This solution was much better, because now our drums were first generation and our tape wasn't dying anymore. We still needed to add our newest overdubs that we had recorded in Miami. What a stroke of luck that we'd just happened to record double basic tracks.

October in Los Angeles is beautiful. The days are warm and clear, and the heat is gone. Often, we get the Santa Ana winds in October. These are wind systems that reverse the normal onshore flow to offshore, blowing the warm, clean desert air out west to the ocean. This usually clears out any smog that we may have. In the worst cases, though, we have our fire season. These fires often happen naturally or by human error, but sometimes they're started by idiot arsonists, who light fires just to see how much damage they can cause. The Santa Ana winds only make the fires worse.

During October, the band was finally beginning to see the light at the end of the tunnel. They had scheduled a ten-day business trip to Europe.

When they returned to the United States, Mick, John, and Christine found that they had immigration problems. Mickey Shapiro had to rush to the airport and straighten things out before the Brits in the group were deported. Another crisis averted.

In October, Mick remarried Jenny and bought a house in Topanga Canyon so that the whole Fleetwood family could live together in the United States.

We planned to leave Heider's in six days, so we had to get down to business. The newly transferred tapes worked perfectly. We retired the old "master" and inserted the new one back in.

In early October, Lindsey recorded the final lead guitar for "I Don't Want to Know," and Christine added the final organ part on the much shorter version of "Silver Springs." Although we had decided to cut "Silver Springs" from the album, we knew it was great and that we'd use it somewhere someday. We figured we'd finish it with the rest of the album, so that we could use it when we needed it. We used it sooner than expected when it became the B-side of the first single, "Go Your Own Way."

The following day, Lindsey found the perfect high acoustic strumming part for "Second Hand News." The next day, Stevie sang the final harmony vocals for "Dreams."

On the personal front, Cheryl and I went out to Malibu a few times, as well as up to Tahoe to see the seasons change. Recently, we had started going out to Malibu just to feel as if we were out of the city and to breathe in the ocean air. We liked to go to Alice's Restaurant out on the Malibu Pier. We took Scooter with us and walked along the pier at the ocean's edge. That was back in the day when you could still take a dog to the beach in Los Angeles. Now they're banned from most beaches.

Some of the most beautiful days in Malibu happen in October. Farther up the coast was Broad Beach, a private beachfront residential area where many stars live. We swam in the surprisingly warm ocean and tossed a Frisbee for Scooter to catch. We enjoyed these days when we could get them, because I could always feel the pressure of the album hanging over me.

The band had grown tired of Heider's, so Richard and I booked two weeks at the Record Plant in Los Angeles. We wanted to be pampered the way we had been in Sausalito. The Record Plant, L.A., was on Third

Street in West Hollywood. In addition, we wanted to mix the album somewhere else, someplace different. We wanted to have a fresh perspective on this labor of love that we'd been working so hard on for all these months.

Like the one in Sausalito, the Record Plant, L.A., was a complete complex with valet parking and runners everywhere, willing to bring us food, booze, or whatever we requested. It had four studios, connected by a long hallway. It also had a Jacuzzi and two bedrooms, in case someone needed to crash or got lucky. It had a reputation for having great sounds, and it had a beer machine, too! Chris Stone, the co-owner of the Record Plant, described the opening: "The official christening of the Record Plant, L.A., was Halloween 1972. We threw a big party, and much of the local rock royalty were in attendance for the festivities. John Lennon and Yoko Ono came dressed as trees. That kind of says it all."

Like its sister studio in Sausalito, the Record Plant, L.A., also had very attractive studio managers—Rose and Jane shared the position. Both women were tall and thin with long hair. Rose was a brunette Asian, and Jane was a blonde. They got a lot of attention from the other bands, and they both liked to do drugs with us.

On our first day at the Record Plant, L.A., Monday, November 1, 1976, I got to the studio early. I stood outside, watching people drive down busy Third Street. Unlike the carefully secluded Northern California Record Plant, this Record Plant was in the heart of the city near La Cienega Boulevard and the famous Beverly Center, which was under construction at the time.

It amazed me that normal people did things during the day while I was locked inside a windowless room in the dark. While I was waiting for the band, I walked east on Third Street. The Record Plant was owned by two guys, one a famous producer-engineer, Gary Kellgren, who had produced Jimi Hendrix. The other was a businessman, Chris Stone. They parked their unmistakable cars side by side in the lot. Gary had a purple Rolls-Royce with GREED on his license plate, and Chris had a two-door sporty Mercedes with DEDUCT on his. Their message wasn't lost on me.

Lindsey pulled into the lot and parked his relatively middle-class older-model BMW next to the owners' cars. He jumped out of his car, excited to see me. It was unusual that Lindsey was genuinely happy about anything. This day could be pretty good, I thought.

Lindsey said he had a great idea. He thought he knew what "Keep Me There" needed to save it. He told me he wanted to make some drastic edits in the song. When the girls arrived, he told them his idea: they would keep Christine's original, incredible ending, but they would rewrite the verses. We had tried to make the verses better, but we just hadn't been able to do it. The verse melody wasn't special enough.

"The Chain" had sat around for quite a while as a different song with a different title, and none of us felt good about it. We all knew that it had potential—it certainly had a great tag, but the chorus was only okay. We needed something equally special for the first half, something that would unite the band and heal their wounds, something written by the whole band for the very first time.

Lindsey wanted to make the verses very sparse, with only a couple of instruments and three-part harmonies as the lead melody. He wanted me to cut out the current verses and give everyone a blank slate to work with. The question was, though, how could I cut in the right amount of blank tape to prepare for what we would need to record? I figured that we would need more than a minute of tape for each verse and, at fifteen inches per second, I would need more than seventy-five feet of tape for each verse.

I decided that the important thing was to have enough tape, so adding more was a good idea. I ran off what I knew would be enough blank tape to fill the intro and the first verse and also enough tape to fill the second verse. I inserted the blank tape where the old verses had been. Then I established the exact tempo of the song, and I created a metronome to play to.

Mick and Lindsey decided they would play together. Mick got his largest kick drum out, and Lindsey decided to play the Dobro because he had already used it at the end of the song.

We got a great sound from Mick's kick. We needed it, because it was going to be sitting exposed, virtually by itself. I wound the tape to where the beginning of the song used to be. I started the click in their headphones, and Lindsey counted it off, "One, two, three, four." Mick played his famous kick lick that we all know as the intro to "The Chain," and Lindsey played his renowned Dobro licks through the intro and the first verse.

I had inserted about thirty seconds of paper leader between the blank tape and the old chorus section just to make sure that I didn't erase anything important. As it turned out, I had inserted about twenty seconds of extra blank tape. After we got to the end of the verse, I marked and cut the tape. I removed the excess and the paper leader and then attached the new first verse to the first chorus. It worked perfectly.

Then we did the same thing for the second verse. I made the appropriate edits, and we had a new song. We still had the original chord structure from the chorus of "Keep Me There," but that was okay because the writers needed to write something to go with the new kick and the old chorus drums. We also needed something that, especially, worked with that great ending. Christine, Lindsey, and Stevie sat around the piano for about an hour and a half, working on ideas while we played back our new creation.

I was amazed at how easy it had been to completely change a song's direction. Stevie said she thought she had a melody that could work for the song. Ultimately, the writers left the studio and went over to Stevie's house to work things out.

Stevie had written another song with a lot of the words that she incorporated into "The Chain." "I'd asked several times before if I could help on that song, and I'd always been told, 'No, no, no. You can't help us,'" Stevie said, but the melody and the chorus of her song went really well with that great ending of Christine's.

So "The Chain" almost didn't exist, because we couldn't figure out how to make the great pieces into an actual song. We had gone over it again and again during the preceding months, trying to think of something that would go with the ending. If Stevie hadn't had that melody and those words, it never would have happened. That's another example of how undervalued she was by the band at this point.

The next morning, Stevie, Lindsey, and Christine came in, and it was clear that they had a plan. Lindsey replayed the Dobro to the appropriate chords for the new version of the song. He had me erase the old chorus chords to fit the new song, all the way to that well-known tag out where John's famous bass riff enters.

"I remember John's great bass solo, 'Doe daaaa doe da da doe doe doe doe da doooooooe.' And it's like the monsters are coming! And we all loved that," Stevie said after we recorded the final version.

So it was quite poetic that the first song we had recorded in the midst of all of that angst eleven months earlier would be the song that brought the band back together near the end.

The control rooms at the Record Plant, L.A., looked the same as those in Sausalito, with wood and colored cloth walls. We also had the same Tom Hidley–designed fifteen-inch equalized speakers.

As usual, we got to know our speakers by doing some rough mixes. The label was getting nervous because the White Album had slipped significantly on the Billboard album chart. The label had requested that we get "Go Your Own Way" mixed and ready to be released as the first single for radio from *Rumours.*

We thought the Record Plant might be the place to mix the single. We spent all day doing rough mixes. As it turned out, we didn't feel that this studio was right for doing a final radio mix. Richard suggested that we try Sound City, where they had recorded and mixed the White Album.

Sound City had an old Neve console that provided a big, open bottom-end-sounding record. I knew we had a great top-end sound with this album, so I said, "Okay. Let's try it."

Richard called Sound City, but they couldn't schedule us to start for two weeks. So that was our target—we wanted to get the finishing touches on this record in the next two weeks at the Record Plant before we moved over to Sound City for the radio edit. We had started *Rumours* at the Record Plant, so it was fitting that we finish it at the Record Plant. "Why don't we put all of our rough mixes into a running order?" I suggested.

It would be great to try to determine the all-important "running order." A running order is, of course, the sequence of the album's songs. The running order is crucial because it can make or break the album's success. If we put too many slow songs next to one another, people could lose interest; if we put too many fast songs together, the same thing could happen. We wanted to make it compelling and tell a story, musically.

Back then, people listened to music on vinyl records. This meant there were two sides, which also meant that there was a break between side one and side two while the listener turned the record over. So, back then, a running order needed to have two acts, unlike CDs or downloads today, where the entire record plays from start to finish without interruption. Trust me, that can dramatically affect how an artist and a producer decide to sequence the songs.

We deliberated about what to do. Should we put all of the fast songs on side one and all of the mellow ones on side two? Should we build side one's intensity until the end so that listeners would be up and excited when they turned over the record? Should we try to guess what the biggest hits would be and put them on first, or should we spread them throughout the album?

We each wrote out our best guess for a running order. That's what they were, guesses. We wouldn't know which one was any good until we actually, physically, took each piece of tape and placed it in that order, spliced it into the reel, and sat down and listened to the entire side.

When you looked at the assembled reel of songs, it appeared similar to the rings of a tree, with the white splicing tape in thin concentric circles, separating each song and also visibly marking its beginning and ending. Choosing the running order became an all-day event.

What would you have done? Here are all of the songs from *Rumours* in alphabetical order:

"The Chain,"	4:28
"Don't Stop,"	3:11
"Dreams,"	4:14
"Go Your Own Way,"	3:38
"Gold Dust Woman,"	4:51
"I Don't Want to Know,"	3:11
"Never Going Back Again,"	2:02
"Oh, Daddy,"	3:54

"Second Hand News,"	2:43
"Silver Springs,"	4:46
"Songbird,"	3:20
"You Make Loving Fun,"	3:31

You'll notice I've left "Silver Springs" in the song list. That's because we were still trying to decide how to save it, even though Mick had told Stevie that it wasn't going to be on the album. Maybe you can figure out how we could have put it on the album. Including it, the total run time would have been 43:46, pushing the limits to the max of the rule that you could put only 44 total minutes on a record back then. Next, you also have to find a way to break the songs so that neither side exceeds twenty-two minutes—virtually impossible. And then the songs you put together on each side have to sound right in sequence. It made much more sense to cut "Silver Springs."

Dear, sweet Judy Wong—"Wongie"—came by the studio to check on her flock of children that day. She saw that we were working on our running order. Without being asked, she sat on the couch and started writing down her ideas. I thought, Oh, Judy, come on. Why are you even doing this? Do you even know these songs well enough to try this? You're their secretary. But I didn't say any of this.

I had everyone else's list, and then Judy gave me hers:

Side One

1.	"Second Hand News,"	2:43
2.	"Dreams,"	4:14
3.	"Never Going Back Again,"	2:02
4.	"Don't Stop,"	3:11
5.	"Go Your Own Way,"	3:38
6.	"Songbird,"	3:20
	Side one total:	19:05

Side Two

7.	"The Chain,"	4:28
8.	"You Make Loving Fun,"	3:31
9.	"I Don't Want to Know,"	3:11

10.	"Oh, Daddy,"	3:54
11.	"Gold Dust Woman,"	4:51
12.	"Silver Springs,"	4:46
	Side two total (with Silver Springs):	24:41
	Side two total (without Silver Springs):	19:55

I looked down at Judy's sheet of paper. It started mid up-tempo, followed by two songs with great emotion, the first being a probable single. The fourth was fast, the fifth, a rocker, and then the sixth was a real tearjerker.

"Wow, Judy," I said, "this looks like a real nice ride from start to finish. Nice one!"

Richard agreed. Stevie took a quick look at the sheet. "That's it. That's the one," she said. "Let's hear it!"

Christine was sipping champagne and smoking a cigarette. She was especially proud of Judy because they were like sisters.

Lindsey was unsure about putting a ballad right after "Go Your Own Way," his lead-single rocker. "But it could work," he acknowledged.

We took each section of tape from our master mix reel and spliced them one after another until we had both sides assembled in Judy's order.

I added up the running times, and we had 19:05 and 19:55 without "Silver Springs." Adding "Silver Springs" would take either side well past the dreaded twenty-two-minute mark.

There's always a lot of anticipation after you finally assemble a running order but before you play it. You want it to sound great, but often it doesn't, for one reason or another. Then it's back to the drawing board. Cris rewound the tape to the head of side one.

Richard recommended that everyone get a drink or whatever they preferred so that their listening experience would be enhanced. The Brits had their cocktails. The Yanks had some pot and beer. We were ready to listen to the completed rough mix of our labor of love in its potential running order.

Richard, Lindsey, and I sat at the console, directly between the speakers. I turned the speakers up nearly all the way. Stevie, Christine, and Judy were on the couch. Mick and John were on the opposite side of the room from them, near Cris and the tape machines, in their rolling chairs. Scooter was at my feet. "Anytime, Cris," I said. We each listened as one song ended and the next began. "Yes! That worked!" We nodded to one another.

By the time we got to "Never Going Back Again," we were all in heaven. When "Don't Stop" started, it was perfect. Then, when "Go Your Own Way" began, we were all cheering. As it ended, we were all standing. When "Songbird" played, we knew it was the perfect way to end side one. Even Lindsey liked it, despite his initial reservations. We all knew we were on the correct path. Side two played perfectly, too. We had our running order. Thank you, Judy!

With our running order set, we put together a plan. We had twelve days left at the Record Plant, so we decided to put up one song each day and try to finish it before we moved over to Sound City. The first song was "Dreams." As we played the song from the top, we noticed that the verse section along with the pre-chorus section didn't build. The instrumentation stayed the same throughout the section. The first rule of good production is that a song needs to grow, bringing new sounds to the listener's ears as it progresses. At the entrance of the pre-chorus (0:48), just as Mick started playing tom accents, we thought a bell-like sound would be great. We tried sparse whole notes on the piano, played on the top of each of the bars, but that was too heavy.

"What about vibes?" said Richard, suggesting we use a Vibraphone, similar to a child's xylophone, played with mallets hitting tuned metal bars, for an additional part.

"Yeah!" I agreed, even though vibes weren't traditionally used in rock songs. Why not? I thought. What the hell? We were already breaking so many of the rules for recording a rock album. Why not another one?

There happened to be a vibes set in one of the other studios, and we brought it in, set it up, and mic'ed it. Christine played the very simple part.

It was perfect for the song. We added a repeat to each strike so that it went *bling, bling* each time in reverb. Now we had a new sound in the pre-chorus and in the high acoustic strumming of the chorus that we had recently added.

The vocals were good but not complete. We went through the vocals with the intent of filling in the established parts with all of the new ideas that we could think to add. Lindsey, Stevie, and Christine sat around the piano, and Lindsey played triad chords, looking for a perfect blend of harmonies. I had worked with the Beach Boys a few years earlier, and they had done the exact same thing. Brian Wilson sat and played, while the rest of the guys stood and sang.

We completed the vocals all the way to the end, using three-part harmony, doubled. Back in those days, the only way to get all of those vocal parts was to sing each of them, even though they were essentially the same part over and over. Now, with digital recording, all that singers have to do is sing the vocals once, and the rest of the song parts can simply be copied, pasted, and even Auto Tuned, if desired.

Next, we decided that some additional percussion would be nice. We didn't have Mick's congas at the Record Plant, though, so we had to send for them, planning to add them the next day.

Then we put up "Go Your Own Way." This song had to be mixed soon to maximize its impact for AM and FM radio (two very different processes back in the seventies), so we wanted to get it perfected. The lead guitar part still wasn't done. We had recorded some great parts at Criteria in Miami, but I still didn't have a completed solo from Lindsey up through the long tag.

We set up Lindsey's Marshall guitar stack in the big studio. Lindsey rolled up and smoked a big joint, had a shot of cognac and a massive toot, and then he let 'er rip. He was playing his Les Paul turned up so loud that I could hear it through the double walls and the double glass of the control room.

I gave him an open track and had him play from the top so that he could get into the vibe of the track, and we recorded one complete guitar pass. Then he wanted to go again. I put my last open track into RECORD. I already had three solo tracks, but I figured that if we got a better one, I could erase some of the others.

"Why don't you play it with more power licks?" Richard suggested. Lindsey obliged.

At that point, I thought we had it. "Let's leave it set up," I suggested, "and we'll listen to it tomorrow with fresh ears." Richard and Lindsey agreed, and we called it a day.

The congas arrived the next morning. Mick tuned them up, and we got our sound on them. We put "Dreams" up again, and Mick played congas for the chorus. After the congas, we added a few tom fills to the end tag.

"Dreams" was starting to feel as if it was finished, too. Next we pulled up "Don't Stop," and we started looking for the perfect lead guitar part. We got it a few hours later.

Stevie and Christine often got bored and left the control room while we were working on guitar solos. I don't know where they went, but they always came back buzzed.

That night was no exception. It was Friday, and it looked as if everyone was ready for another transcension. Great. Jimmy Page came down to hang out with the band that night. Lindsey left. I don't think he wanted to play with Jimmy. That wasn't surprising, because Lindsey rarely stayed late when it was going to be a party night. Mick also left, so Richard played drums, and Ray played acoustic guitar. Surprisingly, they weren't that bad.

On Monday, November 8, we loaded up "Gold Dust Woman." We hadn't done much work on this song since September. We listened to it from the top.

The end always surprised and amazed me. It had this whole vamp rock tag like "The Chain," all seemingly moving around that great John McVie bass line. How did he do that? It sounded as if he was playing fretless again. He slid up the bass, then he ran down. Check it out at 3:21 in the song. I think this may be one of John's finest bass parts on *Rumours*. I really like his chorus slide, too. And how about Mick's toms—especially in the tag? Those toms were all played on the basic track. With his great instincts, we didn't need to overdub them later.

The vibe of "Gold Dust Woman" was always spooky, even on day one. After we tracked it, Stevie went out and sang about five takes of ghostlike "oohs" and "aahs," with a few screams thrown in for good measure. We used some of those in the final mix.

We played the track a few more times. Then we decided to see how far we could take it to the dark side. We called the rental company to see what fun stuff they had for us. They told us that they had just received an electric harpsichord, and, if we wanted wild, they would send over their Jet phaser, which would wash all of the sounds around.

In about an hour, we had our electric harpsichord and phaser thingy. The harpsichord sounds similar to a piano, but instead of felt hammers hitting the strings, the harpsichord uses plastic arms to pluck the steel strings, making it sound like a tack piano, only richer and fuller. Furthermore, the harpsichord was electric so it could be amplified. When you do this, it begins to sound very bright and edgy. When we ran the song through the phaser, it added an effect like a giant wah-wah pedal, but with many random and constantly changing sounds. If my description isn't clear or makes you curious, then you can hear exactly what it sounds like from the start of the song. Listen for its effects at 0:09, 0:25 seconds, and again at 0:28 seconds. You'll hear exactly what the mighty phaser does.

We initially thought that Christine would play the electric harpsichord, but because of the difficulty with timing that instrument, we decided that we should have Mick play it so that we could take advantage of his intuitive feel to get those wild sounds right. The good news was that Mick had a great feel for the timing. The bad news was that he didn't know how to play a piano. We decided that the best sound from the harpsichord wouldn't come from playing chords. Instead, we wanted single notes, stabbed throughout the song.

To get us in the mood to make this wild dark music, we also used the band's favorite instrument: the transcension. Mick was tooting and swigging cognac, washing it down with Heineken. The rest of the boys smoked a few doobs.

When we started, Mick stood over the keyboard, randomly hitting the keys at the timing he desired. When he hit a good note, it was great, but a note in the wrong key was just ugly. I remember Christine laughing hysterically as she watched Mick gyrating in time over the keys. When Mick was in full transcension mode, he was usually so tooted that he would walk around tight-lipped. He would get so beside himself trying to tell you something. He'd pick up some random object, hold it close, and stare into your eyes, speechless.

"What, Mick?" I asked him. "What are you trying to say?" But he couldn't get anything out.

We dedicated three or four tracks to get this part right. That way, we would be able to pick the best parts and combine them later. Finally, we decided to mark all of the correct keys with a piece of black tape so that all Mick had to do was hit one of the pieces of tape, which would make the track sound much better.

Mick had a beer in one hand and headphones on his ears, and his tall body swayed, pulsating around as he stabbed at those black pieces of tape. When he got it right, it sounded great, but, unfortunately, he kept missing the black tape, still hitting bad notes. We all laughed. It was really funny watching him transcend.

Finally, we got white marking tape and taped off all of the keys except for two areas, one below middle C and the other about two octaves above. Now he had only about eight keys to concentrate on. If he felt like making a low growling sound, he'd hit a key in the low area. When he wanted a higher sound, he'd play the upper region.

This whole thing took about three hours to record. We decided to wait to combine the parts the next day when we were more lucid.

Lindsey told us that he wanted to augment his previous Dobro and guitar parts. For the next three or four hours, we added acoustic guitar chord accents. You can hear these at 0:39.

One thing led to another. Lindsey liked his original Dobro, but this song was starting to get too aggressive and tribal. Lindsey knew that he could pull out the stops and accentuate his earlier parts with similar but wilder-sounding parts, carrying more effects. Mick's harpsichord note stabs provided opportunities to answer with some of the other instruments already on the track. Had the harpsichord been on the track initially, then all of the other instruments would have responded to it appropriately.

Next, Lindsey wanted to replay his electric part and add more aggressiveness into it. I thought the problem was that it also needed to be just a little spookier. As this idea grew, we were able to fine-tune the final parts. We matched his old sound and off he went, getting some great licks, such as the ones at 3:51.

By this time, everyone in the band was getting into the act. They tried banging on metal, howling like werewolves. Finally, we decided to bring in sheets of glass and break them on the beat as the song faded out. Fortunately, we didn't have glass available in our transcended state. We would have to wait until the next day. Then we could buy some glass for our final run at "Gold Dust Woman."

The next morning, Ray went to the nearest glass store and bought sheets of glass for us to destroy. Stevie sang a new lead vocal tag from 3:03. Up until that session, she had left the vocal in that part of the song empty. The last two minutes were only instrumental. She wanted to wait until all of the instruments on the track were recorded, so that she could sing along with them spontaneously.

The band had been working their way toward this vocal recording session from the time Stevie had written "Gold Dust Woman." Everything had to be just right so that we could put the frosting on the cake.

Now that we had the new guitar parts and the electric harpsichord, the stage was set to complete the big finish of the song. We worked on some miscellaneous drums, deciding to save the big theatrical piece for that evening.

How do you record someone breaking a sheet of glass? Very carefully, it turns out.

One of the iso booths at the Record Plant was very reverberant or "live." The walls were mirrored and the floor was tiled. Breaking glass in that room would be easy to record. Ray had picked up various-size sheets of glass. The largest one was about three feet by six. Most were about three by four.

We set up a tall wooden ladder in the room. Mick insisted that as the percussionist, he be the one to break the glass. This didn't require any musicianship, but Mick insisted. He stood halfway up the seven-foot ladder, wearing a raincoat, a hat, goggles, and rubber gloves.

Ray handed Mick a sheet of glass, which Mick held in one of his gloved hands. In the other, he held a large carpenter's hammer. We had three mics in the room to get a good stereo recording. The hard part was trying to keep Mick from laughing and ruining the recording.

At first, Mick wanted us to play the music so that he could break the glass at the right time in the music. We soon found out that breaking glass isn't that easy, especially on the beat. On Mick's first attempt, the hammer bounced off the glass. On the second, the glass bounced off the hammer and out of Mick's hand, crashing into a million pieces on the floor. Mick laughed uproariously.

Richard and I decided that we had to narrow Mick's concentration. We told him to break the glass without the music—we'd record it to blank tape and simply play the versions of breaking glass that sounded best onto the song where we wanted them to be.

So, we recorded Mick making small, medium, and large glass crashes. Then we picked up the larger shards of glass and dropped them again, creating a sound as if it was raining glass. It took us three or four hours to get this part of the session right.

"What I remember about recording 'Gold Dust Woman' were the howls at the end, the 'Awwrrchh!' that was that coyote-wolf thing. And we threw down some glass," Stevie told me later.

Soon we had the glass-breaking parts inserted in the track, and it was time to record Stevie's vocal tags. The energy was certainly exciting. We knew we were putting the final touches on "Gold Dust Woman"—and on the whole album, for that matter.

We ordered gourmet Italian food from down the street. I decided to take a walk while we waited for the food to arrive. Richard and Cris were playing with the new sounds and adding delays and reverbs to "Gold Dust Woman."

When I got back, Cheryl and I decided to get a 50-cent beer out of the machine. We got our beers, then I sent her back inside. I wanted to clear my head, so I took a rare stroll down the Record Plant's long hallway, past the "rack room," past bedroom 1, past bedroom 2, past the Jacuzzi room, past studios A and B, and out through the traffic office.

"Hello, ladies," I said to Rose and Jane, without pausing to hear their replies.

I went outside into the Record Plant's east parking lot. I opened my beer and lit my cigarette. It was starting to get cold in L.A. The temperature was probably in the 60s. It was already dark, and the traffic on Third Street was "slow and go" as people headed home from work.

I could never get used to daylight savings time. It had been only a week or so since we had turned back the clocks. I couldn't get used to walking into the studio when the sun was up but walking out when it was dark. Where did the day go?

"If I ever build a studio," I told Cheryl that evening, "it'll have either windows or a big clock."

My ears were still ringing from the loud volume at which we'd been listening, and it felt good just to hear the night sounds of L.A. Rose and Jane came out and told me that our food had been delivered. They both looked hot in their tight pants.

But I thought that Cheryl was definitely hotter. The three of us stood there for a moment, smoking our cigarettes in the parking lot. It was filled with expensive new Mercedes and Gary Kellgren's purple Rolls-Royce. I guess that was a seventies L.A. moment.

Back inside studio C, everyone was eating. Stevie sat on the couch with a plate in her lap. Christine, Mick, and John were out in the lounge, and Lindsey was eating with Richard at the console. Cris Morris brought my dinner to me, and I sat down at the console, too.

I could feel someone staring at me. I turned to my right and saw that it was Scooter, his beagle ears up in full begging position. I cut off a piece of my chicken and held it at the end of my fork. He took it right off the end and swallowed it whole.

After Scooter and I finished my dinner, I made my way over to the couch. "Stevie, how do you feel about singing?" I asked.

"I think I'll be ready in about an hour," she said. Cheryl and Stevie were chatting together on the sofa.

"Okay," I said. "I'll work on the mix for a while."

A little while later, Stevie was ready. A small bump, a joint, and some Courvoisier in her tea had moved up the timetable. Stevie was ready to perform. During dinner, a journalist named Jim Grissim had come to the studio to interview Stevie. He seemed like a nice enough guy. Somehow, he seemed to know that Stevie was going to perform that night. In *Crawdaddy* magazine, he wrote,

Stevie did the first take standing in a fully lit studio. The song required a lot of power and an equal measure of feeling. As take followed take, Stevie gradually withdrew. The lights were turned down; a chair was brought in for her, and she wrapped herself in an oversized cardigan to keep warm. Forty minutes later she was barely visible in the darkness—a mere waif wearing flight-deck earphones, huddled in a chair while next to her on a stool sat a convalescent stash of Kleenex, a Vicks inhaler, a bottle of Calistoga mineral water and a box of throat lozenges. Stevie had achieved an astonishing command of the material and on the eighth take she sang the song straight through, nailing it perfectly.

At the end of the song, Stevie was howling like a witch on fire. Cheryl looked at me and nodded. I knew what she was thinking: I told you she was a witch! I could see it in her eyes, but I didn't care. At that time, I still thought Stevie was great—just a very cool gal.

The label continued to pressure us to get "Go Your Own Way" ready for release. When we put out "Go Your Own Way" as a single, then we'd have to use another song on the other side. Someone suggested "Silver Springs." I don't remember whose idea that was. In those days, singles were released as 45 rpm records, which were about six inches in diameter, with a second song on the other side.

We went to Sound City to mix *Rumours*. This was where the band had recorded their previous album. Sound City was an older studio and somewhat rundown. It was out in the middle of the San Fernando Valley and was definitely a longer drive for most of us than to any of the other studios where we had worked.

Sound City had old Neve consoles, which should have sounded excellent with our music. We tried mixing "Go Your Own Way" and "Never Going Back Again," but the EQ wasn't as precise as we wanted. Then Lindsey, frustrated as the rest of us were, suggested that we had had such good luck mixing "Rhiannon" at Heider's that we should go back there to mix *Rumours*. So back to Heider's we all went.

It was mid-November when we returned to Heider's, to mix the mono and stereo versions of "Go Your Own Way" and "Silver Springs." We were back where we had started at the beginning of 1976, almost a year earlier.

I walked into good old studio 1 at Heider's. "Hello, old friend," I said to the room. Richard and Cris came in a few minutes later.

"This is where it all started, Cutlass," Richard said.

Cris followed up with his usual sarcasm. "You guys actually mixed 'Rhiannon' in this hole?" I didn't point out the fact that "Rhiannon" had been a success, peaking at number 11 on the U.S. singles charts in June of that year and helping to drive the White Album to number 1.

Cris aligned the tape machine to the tape's tones. I set up all of my outboard mixing gear, special sound compressors, effects processors, and

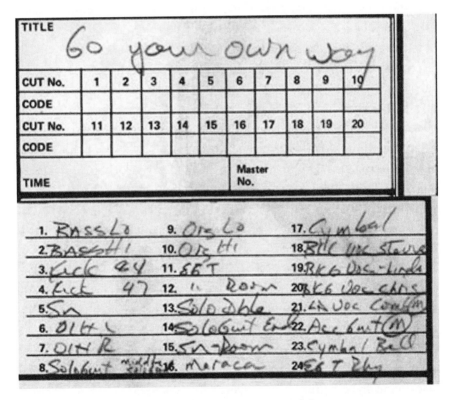

Here's our "Go Your Own Way" tracksheet.

EQ boxes. We put down new masking tape on the console and marked each channel with the instrument that would be playing through it.

The reason we were making new mixes of these songs was that back then, most singles played on AM mono radio stations. We had to mix the song in mono because we could never be certain what a stereo song would sound like when it was played in mono. So we had to make a mix that sounded as good as possible in both stereo and mono when coming through an AM mono car radio speaker, such as the ones in the center of the dashboards in seventies cars.

The worst thing about making those mixes was that we had to listen to them on tiny, crappy, four-inch Aura tone speakers. Usually, the radio stations wouldn't play songs that were longer than three and a half minutes, either, so we had to shorten both songs considerably for airplay. We had edited "Go Your Own Way" down to 3:34. The FM stations would play shortened stereo mixes of the 45-rpm singles if the album versions weren't available.

It took us about six hours to get this mix close, always stopping to listen to another crappy speaker or going out to one of our cars to listen to a cassette. We were constantly making small adjustments to the tone of the track or the vocal level. Today, of course, we don't worry about any of this because we live in a stereo world. Back then, I could only dream of a day when everything would be broadcast in stereo. Hello, future! Hello, now!

Lindsey stayed with us the whole day while we worked on the radio edits. Mick and John came down around dinnertime to hear how the songs were sounding.

Finally, we were ready. Cris loaded a fresh roll of one-quarter-inch tape on the recorder and one on the old mono one-quarter-inch recorder. We were making both the AM and the FM versions at the same time. The first would be a stereo mix that would fold down to mono perfectly and the other would be a full mono mix made especially for cheap TV speakers.

All of the lads had learned their moves on the console, each making adjustments to his assigned fader or volume level to keep his assigned instrument from getting lost as everything was joined together. Then a joint was passed around the room, followed by a midsize hit of coke—just enough to inspire without confusing.

"Roll 'em, Cris," I said.

"Rolling, Sire," he responded.

I reached over and hit the slate button on the console. "'Go Your Own Way,' single mix, take one," I said and pressed PLAY on the 24-track remote at my side.

Lindsey rubbed his hands together, excited and ready for his baby to be born. As the song played from the top, we all hunched over the console, making our moves like precision machines. Of course, the guitar solos were all mine, because all of the components of the solos had to be performed by me with just the right amount of flair and style. As I made the last moves on the lead guitar lick at 3:21, "Dicky Dash" was eloquent in pulling down the master fader, taking the end of the song to silence.

Lindsey slapped Richard and me on the back, "Yeah!" he exclaimed.

"Anybody hear any problems?" I asked. No one had any complaints. Cris leadered the two master tapes.

"Should we do one more for insurance?" I asked.

"No, we nailed it," Lindsey said.

Cris gave a cassette to each of us to listen to at home. We left the board set up in case we needed to make changes to the mix in the morning. We got out of the studio fairly early that evening.

The next day we mixed "Silver Springs," finally! Stevie, Lindsey, and Mick were there the whole day. John came later. Mick wanted to make sure that everything went smoothly and that Stevie was happy after all she had gone through with her song.

We got the stereo and mono mixes made before it got dark. We all went home happy that night. I felt as if it was the beginning of the end. When I got home, Cheryl told me that she had heard on the news that Patty Hearst had been released from prison on bail the day before. I remember thinking, Well, at least someone got out of jail. I still had some time to go before I'd be free.

Nevertheless, I was beginning to see the light at the end of the tunnel.

14

The Final Mix

Years later, Peter Green told me that he wasn't sure about me until he heard my guitar solo on "Go Your Own Way."

—*Lindsey Buckingham*

It was the first of December, and we were about to start the final phase of making an album—the mix. The mixing process can make or break an album. After all of the hard work and time we'd spent recording this album, we wanted to squeeze every drop of sonic power and emotion out of each song.

Several months earlier, our friend Billy Youdelman had told Richard about a studio called Producer's Workshop up on Hollywood Boulevard. The studio had been built by a tech, and it was supposed to have all custom equipment that had been cleaned up to sound fantastic. It had specially modified 24-track tape machines with all of the transformers removed so that the sound came out pure and open.

Not only was all of the gear simplified and cleaned out of anything that could hurt the sound, but the rooms were built like big acoustic microscopes where we could hear each and every aspect of our sounds, enabling us to work on them the way a surgeon uses a scalpel.

Richard and I were very excited when we first heard about this studio. We drove over with Cris to check it out. Producer's Workshop was up on Hollywood Boulevard, east of the famous part, at the edge of the broken part, in a single-story building that had two studios inside.

From the outside, it looked ordinary and modest. The parking was in the rear of the building. We drove up the driveway and turned left, then parked by the studio door. As I got out, I looked up at the nearby foothills and saw that the Hollywood sign was much bigger than I was used to seeing it. The Hollywood sign had been erected on the side of the Hollywood Hills. Just below the sign was a private reservoir, Lake Hollywood, which had played a significant role in the movie *Earthquake* a few years earlier. In the movie, a giant 8.3 earthquake cracked the lake's 210-foot-tall, 50-year-old concrete dam, and a 300-foot wave cascaded into the canyons above Hollywood, washing most of Hollywood out into the Pacific Ocean. Sounds tragic, but I wouldn't be surprised if some people in America think that would be a good thing,

Producer's Workshop was directly below the reservoir. I knew that scene in the movie would become a source of tension and laughter if we told Mick about it when he was sufficiently high.

We walked into the studio, and the studio receptionist, Carol Harris, greeted us. She was beautiful and had long blond hair and deep dark eyes. Richard and I exchanged a glance. I love this place already! I thought.

Richard pretended to trip over his feet. He laughed and looked up at Carol. "A guy could fall for you, honey," he said, sounding a little like Rodney Dangerfield.

"Let me show you around the studio," Carol said.

Just then Dave Lebarre, the chief tech, came in. "I can show them around," he said to Carol, and she went back to her reception desk. Damn!

"Bye! Call me!" Richard yelled back at Carol, as Dave led us into the mix room.

When Dave pulled open the door to the studio, we noticed that it wasn't a rectangle. The door was cut wider at the bottom than at the top, and it opened up and out toward us because the wall was angled.

Richard, Lindsey, and Carol—guess which guy won the girl.

I held the first door open because there was a second door to go through. All good studios have double doors, each made of solid wood. Between the two doors, there is usually about six inches of space to provide an air lock—a sound lock, really. The second door opened the opposite way, up and away from us. So Dave actually pushed the door uphill to go inside the specially built mix room.

The room was small, about fifteen-by-twenty-feet, but it had reasonably high, ten-foot ceilings. Yet no wall was parallel to another. Every wall was either angled up or had a peak in the middle. Parallel walls are bad news for creating clear sound, because the sound waves produced by the big fifteen-inch speakers just reflect back and forth off each of the opposing walls, creating bumps or dips in the sound, fooling the listener.

Dave had designed the room so that none of these walls reflected back on another. He had also built a flat, absorbent acoustic panel that hung over the flat portion of the mixing board so that nothing bounced off it and back into the mixer's face. This studio was a real hot rod.

Cris gave Dave our 24-track master reel so that we could do a test mix. Because we had just mixed "Silver Springs" at Wally Heider's, we decided to mix it here and compare the two versions. Dave put the two-inch tape on the specially modified Stevens 24-track machine. He rewound the tape to the tones section so that he could align the machine's low and high frequency output to our norms.

I had decided at the beginning of this project to do something unusual in the business. These 24-track machines had two speed choices: fifteen inches per second and thirty inches per second. It was common knowledge that 30 ips sounded better and quieter. It was better because the faster a tape moves over the head when it records, the better the high frequency response. It's quieter because the faster it moves, the less tape hiss is heard. At 30 ips, however, the bottom end gets a little washed out.

It seems I always have to be different. I decided to use the lower speed and record the whole album at 15 ips to get a tighter bottom end. To compensate for the reduced high end and the increased noise, I had recorded every track through a 24-track rack of Dolby Noise Reduction, which allowed me to lower my recording level by three decibels. This meant that I wasn't doing the usual oversaturation of the tape, which disfigures the high frequency transients.

As a result, we got lower noise and a cleaner top end than if we had recorded at 30 ips, the way everyone else did. We also used 50 percent less tape. Genius!

So, while Dave and Cris were aligning the machine to our tones, Richard and I escaped from the studio and made our way over to the front desk to talk to Carol for the next fifteen minutes or so until the alignment was done. Dave buzzed Carol over the intercom and said he was ready for us.

I went back to the studio, and Richard told me that he'd be in soon. As I pulled the first heavy door open, I heard Richard say, "Now where were we, my darling?"

I pushed the inside door open and jumped out of the way as they both closed, sealing us inside the mixing room. I was very excited to hear how our songs sounded in this room.

Cris had rewound the tape to the top of "Silver Springs." I pulled up the expensive ergonomic rolling desk chair, sat down, and rolled up to the console. Dave was standing over me to help if I had any questions about the console. He pointed to the volume control to my right. I turned the volume up about halfway and pressed PLAY on the remote.

The meters started to move. I pushed up the first eight faders, containing the bass and the drums. They immediately blasted out of the speakers. I reached up and positioned the pan pots in their proper positions. This console had buttons and a panner. If I wanted a sound to come out of the left speaker, I pushed the left button, and I pushed the right button for the right speaker. If I wanted the sound to come out of the center, then I pushed both buttons. If I wanted a sound to come out slightly left or right of center, however, only then would I engage the pan to place the sound anywhere in between, left or right. I quickly found the proper balance for the first eight faders. It sounded great!

Since I had jumped the gun and started playing the tape before Cris could mark all of the faders with their correct instrument names, I rolled away and let him take care of that. Cris took a one-inch piece of white masking tape and stretched it above the faders and just below the mute buttons in the space provided for this tape by the console manufacturer.

Then he wrote the name of the instrument and the song title at one end, so that Richard and I could quickly locate all of the song parts, and the tape could be saved in case we needed to remix a song later. Cris copied the instruments off the master track sheet and onto the tape.

Mixing is a make-or-break part of the recording process. A good mix can make a song; a bad one will kill it. I always picture my speakers as my canvas and my console as the tool that helps me create a sonic image that's as high, wide, and deep as possible. The way I see it, there's a mix space extending about eight feet beyond the speakers. My sound field extends up to the ceiling and down to the floor, with the bass and the kick drum down at floor level, and the cymbals and the guitar harmonics at the ceiling.

So, if the speakers are ten feet apart, the mixer has about eighty square feet of space to work with. The consoles allow you to adjust each

This was our master track sheet for "Silver Springs."

instrument's or track's volume in real time, its speaker position, and the amount of bass, midrange, or treble that an instrument has (which becomes the sound's character). You can add effects to a track, too, such as reverb to a vocal to make it sound angelic or a delay to the echo to make it more pronounced. You can also add delay to an electric guitar and place the delay on the opposite speaker from the guitar, to make it seem much wider and more powerful.

You can even add multiple effects at the same time. For instance, sometimes I add high frequency to a snare drum to make it *sss-nap* or add bottom end so that it has more impact together with the kick drum. I helped make the character of "Dreams" darker by placing more emphasis on most of the instruments so that they had more bottom end. Then I could give some instruments more top end to make them stand out, such as the phasing on Mick's high hat or the sibilance of Stevie's vocal.

Most of the time, an instrument also has a rough spot that needs to be taken down a little. For instance, in "Silver Springs" the kick drum was always powerful, but it had an annoying bump in its upper bottom that caused the speaker to make a nasty popping sound when it was turned up too loud. Picture all of the instruments as brush strokes, and EQ can change the shape and color of each stroke so that everything fits perfectly together and jumps out at you and becomes a symphony to your ears.

Finally—and most important—there are the song's dynamics. As instruments are added to a song, their relationships change. Some instruments' volume or dynamics need to be controlled. That is why the closest thing to an engineer on the console is the faders. This allows the engineer to "ride levels," which means that he can reach out and move the volume sliders up and down as he sees fit. For me, this is the most fun part of mixing, and it's what kept Kelly Kotera from getting this gig. Kelly had relied on computer-assisted faders to remember his moves that first day and make them for him, but when his computer died, he was in trouble, and I got this gig.

A good mix is rarely static. It's fluid, always changing. Back then, when I started learning to mix, a lot of the fun came from the fact that we didn't have computers to help us ride levels or to move faders for us. Like everyone who'd come before me, I had to learn how to do it myself.

When it came to mixing, it took us a long time to perfect each song. We'd listen to each one for six to eight hours, and everyone in the band offered suggestions. When the EQ, the effects, and the panning were perfect, and we had all listened to the four-minute song over and over, each of us—including every member of the band—made suggestions, such as, "Ken, where the beef in my kick?" which Mick may have asked. Or, "I don't like my vocal sound," Christine may have said. Or, "Ken, can you add some more fairy dust to my vocal?" Stevie may have requested. We weren't finished with a song until all of the complaints were resolved, and everyone was happy with absolutely everything.

By this time, we had all of the faders marked in their optimal positions, and it was time to play the console. I usually handled guitar and vocal levels, and Richard handled the drums and the bass. Each of us kept those instruments prominent so that they didn't get lost in the mix. Then, when we were ready, we hit PLAY, and I would ride the vocal up if one of the words got buried when a hot guitar lick came in during the first chorus.

I pushed it up loudly to make it jump. Then Richard answered back with one of Mick's tom fills or John's bass lines. When the guitar solo started, I tried to make it tear off everyone's heads. Richard pushed up the rhythm section. With my other hand, I supported the guitar solo with Christine's keyboards. By the next chorus, everything was back at its starting mark, and I shoved up the tag chorus vocal for a big finish.

On some mixes, we needed more hands. Mick, Lindsey, or Christine would reach in and help. Richard conducted. "Okay, Chris, mute that key part," he said. "Mick, now here it comes—ready, three, two, one."

When we all had our performances and the high-fives were flying, we'd load up a two-track and record the mixes, stopping when someone made a mistake or pushed something up too far. Eventually, we got it right. Then we listened to it to see if we liked it. During these sessions, the band tended to avoid booze and drugs. There was an occasional hit of pot—at least by me—but otherwise mixing got too complicated.

That's what mixing *Rumours* was like. Of course, today computers assist engineers, remembering each of the rides so that the engineer can work on other aspects of the mixing process. Yet computers can't replace how dedicated we were to our music. After we finished each song, we usually made cassettes for each of the band members so they could listen to them in their cars or at home. We left the mix set up for the next day so that we could listen to it with fresh ears, fixing any small problems in the morning before going on to the next song.

On that first day, Richard finally came back into the studio after chatting up Carol. By that point, Cris had finished labeling the board.

"How'd you do?" I asked him.

"Not bad," he said. "I made her laugh." She really wants *me*, I thought, smiling at Richard.

We started to mix "Silver Springs." The console was amazing. I could hear everything so well that we were able to smooth out the rough edges in about an hour. But "Silver Springs" was an easy mix. All we needed to do was push up the vocals, enhance the acoustic accents, ride the bass licks, and slightly adjust the tag background vocals.

Richard called Lindsey and Mick, telling them that the mixing on "Silver Springs" had gone really well. "We really want to work here," Richard told them, inviting them to come down and listen.

Mick and Lindsey arrived at Producer's Workshop about an hour later, and they loved what we had done. Lindsey proved the point, rubbing his hands together again. We had found the studio where we were going to finish mixing our baby.

Richard and I went outside for a smoke, waiting for Lindsey, but he didn't come out to join us. Finally, we went back into the studio to find him, and he was talking to Carol. Neither of them seemed to notice that Richard and I had walked back into the building. Carol and Lindsey would eventually become a couple, and after their relationship ended, she would write a book about Fleetwood Mac and how Lindsey had abused her. Interestingly, at the time of this writing, Lindsey has done some interviews saying that he's finally able to relax and enjoy himself because of his children and home life. Congratulations, Lindsey! Welcome to the club.

At the end of that day, Richard and I headed home, happy about our work, but he was a little dejected personally. "Great job, today," he said.

"Yeah." I agreed. "Have a good night." I drove home without any music.

Herbie Worthington had done the cover shoot for *Rumours* in November, which also created a controversy within the band. By this point in December, the proofs from the photo shoot had come back, and the band was making the all-important decision about which shot to use. Although they all agreed about which shot from that session was best, some weren't happy about the fact that the shot was an artistic one, instead of a photo that included all of Fleetwood Mac's members.

The title, *Rumours*, had been chosen because it didn't reflect a particular song, yet it managed to capture the entire vibe of the album.

I think the album's cover achieves the same effect. Herbie had shot the cover of the White Album, and because of the ultimate success of that record, he was asked to come back and shoot the cover of *Rumours*. Instead of shooting a standard photo, Herbie had focused on a couple of members of the band to capture the essence of the music that they were producing. It was also an artistic extension of the cover shot of *Fleetwood Mac*, where John McVie was subserviently trying to catch a large bubble from Mick Fleetwood's aristocratic champagne glass.

The result of the *Rumours* photo shoot was the iconic shot of Stevie Nicks and Mick Fleetwood, each wearing their idiosyncratic stage garb that evokes a different time—past or future, it's hard to say. Mick wears his balls below his waist, and Stevie has on one of her famous twirling outfits. The cover shot of this book is one of the photos from that session. Herbie told me that Mick wanted the *Rumours* cover to be something special—a work of art. Herbie decided to shoot Mick and Stevie together because Mick wanted something "Shakespearean."

Later, Herbie told me that he had picked the cover shot before he showed the band the rest of the shots. "I knew immediately which shot it should be," Herbie said. "I blew it up to album-cover size before anyone in the band saw the shots. When I gave them the contact sheet, they chose the same shot that I had. I knew they would choose that one because it was so perfect *for Rumours.*

"Lindsey has never forgiven me for not being on the *Rumours* cover," Herbie told me later. "Lindsey came up to me and said, 'I wish I could have been on my own cover.'"

Herbie had tried to explain to Lindsey that the cover idea was about trying to create a piece of art. It wasn't about trying to promote individual members of the band. I'm still close friends with Herbie, and over the years, we've talked about this many times.

Cover jealousy wasn't limited to Lindsey, though. When we finished *Tusk* in 1979, the only shot on the cover was one of Scooter biting my shoe. Stevie wasn't happy about that at all. Of course, she had been fine being only one of the two band members on the cover of *Rumours*. She had not suggested that Lindsey, Christine, and John be included on that cover.

When the band decided that the cover of *Tusk* should be a picture of Scooter biting my foot, Stevie told me that she had put a hex on Scooter. Then, when he died four years later in 1983, Stevie said, "I'm glad, Ken. Your dog had that album cover that should have been mine."

It seemed a little brutal to me, but Stevie and Christine had never liked Scooter much, maybe because he was too much of a guy, always pestering their little dogs. All of the guys in the band really liked Scooter, though. Maybe that's part of the reason that the guys approved the *Tusk* cover. It was a subtle victory in the battle of the sexes within the band.

We launched into the full-on mixing the following week.

As I drove in to the studio, I saw that the city of Hollywood was hanging lighted Christmas decorations over the street. They looked a little out of place in this rundown part of town.

At this point, we had already put in nearly a year of work—almost three thousand hours for me, which was more than sixty hours a week on average. But I had had a few weeks off here and there, so during the weeks when we worked, I was often putting in an average of seventy to eighty hours a week. And, of course, there had been those weeks where I'd racked up more than a hundred hours.

We had two weeks left, which gave us about one day to mix each song. After finishing "Silver Springs," we decided to work on "Don't Stop" next.

That day Cris, Richard, and I were the first ones to the studio, as usual, but we liked it that way. We preferred to have the first couple of hours alone with the mix before any of the band members arrived. In fact, when I start mixing, I usually ask the artist to leave the room for an hour or two while I reestablish contact with the heart of the song. A lot of artists are reluctant to give their engineers this time, but I've learned over the years not to accept no for an answer.

So, if you're an up-and-coming recording engineer, then you've got to learn how to tell your artist something like, "I can't listen with your ears. I have to listen with my ears. And when you talk, it makes it hard for me to listen with mine. So, you have to let me do this my way."

The track sheet for "Don't Stop."

Richard left me alone to play with the sounds on "Don't Stop." The console had the ability to do wonders with our sounds. "Silver Springs" sounded fantastic when I played it at home.

Stevie called me to say how excited she was after she had listened to her song. "It's like I'm hearing it for the first time," she said to me. She was right. With the console and the speakers at Producer's Workshop, it seemed as if we could disassemble and reassemble each song in a way that made all of them more powerful and exciting.

After I had worked on "Don't Stop" for about an hour, Richard came back into the control room. He stood and listened. "Sounds great, Cutlass! Now get out! It's my turn."

During those two weeks, Richard and I did this often, trading off to improve the mix. I would move the song in a direction, and my ideas would inspire him. I'd go away for an hour or so, and he'd polish the sounds in his unique way. At this point, the artists turned their creative work over to the mixers, trusting us to enhance their sonic vision. However, they frequently came into the room and gave us feedback. The mix wasn't done until everyone was happy.

When I was able to leave the studio because Richard was mixing, I passed the time talking to Carol. She told me that she had already finished her Christmas shopping. I hadn't had time to give the holiday a thought. It was nice talking to Carol. With Richard and me trading off, I could finally find time to flirt with a girl outside the studio. I wish I could have done that with Nina back in Sausalito. It was great to talk to someone about something other than the album. Cheryl came down and hung out with Carol, too.

Lindsey frequently spent time with Carol, speaking quietly to her, with their heads close together when Stevie was there. I think he was trying to avoid any more trouble with his ex-girlfriend while they were so close to finishing the album.

Despite how well the mixing was going, the album continued to take its toll on us. It was always on our minds, calling to us, nagging at us, like a spoiled child who needed constant attention.

When I drove to and from the studio, I continued to notice all of the Christmas decorations. I was having trouble accepting that it was already the Christmas season, again. I was numb and exhausted. I had no idea whether this album was even any good.

"The two songs I've heard sound fantastic," Carol told me on one of my mini-breaks. "I especially like . . ."

Then Lindsey walked in the door, and Carol's eyes lit up. She didn't even finish her sentence. Instead, she greeted Lindsey. I never learned which song she especially liked.

Lindsey was also happy to see Carol. They talked for a moment, then he turned to me. "Hey, Ken. How's it going in the studio?"

"Really good," I said. "Richard's working on the mix of 'Don't Stop' now."

"Would you like a brandy coffee or spiced cider?" Carol asked Lindsey.

"You choose," he said.

I went back to the control room. Richard was playing with the EQ on "Don't Stop," and it sounded great. He had compressed a few instruments.

Christine walked in and sat next to Richard, listening. "It sounds fucking great, Richard!" she said. It did. Richard slid over to make room for me.

I remember Christine remarking on how we were all bored to death with our songs after a year of working on them, but then something amazing happened during the mixing process. By the time we finished mixing the album, we knew there was something really exciting about it. Everybody was high because it just sounded so good, so good.

One by one, we put our finished mixes on the shelf. As Christmas approached, we started to relax. By the time we were ready to break for Christmas, we had averaged one song a day. We had finished "The Chain," "Dreams," "Oh, Daddy," "Songbird," "You Make Loving Fun," and "Second Hand News." Our nicknames for the songs fell away as our stereo master reel got bigger.

With "Songbird," I experimented with putting in Lindsey's acoustic guitar part and acoustic solo, along with John's bass. They sounded pretty good, but in the end we decided to cut those parts and leave it open.

One day, as I was mixing the song alone, I put on a set of headphones and sang along to the mix. I got a strange feeling that I was being watched. I slowly turned around to see the entire band standing behind me, laughing at my horrible voice! I never did that again.

The band took off the week before Christmas. We decided to resume mixing on December 27. We had seven songs mixed, and we were in the home stretch.

Cheryl and I spent a white Christmas at Lake Tahoe with my folks. The Brits in the band went to England for the holiday. Lindsey went to Northern California, and Stevie went east to see her parents. Richard stayed in Los Angeles, and Cris went back to the East Coast.

While Cheryl and I were at Lake Tahoe, that area had one of the biggest snowstorms in years. It snowed eight feet in two days. Cheryl and I were stuck in Tahoe and couldn't get back to Los Angeles.

I called the studio on the next mix day to let the band know that I was trapped in Tahoe because the roads in the area were all closed. I talked to

Cris, who told me that they had decided to mix "I Don't Want to Know" next, and that it was sounding pretty good. They told me not to worry.

The next day the snow was supposed to stop, so I thought that Cheryl and I would be able to make it home. The sky did clear as we headed out at eight in the morning. Unfortunately, we had to drive with chains on our tires most of the way. By the time we got home, it was nearly midnight.

When I reached my place, I called the studio. Richard had a frantic tone in his voice. They were trying to mix "Go Your Own Way," but they hadn't been able to duplicate my moves on Lindsey's lead guitar tag-out.

I had built that tag from assorted guitar parts. I thought that I had made the fader moves transparent, but this was when I learned the truth about Lindsey's and my famous guitar solo. I had actually played the console as if it were a musical instrument. In fact, I learned that it was. I almost felt as if I was one of the musicians in the band.

Richard and Lindsey begged me to come down to the studio, even though it was already after midnight. I drove the twenty minutes from Burbank to Hollywood. When I got to the studio, everyone in the band was still there, and they were certainly happy to see me.

The track sounded amazing, but I made a few tweaks to the mix. Then I hit RECORD on the mix machine and played Lindsey's solo in the tag. You can hear a couple of my transitions to his many solo ideas at 2:53 and 3:14. At 3:22, there's a lick where I rode up especially high. To this day, Mick says that that's his favorite part of "Go Your Own Way."

When I was done mixing the song, Lindsey grabbed me and lifted me up with both of his arms. "Caillat, you're worth your weight in gold!" he said.

We got the mix that night, and, for the live tour, Lindsey listened to our mix over and over, learning to play the solo the way I had put his brilliant licks together. He made it sound even better than the record because, at that point, it really was his performance. All I had done was remember where all of the pieces were that he had played, and I assembled them in the right order for him. That's teamwork.

That week we finished "Go Your Own Way," "I Don't Want to Know," and "Never Going Back Again." We worked right up to New Year's Eve.

We still hadn't mixed "Gold Dust Woman," so we finished it on the day after New Year's. Then we decided that we wanted to try to improve on our first mix of "Don't Stop." We did that in about four hours. Next, we finally put together the running order that Judy had suggested back in November, only without "Silver Springs." At least it was already on the B side of "Go Your Own Way."

So, on January 4, 1977, twenty-four days short of a year since the day I had left home to start this wonderful, exhausting, life-changing adventure, our songs were mixed and sequenced. Now, all we had to do was choose the correct spreads between the songs. We considered it an art to select the precise number of seconds of silence to put between one song and another. If the break was too short, the transition would feel too abrupt, and that would disturb the flow. If it was too long, the listener's mood could be broken. By Friday, I had made copies of the final album for everyone in the band so that they could take a cassette home and listen until their hearts were content.

Stevie's brother, Chris, lived in the Hollywood Hills above the Hollywood Bowl in an old area called Whitley Terrace, and Stevie wanted to have an end-of-album party. She invited all of us to come up to Chris's house so that she could play the album for the first time for our friends.

I invited my friend Chiggy and his wife to the party. Up to that point, none of my friends had heard the album. Stevie had also arranged for a screening of *Snow White and the Seven Dwarfs*, because the label had given her a copy of the film. It looked as if it was going to be a great night.

We all arrived around seven that evening and had a drink or two and maybe a hit or two of pot. When the time came to play the album, I got out my Revox two-track and hooked it into Chris Nicks's stereo system and rewound the tape to the beginning. Chris suggested that we should all get comfortable while we listened to the new album. Everyone settled in with another drink. I pressed PLAY. Then I took a seat next to Cheryl.

I always clench up a little when I play back anything that I've produced for strangers to listen to, especially when it's going to play on someone else's home speakers. The album wouldn't be mastered until the next week, but I still thought it sounded pretty good.

After the first side was finished, everyone applauded. When side two finished, the guests whistled and applauded.

Richard, Cheryl, and I went outside and joined Mick and Lindsey, who were looking at the view of the city below. Chiggy came out, but he didn't say anything to us.

"Well, what did you think, Chiggy?" I finally asked him.

"To be honest with you, I didn't hear a hit." He took a swig from his drink and looked away from me, out over the city.

All of us who had worked so hard on the record looked at one another in disbelief. No hits? How could that be? I was devastated.

To this day, I still love this story because it reveals so much about musicians and engineers and our relationships with our music. We had four top-ten singles—the first album in history to achieve that. Every song from *Rumours* got airplay on the radio. You would have thought that one of us would have said, "Chig, you're crazy. Get out of here." But we were so close to the album, and we were all so exhausted that we were simply devastated. We had no idea what we had created.

It was mid-January again in Southern California, mid-January 1977, to be exact. Winter, spring, summer, fall, Thanksgiving, Christmas, that's all I remembered from 1976 beyond working on the album. Now it was winter again. Exactly this time a year earlier, I had packed my Audi, and Scooter and I had started our amazing adventure. I didn't know it then, but my life was on the verge of changing forever.

During the last few days, I had finished mixing and mastering the album. We were about to start the process of pressing the LPs.

In mastering, we assembled all of the songs in their proper running order on two reels, sides one and two. We adjusted the levels of each song so that they would play in a uniform way, maximized for volume, bass, and treble. We used Capital Records' Mastering Studio and their engineer, Ken Perry, to perfect the album.

In the days of vinyl records, the mastering engineer had to play the tape through his console and turn all of the knobs precisely on cue to make the required adjustments in real time. This sent the final stereo

This is a shot of the cutting lathe that was used to make the lacquer disks from which the vinyl records were ultimately made.

mix out of the mastering console to a large lathe, which had a sharp blade that vibrated and converted the sound waves into grooves in the disk. It literally cut the grooves into the rotating blank virgin lacquer to make an actual long-playing (LP) record. When people played the disks on their turntables at home, their record players each had a diamond needle that would sit in the groove. As the disk turned, the tiny bumps down in the cut groove would convert back into sound that could be played out of the speakers.

Then the mastering engineer had to reload the lathe with new blank lacquer, put side two of the tape onto the tape machine, and repeat the process with different cues for side two. After both sides were cut, the mastering engineer placed the lacquer parts in a box to be shipped out to the local pressing plant, where each vinyl disk was placed in a bath that coated the lacquer disks with silver. These metal images became the master "impressions" from which other vinyl versions would be created.

This is what a blank disk looks like before cutting.

Ultimately, these metal versions were made into metal "stampers." The metal stampers would literally stamp the grooves into hot vinyl. Then more vinyl copies could be stamped out, producing LPs for the world to play.

Richard and I watched Ken Perry cut these lacquer masters. Each one took place in real time, in other words, a little less than twenty-two minutes per side.

The initial orders for *Rumours* were so large that we needed to cut 146 of these lacquer master disks, which would be shipped to pressing plants around the world. As the day wore on, "our babies" just piled up on the floor, waiting for the evening messenger to pick them up and ship them out.

"Is it okay if these masters just sit in this cold room?" I asked him.

"It's standard procedure," Ken Perry explained. "The quality isn't compromised much."

That didn't really answer my question. "Much?" I demanded. "Is there a better way?" What a pain in the ass I was.

Ken explained that after the grooves were cut into the lacquer, they were perfect, but as the hours passed, the grooves would tend to "spring back" toward their original state, somewhat. I was horrified!

And this is what the disk looks like after it has been cut.

"So, if we got them into the bath sooner, then they'd have better quality?" I asked. Ken acknowledged that this was true. "Is there any way to get them into the bath faster?" I asked.

"Well, there's a small shop that's less than a mile from here that specializes in making custom parts, and it has a bath tank," Ken said. "But I doubt that your label will let you use them. Their contracts are with plants that are farther away."

I immediately called Ed Outwater in Quality Control at Warner Records and told him about this potential problem. Within an hour, Ed had cleared all of the red tape so that each vinyl part could be taken to the local bath tank as soon as it came off the lathe. God bless him, I thought.

Guess who got the job of delivering the original lacquers to the shop down the street? Yep, the producers of the album: Richard and me. If they gave out a Grammy for best delivery boy, then Richard and I should have shared that one, too.

We spent nearly two weeks driving back and forth from the lathe to the bath. We started at 8 a.m. and finished around 6 p.m. Each run took us about thirty minutes. Every time Richard and I passed each other, I could see him thinking, I'll get you for this, Caillat!

Later, I learned that this effort probably increased the quality of each of the multiple millions of vinyl records sold by about 5 percent. Who knows if—or how much—that affected the final sales figures?

After five days of this, we had dipped all of the vinyl masters into the bath, and the quality of our work was preserved. That was my last effort for the album. I had made my final sacrifice for *Rumours*. The record was complete. I was done.

Epilogue

My days were finally my own again. I called my old friends. I took Scooter to the park, and I started taking care of long overdue business. There were so many things I had neglected that I didn't know where to start. I decided I wouldn't drive myself crazy—I'd just get to each of these tasks as I needed to.

One thing that had been bothering me was that my 35-mm camera shutter was sticking, so I took it to Studio City Camera in a small suburb in the valley. It was a beautiful Southern California day, and I was happy to be out of the studio.

I parked my Audi across the street from the store, took my camera in, and dropped it off to be repaired. When I left the store, I smiled and inhaled deeply, enjoying the sunny winter day and the fresh air. I got in the car and turned the key, and the radio came on.

Before I turned over the engine, the DJ said, "Folks, I have a real treat for you today for our lunch-hour special. I'm going to play the new Fleetwood Mac album. I want you to turn up your speakers, because it sounds absolutely fantastic! I'm going to play the whole thing without interruption. So, sit back and enjoy!" I followed his instructions, and, suddenly, I heard *my* music being played over the radio. He was certainly right. It sounded fantastic! Scooter and I sat in the car until side one ended. I didn't want to interrupt the music by starting the car. Then, after "Songbird" finished, side two began, and "The Chain" played as Scooter and I drove off into the California sun. I had a huge smile on my face, feeling such satisfaction. I would have done it all over again just to experience that one moment.

In some ways, I wish that I had had a cell phone back then to share the moment with someone, but the moment was Scooter's and mine alone, just the way we had started this adventure twelve months earlier. We pulled over at the park and listened to the rest of the album with the car windows down as side two finished.

I had no idea what the future was going to offer. The band had officially made me a producer on a handshake and good faith. There had been no heavily negotiated contracts by lawyers, just friends working with friends. I truly felt that we were all family, looking out for one another's best interests. I had made a lot of new friends—Ray, Rhino, Richard, Cris, Nina, Cheryl, the attorneys, the label people, Judy, and Gabby. Nina and I never got together again, but we've talked, and I respect her deeply. Cheryl and I continued to be hot and heavy, but we eventually ended our relationship. We're all still friends to this day.

Whenever I see anyone else from that time, we admit that we experienced something extraordinary, something bigger than all of us. As time went on, though, fame took the members of the band further away from those of us who worked with them at the beginning. That happens in rock and roll.

When the royalty checks started rolling in later in 1977, I got a new top for my little '56 Mercedes. Richard bought a little red Ferrari. I sold the Audi and eventually moved to Malibu and bought a blue Ferrari. The '77 Grammys were a year away, held in February '78. We won the top award—Album of the Year—which went to the producers, Richard and me. I went from being a San Jose wannabe-songwriter to Producer of the Year. Not bad for twelve months of work.

After that, I would go on to do three more albums with Fleetwood Mac—*Tusk*, *Mirage*, and *Live*. Richard would do four. Each was more intense, more expensive, and more complicated than the one before it. Lindsey became even more difficult for everyone to work with, including Richard and me.

But that's another story . . .

Acknowledgments

First my deepest thanks go out to Fleetwood Mac for seeing my potential and giving me the opportunity to make their music better, thereby forever changing my life. I'd especially like to thank the following people for their help in making this book possible:

- Richard Dashut, for being my friend from the beginning, through the good times and bad.
- Nina Urban Bombardier and Cheryl Geary Bird, for their patience, understanding, and sweetness through the years and their invaluable help with the photos in this book.
- David Elliot and Michela Angelini, for convincing me that I could be an author.
- My wife, Diane Caillat, for indulging my many trips down memory lane.
- My parents, Beryl and Ken Caillat, for printing and reading so many versions of this book and not judging me too harshly for the things they found out about me.
- My daughters, Morgan and Colbie, for their support and (I hope) understanding that their dad is not perfect.

- My editor, Stephen S. Power; my agent, Jennifer de la Fuente; my consultant Jennifer Wilkov; and Lane Shefter Bishop, my friend and wise adviser, for seeing the potential in my story.
- Steve Stiefel, for becoming my trusted friend and cowriter and who came in to help me finish my book, to expand, clarify, and polish my thoughts. He has great wisdom and professionalism and an attention to detail that I needed.
- Herbie Worthington, for your great photos and your friendship and insights.
- Cris Morris, Christina Conte, Ray Lindsey, Curry Grant, Ron Penny, and Leo Rossi, for your good memories in helping me recall details included in the book.
- Richard Arlook and Biff Dawes, for helping me find my agent, and a deep thank you, Biff, for finding Cheryl for me and for those great pictures from the past.
- Big thanks to the guys from the Warner Tape Vault who made my research so complete: Steve Lang, Mike Johnson, and Mike Wilson.
- Jackie Denny, Ilyce Dawes, Dennis Mays, Chris Chigaritas, Tina Cerventes, and Marley Knoles, for their very excellent support.
- Dan Hoffeins, for his great research and friendship; Tanner Colby and Peter McGuigan, for getting the ball rolling
- Those sixty-plus friends who gave their valuable time for our extensive interviews, which can be read in their entirety on my book's companion website, www.makingrumours.com.
- Especially to Wally Heider, for teaching me that no corner is worth cutting.

In Memoriam

For those who are no longer with us, I'd like to celebrate their lives:

- My mentor, Wally Heider; my friends Scooter Brown, Judy Wong, Gary Lubow, Terry Stark, and Jerry Stroud; my grandparents, Norine and Sheldon Cronk and Ken and Ruth Priestley.

- Of course Grace Geary, Robin Snyder, Bob Weston (Fleetwood Mac guitarist), Bill Pastenbach, Bob Regehr (Artists Development, Warners), Colonel John Joseph Kells Fleetwood, Garney Geary, Greg Buckingham, Barbara Nicks, Jess Nicks, Susan Fleetwood, and Steve Ross (CEO Warners).

—Ken Caillat

First and foremost, Lane Shefter Bishop and Andy Bishop deserve my humble prostrations for introducing me to Ken Caillat. Lane had read Ken's first draft of his oral history of the band, and she thought we would make a great team to turn that version into this memoir. For their help during the process, I'd like to thank my readers and moral support team. These include Jeff O'Connell, Karen Orsi, Anne Russell, Jim Sullivan, Jodi Teti, and many others. They helped keep me as sane as they could. They bear no responsibility, however, for any of my moral failings. As Ken will surely agree, this process was creatively rewarding but quite vexing when it came to dealing with the business changes occurring in the publishing industry. Thankfully our agent, Jennifer de la Fuente, and our editor, Stephen S. Power, threw themselves in our path and expressed enthusiasm for the project. Then they made it happen. Finally, I'd like to thank Ken for living the fascinating life he has led. It's been a thrill to be his "with," along for the ride in the side scooter.

—Steven Stiefel

Index